The Maldives

Color Edition

Lionel Bolnet

Author and self-publisher:
Lionel Bolnet

Distributor:
www.lulu.com

Miscellaneous warnings:
(1) This book is not a travel guide and therefore no date, no prices, no address, no schedule mentioned in this book should be taken into account to organize a stay. The readers are invited to check for themselves.
(2) The author of this book is not affiliated with anybody in the Maldives. This book is not an advertising brochure.
(3) This book is translated from French. Thus, temperatures, lengths, capacities and surfaces are expressed in the metric system. Many comparisons between France and the Maldives occur throughout the book.

Table of Contents

Foreword

In the distant future, as a result of global warming that caused the ice to melt, the Earth will be completely covered with water by a huge and high flood. Humanity now lives on artificial atolls. However, a legend is circulating: that of Dryland, which is said to be the only land that is still emerged. A mutant half human and half fish, accompanied by a young woman and a little girl, are going to leave to find Dryland. They face and confront bloodthirsty pirates, named the Smokers and led by the deacon who is a bloodthirsty barbarian.

Synopsis of the Hollywood film Waterworld, released in 1995.

The film Waterworld is a fiction, but the history, geography, domestic politics and future of the Maldives come very close.

In just a few decades a tiny state has managed the feat of making itself famous in the eyes of the whole world as the example of paradise on Earth, dethroning the Seychelles or Bora-Bora. The Maldives is the kind of country that nobody knows how to position on a world map but whose name is well known to everyone. We don't even know who told us about it the first time. A couple of friends returning from a honeymoon? An advertisement in the subway? A ranking of the most beautiful beaches in the world? Or one of those Powerpoint files of photos of blue lagoons that people exchanged by e-mail at the beginning of the internet?

In the popular imagination, the Maldives, we never go there. It is too expensive. And then will paradise be up to the task? The most informed among us wonder why a supposedly paradisiacal country is so often prey to political violence and religious fundamentalism. The greener ones wonder whether a landscape that is proclaimed paradise should be a natural territory preserved with coral or a tourist counterfeit.

This book offers a 360° panorama of the history, geography and culture of the Maldives.

Identity card

Name	The Maldives
Full name of the country	Republic of Maldives
Local country name	Dhivehi Raa'jeyge Jumhooriyya
National Currency	In national unity we salute our nation.
National Anthem	In national unity we salute our nation.
Form of State	Republic
President (as of the date of writing of this book)	Abdulla Yameen Abdul Gayoom
Official Language	The Maldivian or Divehi
Capital	Malé
Largest city	Malé
Area	298 km² (298 km²)
Surface of water bodies	0,12 km² (0,12 km²)
Time Zone	UTC +5
Independence	From the United Kingdom 26/07/1965
Gentile	Maldivian

Total population in 2018	512,038 inhabitants
Density	1,318 inhabitants/km².
Human Development Index (2018)	0,712
Currency	Rufiyaa (1 = 0.055 EUR) (1 = 0.065 USD)
Internet Domain	.mv
ISO 3166-1 Code	MDV, MV
State religion	Islam
Telephone code	+960
Driving	On the left
Nominal GDP	4,825 billion US dollars
Nominal GDP per capita	13,196 U.S. dollars

Flag

The current flag of Maldives is a white crescent on a green rectangular background framed by another red rectangle. It was adopted at the independence of the country on July 26, 1965. The white crescent and the green background are symbolic of Islam. The red bottom does not have a particular symbolism: it seems that for centuries, the Maldivian boats had a red flag simply because it contrasts well with the beautiful turquoise waters of the country. Before being the flag of the Maldives, the red background was the emblem of the Maldivian royal family.

Figure 1: Flag of Maldives

The old flags are described in the following table.

Old flag	Start	End	Description
	1796	1903	Red Rectangle
	1903	1926	Red rectangle + black and white stripes
	1926	1953	Same + white crescent
	1953	1954	White crescent on green rectangle on red rectangle + stripes

	1954	1965	Inversion of the crescent direction
	1954	1965	Adding a star
	1965	1968	Scratch removal

Then the white star was removed in 1968.

The black and white stripes present on the flags from 1903 to 1965 do not mean that the country is under British protectorate. It is just a fantasy that has no particular symbolism.

Toponymy

The etymology of the name of the country in French, "Maldives", is the subject of controversy. One of the explanations seems to refer precisely to the geomorphological disposition of the archipelago or the extremely high number of islands that compose it; it would come from the Sanskrit malodheep (garland) or mal dvipa (thousand islands), dvipa (island). It is also said that women from Sri Lanka settled there, hence the name Mahiladipa, meaning islands of women, which gave the name "Maldives".

Another explanation would have been given by the Arab geographer and historian Ibn Battûta who was cadi (judge) there and married several daughters of viziers. He claimed that the archipelago was named after the island where the sultan's official residence was located, al-Mahal meaning "the palace. Thus, in Arabic, Dhibat al-Mahal (Palace Island) was, according to him, the whole of the Maldives in the broadest sense (dhibat being an Arabic borrowing of the term dvipa). In the narrower sense, it referred only to the island of Malé, the capital of the state, the toponym of the city being itself directly derived from the term Mahal.

Maldivian atolls are often indicated by two names, one of which corresponds to the traditional geographical name while the other indicates the administrative district in which the atoll is located.

The names of localities frequently consist of terms that indicate particular geographical features: for example, finolhu refers to an island with few coconut palms, fushi to a large island near the outer reef and thila to a coral reef located a few meters below the sea surface.

One must always be careful when looking at the islands of the Maldives because they often have homonyms in other atolls. For example, "Villingili" can designate:

- A deserted island in the atoll Alif Dhaal,
- An inhabited island in the Gaafu Alif atoll,
- An inhabited island in the Kaafu atoll,
- An island resort in Seenu atoll.

Geography

The Maldives is an island state in the Indian Ocean located 599 kilometers southwest of the state of Kerala, India, and 755 kilometers west-southwest of Sri Lanka. The country, made up of 26 atolls and three isolated islands, is divided into twenty administrative regions with a total of 1,199 islands, of which just over 200 are permanently inhabited, and stretches from north to south between the Lakshadweep and the British Indian Ocean Territory (Chagos Archipelago). The archipelago separates the Arabian Sea in the west from the Lakshadweep in the east.

This myriad of islands and islets is scattered over an extremely vast area, almost 90,000 km², extending over 868 kilometers in the longitudinal direction and 130 kilometers in the latitudinal direction. The Maldives is seen as a tiny archipelago, while the maximum distance between two islands is equal to the distance between Calais and Carcassonne.

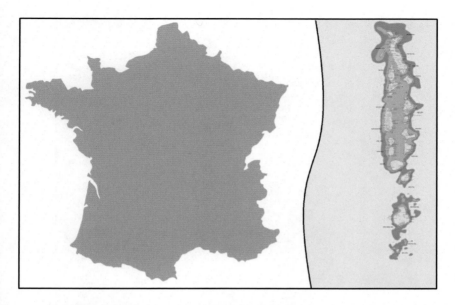

Figure 2: Comparison between Metropolitan France and the Maldives

Geology

The Maldives is an archipelago of 1,199 coral islands grouped into 26 atolls. An atoll is a type of low coral island in the tropical oceans. The atolls consist of a barrier reef, one or more islets called motu formed by accumulation of sand at the back of this reef, and surrounding a central depression. The depression may be part of the emergent island or part of the sea i.e. a lagoon or, more rarely, a closed enclosure filled with fresh, brackish or highly saline water. The term was popularized by the English naturalist Charles Darwin, who described atolls as a subset in a special class of islands, whose only property is the presence of an organic reef.

Figure 3: Location of the Maldives

And besides, the word atoll comes from the Maldivian word "atolu". Its first trace of use in European languages dates back to 1619: the term atoll is used several times by François Pyrard to describe the Maldivian atolls in his book Voyage de François Pyrard de Laval containing his navigation in the East Indies, Maldives, Moluccas, and Brazil.

Thus, the word atoll is almost the only Maldivian borrowing present in the French language.

The country is totally flat. Its maximum altitude is a 5.1-meter high "mountain", Mount Villingili, located on the island of the same name in the atoll of Seenu.

Figure 4: Mount Villingili

The archipelago is all in length: the country looks like a handful of confetti spread vertically.

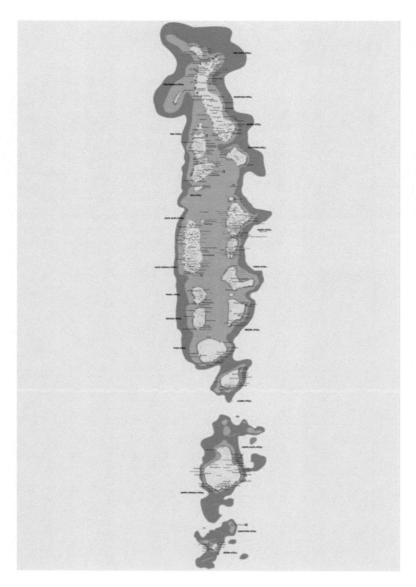

Figure 5: Entire map of the Maldives

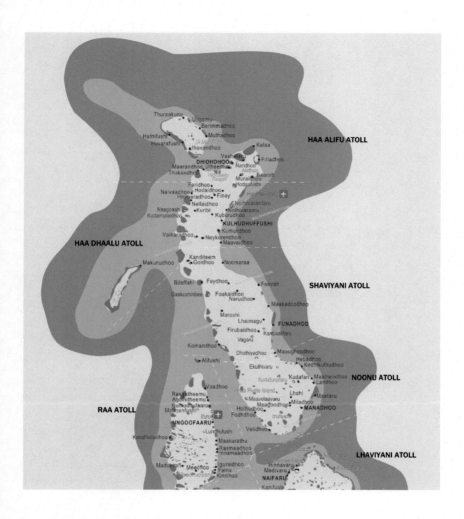

Thuraakunu
Uligamu
Berimmadhoo
Hathifushi Mulhadhoo
Huvarafushi JA Manafaru
Ihavandhoo
Kelaa
HAA ALIFU ATOLL
Vashafaru
DHIDHDHOO Nandhoo
Maarandhoo Utheemu Filladhoo
Thakandhoo Hideaway Aidhoo
Resort
Baarah
Muraidhoo
Hodaafushi
Faridhoo
Naivaadhoo Hodaidhoo
Hirimaradhoo Finey Nolhivaranfaru
Nellaidhoo
Naagoashi Kuribi Nolhivaramu
Kudamuraidhoo Kuburudhoo
KULHUDHUFFUSHI
Kumundhoo
Vaikaradhoo Neykurendhoo
Maavaidhoo
HAA DHAALU ATOLL
Kanditeem
Makunudhoo Goidhoo Noomaraa

Bileffahi Feydhoo
Feevah
Gaakoshinbee Foakaidhoo
SHAVIYANI ATOLL
Narudhoo
Maakadoodhoo
Maroshi
Lhaimagu
Firubaidhoo Kanbaalifaru FUNADHOO
Vagaru
Komandhoo Maaughoodhoo
Dholhiyadhoo
Hebadhoo
Alifushi Ekulhivaru Kedhikulhudhoo
Kudafari Maalhendhoo NOONU ATOLL
Kudafunafaru Landhoo
Waadhoo Lhohi Maafaru
Rasgetheemu Maavelaavaru Miladhoo
Angolhitheemu Maaboodhoo MANADHOO
Hulhudhuffaaru Holhudhoo Irufushi
Maafaru
Fodhdhoo
RAA ATOLL Maamigili
UNGOOFAARU
Lundhufushi Velidhoo
Kandholudhoo
Maakurathu
Rasmaadhoo
Innamaadhoo
LHAVIYANI ATOLL
Madulvari Meedhoo Iguraidhoo Hinnavaru
Fainu Medivaru
Meedhuppaaru Kinolhas NAIFARU
Kanifushi

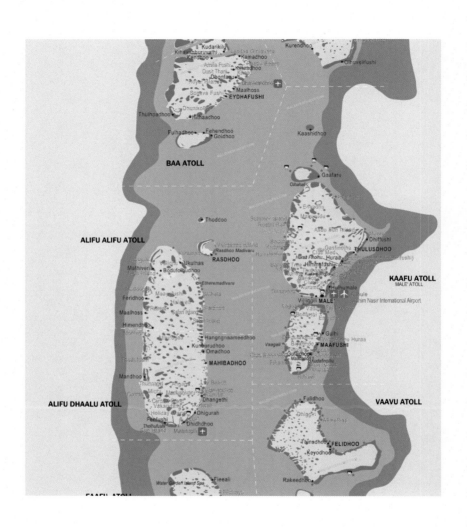

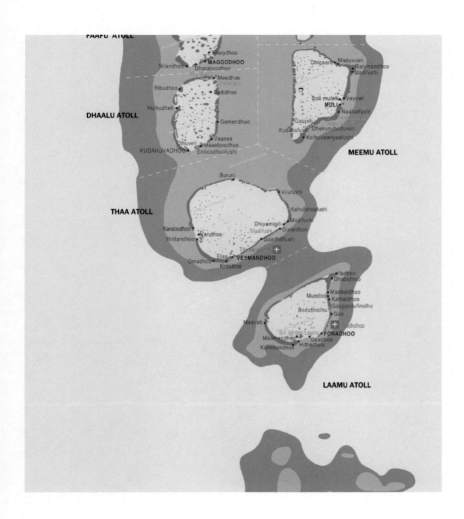

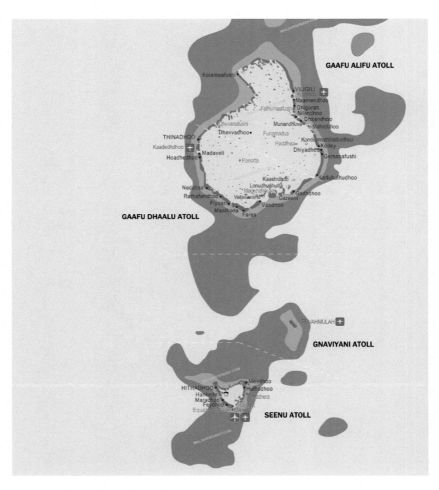

Figure 6: Detailed map of the Maldives

The atolls of the Maldives form the majority of the land mass of this Indian Ocean state. To these 22 atolls, we must add three isolated islands which are Kaashidhoo, Thoddoo and Fuvahmulah as well as the non-emerged atoll of the Vattaru reef. With the exception of Addu (Seenu), all atolls are in the northern hemisphere.

Administrative division

The administrative subdivisions of the Maldives are on two levels: seven provinces divided into twenty divisions called atolls but which do not necessarily coincide with the geographical entity. Thus, a division can be spread over part of an atoll, over several atolls or over a single atoll, with the administrative entity superimposed on the geographical entity in the latter case. To these provinces and atolls must be added Malé, the capital, which is not included in any province or atoll.

Administrative Atoll	Geographic atoll(s) and/or island(s)	Province
-	Malé	-
Gnaviyani	Fuvahmulah	Dhekunu
Seenu	Atoll Addu	Dhekunu
Laamu	Hadhdhunmathi Atoll	Mathi-Dhekunu
Thaa	Kolhumadulu Atoll	Mathi-Dhekunu
Haa Alifu	Ihavandippolhu Atoll and Thilandhunmathi Atoll	Mathi-Uthuru
Haa Dhaalu	Makunudhoo Atoll and Thilandhunmathi Atoll	Mathi-Uthuru
Shaviyani	Miladummadulu Atoll	Mathi-Uthuru
Dhaalu	South Nilandhe Atoll	Medhu
Faafu	North Nilandhe	Medhu

	Atoll	
Meemu	Mulaku Atoll	Medhu
Gaafu Alif	Huvadhu Atoll	Medhu-Dhekunu
Gaafu Dhaalu	Huvadhu Atoll	Medhu-Dhekunu
Alif Alif	Ari Atoll, Rasdu Atoll and Thoddoo Atoll	Medhu-Uthuru
Alif Dhaal	Ari Atoll	Medhu-Uthuru
Kaafu	Gaafaru Atoll, North Malé Atoll (except Malé), South Malé Atoll and Kaashidhoo	Medhu-Uthuru
Vaavu	Felidhu Atoll and Vattaru Reef	Medhu-Uthuru
Baa	Goidhoo Atoll and Maalhosmadulu South Atoll	Uthuru
Lhaviyani	Faadhippolhu Atoll	Uthuru
Noonu	Miladummadulu Atoll	Uthuru
Raa	Maalhosmadulu North Atoll and Alifushi Atoll	Uthuru

The Maldives is divided into four types of islands:

- The capital **Malé**,
- The **inhabited islands**: the rural Maldives, "the regions or the province" as they would say in French.
- **Island hotels** exclusively for tourists.
- **Uninhabited**, deserted **islands**.

Climate

The climate of the Maldives is one of the major reasons for the fame of this country: on the whole, the climate of the Maldives can be defined as hot and humid. Temperatures average between 26°C and 28°C at night and between 30°C and 32°C during the day. The proximity to the equator and the ocean maintains a humidity between 70% and 90%. The temperature felt, also called Humidex Index, therefore often exceeds 40 °C, however, the heat is tempered by the constant presence of light sea breezes which make tourist stays extremely pleasant. The same can be said of sea water which, with its qualities of transparency and color, combines a temperature that never drops below 27°C and thus allows the existence of a flourishing underwater life. The temperature of the water, generally higher than that of the ocean that surrounds the archipelago thanks to the strong sunshine of the low waters of the lagoons, favors the presence of underwater flora and fauna as numerous as it is luxuriant.

However, the tourist who wishes to avoid the rain will prefer a stay between November and March. In February, it rains for a maximum of three days in a month.

Month	Jan	Feb	Mar	Apr	May	Jun	Jul	Aug	Sep	Oct	Nov	Dec	Year
Average high °C (°F)	30.3 (86.5)	30.7 (87.3)	31.4 (88.5)	31.6 (88.9)	31.2 (88.2)	30.6 (87.1)	30.5 (86.9)	30.4 (86.7)	30.2 (86.4)	30.2 (86.4)	30.1 (86.2)	30.1 (86.2)	30.6 (87.1)
Daily mean °C (°F)	28.0 (82.4)	28.3 (82.9)	28.9 (84.0)	29.2 (84.6)	28.8 (83.8)	28.3 (82.9)	28.2 (82.8)	28.0 (82.4)	27.8 (82.0)	27.8 (82.0)	27.7 (81.9)	27.8 (82.0)	28.2 (82.8)
Average low °C (°F)	25.7 (78.3)	25.9 (78.6)	26.4 (79.5)	26.8 (80.2)	26.3 (79.3)	26.0 (78.8)	25.8 (78.4)	25.5 (77.9)	25.3 (77.5)	25.4 (77.7)	25.2 (77.4)	25.4 (77.7)	25.8 (78.4)
Average rainfall mm (inches)	114.2 (4.50)	38.1 (1.50)	73.9 (2.91)	122.5 (4.82)	218.9 (8.62)	167.3 (6.59)	149.9 (5.90)	175.5 (6.91)	199.0 (7.83)	194.2 (7.65)	231.1 (9.10)	216.8 (8.54)	1,901.4 (74.86)
Average precipitation days (≥ 1.0 mm)	6	3	5	9	15	13	12	13	15	15	13	12	131
Average relative humidity (%)	78.0	77.0	76.9	78.1	80.8	80.7	79.1	80.5	81.0	81.7	82.2	80.9	79.7
Mean monthly sunshine hours	248.4	257.8	279.6	246.8	223.2	202.3	226.6	211.5	200.4	234.8	226.1	220.7	2,778.2

Figure 7: Table of Maldivian climate

Lakes

The only two bodies of unsalted water in the Maldives are the Dhadimagi Kilhi and the Bandaara Kilhi. Kilhi means lake. They are located on the island of Fuvahmulah.

Bandaara Kilhi has a surface area of 58,000 m² and a depth of 3.6 meters making it the largest lake in the Maldives and therefore the most beautiful freshwater reserve in the country. It is surrounded by ferns, pandanus, badamiers, nono (dog-apple tree), banana trees, coconut trees, taro fields and mango trees. One can see white-breasted rales (amaurornis phoenicurus).

Figure 8: White-breasted Rail

In the past, people used to fish in this lake. Nowadays, no one does it anymore. The locals don't swim in this lake either because it is muddy and shallow.

In 2003, a pier and an observation post were built at the same time as the port of Fuvahmulah. Then, in 2011, the place is modified to include two straw huts and a restaurant whose architecture respects the Maldivian style.

Figure 9: Lake and observation post

Tourists have the opportunity to feed the tilapia and other creatures living in the lake, but they cannot fish or eat them.

The other lake, the Dhadimagi Kilhi has a surface area of 63,700 square meters and a depth of just 120 centimeters. In its surroundings, it is possible to see pink flamingos, herons and white gygis. It is a bird whose enigmatic elegance is worthy of special attention.

The government of the Maldives has been protecting these two lakes since June 12, 2012.

Fauna and Flora

Flore

The terrain of the Maldivian islands, largely made up of sand and marine residues, is not particularly favorable for the development of many plant species. However, many islands are covered with a rich vegetation of tropical plants, perfectly adapted to poor soils and warm climates.

One of the few books listing the plant species of the Maldives, "Common Plants of Maldives", describes 270 of them.

Although air and water temperatures remain fairly high throughout the year, the coral islands that make up the Maldives archipelago only have lush vegetation in some places: The scarcity of vegetal soil and the virtual absence of fresh water on the surface (lakes and rivers) and underground (springs), combined with the small size of the islands (most of which measure less than one km²) and the very nature of the islands' coral banks, strongly limit the growth of spectacular plants, with the exception of the magnificent coconut palms that line the lagoons, the ficus, the mangroves and some areas of rainforest that produce precious woods.

In smaller quantities than coconut trees, we will find pandanus, walnut trees from Oceania, velvets, green velvets, balambala (still called black coffee), takamakas, pemphis acidula and melanthera biflora.

Figure 10: Book devoted to the flora of the Maldives

Figure 11: Pandanus

Figure 12: Takamaka

Scholarly name	Other names
Pandanus tectorius	Pandanus, screwpine, hala
Pandanus odorifer	Pandanus, screwpine, kewda, umbrella tree, adan, al-kadi.
Cordia subcordata	Oceania walnut, false ebony, tou, manjak
Heliotropium foertherianum	Velvet maker, tournefortia argentea
Scaevola taccada	Green veloutier, brown cassava seafront, magoo, sea lettuce, naupaka, sea cabbage
Cocos nucifera	Coconut tree
Senna occidentalis	Fake kinkeliba, negro coffee, balambala, female mocha coffee, stinking coffee, zepyant, bentamaré, bastard coffee, stink-buster, dartrier.
Calophyllum inophyllum	Takamaka, mahogany of Borneo, funa
Caesalpinia pulcherrima	Fathangumaa, flamboyant, pride of China
Pemphis acidula	Miki miki, wood sailor, pemphis, kuredhi
Melanthera biflora	Mirihi

The largest tree in the Maldives is the ficus benghalensis, also called banyan, nika or kirigas. It is a ficus that grows up to 30 meters high.

The arable land is so small that it is unable to meet the food needs of the inhabitants. For this reason, and also to meet the high demand for food due to tourist activities, large quantities of agricultural products are imported from abroad. From the point of view of arable land, the most fertile island is Fuvahmulah, in the southernmost part of the archipelago, whose vast plantations include crops of tropical fruits such as mangoes and pineapples.

The coconut tree is part of the national emblem of the Maldives and is explicitly named dhivehi ruh, i.e. the palm tree of the Maldives.

Figure 13: Emblem of the Maldives

Land wildlife

A wide variety of land animals are not found on the islands. As the islands are very small, land reptiles are rare. However, there are several species of gecko as well as a species of lizard: the agama. It is a terrestrial and diurnal lizard that feeds mainly on insects and fruits. Like the chameleon, it can change color from dark green to brick red. It uses its inflatable chin pouch during courtship or to impress its enemies. It measures about twenty centimeters.

Figure 14: Agama

In the Maldives, there is a species of saurian, the lygosoma albopunctata, still called the soft skink with white dots. The proximity of the Maldives to India also explains the existence of the lycodon aulicus also called indian wolf snake. Lycodon aulicus measures on average 51 cm including 11 cm for the tail; the females being generally larger than the males. Its coloration varies according to its geographical origin. Its back is brown or grayish brown either uniform or with white cross-linking or cross bands, and with or without white collar. It is a nocturnal snake that feeds on lizards, mice and amphibians. Females are oviparous and lay four to eleven eggs.

There is also a harmless and blind snake, the poor indotyphlops braminus also called brahminy blind snake. It has the appearance and behavior of an earthworm and measures a maximum of only ten centimeters.

It is difficult to see them and it is better but some marine crocodiles have taken up residence in the swampy areas of the Maldives, probably only close to uninhabited islands.

Amphibians include sphaerotheca rolandae (Sri Lanka bullfrog, roland's burrowing frog, southern burrowing frog, marble sand frog) and toads of the species duttaphrynus melanostictus called masked toad because of its bony ridges, along the edge of the muzzle (rostral ridge), in front of the eye (pre-orbital), above the eye (supra-orbital), behind the eye (post-orbital), and a short one between the eye and the ear (orbito-tympanic).

Concerning mammals, there are really very few species. There are only two mammals that can be considered as endemic: the shrew, a kind of mouse with a long snout but which, in fact, is not a rodent but rather a kind of mole, and the "flying bat". They are very large fruit bats, without a visible tail, with an often-reddish mane (hence their French name) around their neck. Their head resembles that of a dog, and in several languages, they are nicknamed flying foxes (for example in English: flying foxes and in Portuguese: raposa-voadora). They spend the hot hours of the day sleeping in the trees, often in very large groups. They are mainly active at dawn and dusk. Tourists can see them in the trees of the resort islands.

Figure 15: Fruit Bats

Non-endemic mammals such as cats, rats and mice have been accidentally introduced by transient humans. Dogs, for their part, are strictly forbidden throughout the country.

In the opinion of zoologists, the small size and isolation of the Maldives leads to an extremely small bird population. Yet some books mention up to 122 species of birds on the Maldives.

Amur falcon, Falco amurensis	Isabelline shrike, Lanius isabellinus
Asian koel, Eudynamys scolopacea	Kentish plover, Charadrius alexandrinus
Barn swallow, Hirundo rustica	Lesser crested tern, Thalasseus bengalensis
Bar-tailed godwit, Limosa lapponica	Lesser kestrel, Falco naumanni
Black bittern, Dupetor flavicollis	Lesser sand plover, Charadrius mongolus
Black-crowned night heron, Nycticorax nycticorax	Little egret, Egretta garzetta
Black-headed gull, Chroicocephalus ridibundus	Little ringed plover, Charadrius dubius
Black-naped tern, Sterna sumatrana	Little stint, Calidris minuta
Black-tailed godwit, Limosa limosa	Little tern, Sternula albifrons

Black-winged stilt, Himantopus himantopus
Bridled tern, Onychoprion anaethetus
Brown booby, Sula leucogaster
Brown noddy, Anous stolidus
Brown shrike, Lanius cristatus
Bulwer's petrel, Bulweria bulwerii
Caspian gull, Larus cachinnans
Caspian plover, Charadrius asiaticus
Caspian tern, Water hydrangea caspia
Cattle egret, Bubulcus ibis
Cinnamon bittern, Ixobrychus cinnamomeus
Common buzzard, Buteo buteo
Common coot, Fulica atra
Common cuckoo, Cuculus canorus
Common house martin, Delichon urbica
Common kestrel, Falco tinnunculus
Common moorhen, Gallinula chloropus
Common myna, Acridotheres tristis
Common redshank, Tringa totanus
Common sandpiper, Actitis hypoleucos
Common snipe, Gallinago gallinago
Common swift, Apus apus
Common teal, Anas crecca
Common tern, Sterna hirundo
Crab-plover, Dromas ardeola
Curlew sandpiper, Calidris ferruginea
Dunlin, Calidris alpina
Eastern great egret, Ardea modesta
Eurasian curlew, Numenius arquata
Eurasian hobby, Falco subbuteo
European bee-eater, Merops apiaster
Ferruginous duck, Aythya nyroca
Flesh-footed shearwater, Puffinus carneipes
Garganey, Spatula querquedula
Glossy ibis, Plegadis falcinellus
Great bittern, Botaurus stellaris
Great crested tern, Thalasseus bergii
Great frigatebird, Fregata minor
Great white pelican, Pelecanus onocrotalus
Greater sand plover, Charadrius leschenaultii
Greenshank, Tringa nebularia
Grey heron, Ardea cinerea
Grey plover, Pluvialis squatarola
Grey wagtail, Motacilla cinerea
Gull-billed tern, Gelochelidon nilotica
Heuglin's gull, Larus heuglini
Hoopoe, Upupa epops
House crow, Corvus splendens
House sparrow, Passer domesticus
House swift, Apus affinis
Indian pond heron, Ardeola grayii
Indian roller, Coracias benghalensis

Long-toed stint, Calidris subminuta
Marsh harrier, Circus aeruginosus
Marsh sandpiper, Tringa stagnatilis
Masked booby, Sula dactylatra
Montague's harrier, Circus pygargus
Northern pintail, Anas acuta
Northern shoveler, Spatula clypeata
Oriental honey buzzard, Ptilorhyncus pencil
Oriental pratincole, Glareola maldivarum
Osprey, Pandion haliaetus
Pacific golden plover, Pluvialis fulva
Pallas's gull, Ichthyaetus ichthyaetus
Pallid harrier, Circus macrourus
Pallid swift, Apus pallidus
Pintail snipe, Gallinago stenura
Purple heron, Ardea purpurea
Red-throated pipit, Anthus cervinus
Ringed plover, Charadrius hiaticula
Rock pigeon, Columba livia
Roseate tern, Sterna dougallii
Ruddy turnstone, Arenaria interpres
Ruff, 'Calidris' pugnax
Rufous turtle dove, Streptopelia orientalis
Sand martin, Riparia riparia
Sanderling, Calidris alba
Saunders's tern, Sternula saundersi
Short-eared owl, Asio flammeus
Sociable lapwing, Vanellus gregarius
Sooty tern, Onychoprion fuscatus
Streaked shearwater, Calonectris leucomelas
Striated heron, Butorides striatus
Swinhoe's snipe, Gallinago megala
Temminck's stint, Calidris temminckii
Terek sandpiper, Xenus cinereus
Tree pipit, Anthus trivialis
Tropical shearwater, Puffinus bailloni
Tufted duck, Aythya fuligula
Turtle dove, Streptopelia turtur
Watercock, Gallicrex cinerea
Wedge-tailed shearwater, Puffinus pacificus
Whimbrel, Numenius phaeopus
White tern, Gygis alba
White-breasted waterhen, Amaurornis phoenicurus
White-eyed gull, Ichthyaetus leucophthalmus
White-faced storm petrel, Pelagodroma marina
White-tailed tropicbird, Phaethon lepturus
White-throated needletail, Hirundapus caudacutus
White-winged black tern, Chlidonias leucopterus
Wilson's petrel, Oceanites oceanicus
Wood sandpiper, Tringa glareola
Yellow bittern, Ixobrychus sinensis
Yellow wagtail, Motacilla flava

If we stick to the best known, we find the grey heron, which is characterized by a long neck, a long, pointed beak and long legs. It has an excellent lateral panoramic view and a very good frontal binocular vision. Its hearing, also very developed, makes it react to the slightest suspicious noise. It generally reaches a height of 95 cm and a wingspan of 1.85 m for a mass of 1.5 to 2 kg.

There is also the frigate. Frigates have long wings (their wingspan can reach 2.3 meters in males), a pointed and forked tail, and a long, hooked beak. The female usually has a white neck. The male has a red pouch, more precisely a gular bag under the throat, which he inflates during the mating season to attract females. These birds do not swim, walk rather badly, and cannot take off from a flat surface. They have one of the highest wingspan to body weight ratios, and can therefore fly for a long time without getting tired. They are able to fly for several months without landing.

Then come the gallinula: a genus of birds of the family rallidae. Its species have the standardized name gallinule. They are often known as water hens.

Last remarkable bird: the white gygis (gygis alba) is a species of seabird found in much of the tropics. It is a bird whose enigmatic elegance is worthy of special attention.

Figure 16: White Gygis

Arthropods are represented by four species of lobster and several different species of crabs among them, the ghost crab. This type of crab spends all its life on beaches, in or on wet sand. The fiddler crab, so called because of its particularly large claw compared to the other in the male, lives in swamps or mangroves. The hermit crab lives under dead leaves on beaches. Another type of crab, the earth crab is a nuisance because it can pinch very hard and damages houses.

Tourists are not particularly interested but there is also on the archipelago, a type of millipede, a species of scorpion and some species of spiders. There are several species of spiders in the Maldives. They show a remarkable resemblance with the species of southwest India or Sri Lanka. An inventory of spiders in the Maldives was carried out by R. I. Pocock in 1904 in his book "Fauna and Geography of Maldives". The heteropoda venatoria, the plexippus paykulli, the argiope anasuja, the lynx spider and black widow spiders are sometimes seen on Hulhumale Island near the international airport.

Aquatic fauna

The underwater fauna of the Maldives is very famous: there are 250 varieties of corals, 2,000 species of fish including sharks and rays, five species of turtles. Octopus, squid, starfish, sea cucumbers, sea urchins and clams complete the picture.

Among the turtles, it is necessary to mention the green turtle, chelonia mydas still called the hawksbill turtle. This sea turtle is the largest of the cheloniidae. The carapace measures on average 110 cm and the animal weighs between 80 and 130 kg. Some specimens can reach a weight of 300 kg for a carapace length of 1.5 m. Its oval carapace is flattened for better hydrodynamics, its width is about 88% of its length. Its head is small and represents about 20% of the carapace length. It has only one pair of prefrontal scales. The edge of its lower jaw is coarsely toothed while the upper jaw has strong ridges on the inside. The upper surface is olive brown, the shiny plates with yellow, green and black radial spots, the plastron is pale yellow, cream or whitish. Tourists who try to touch it while swimming in the lagoons will realize that it is the fastest of the sea turtles: it can reach a speed of almost 35 km/h.

Another sea turtle, the hawksbill turtle, hawksbill turtle, loggerhead turtle or loggerhead can be seen in the Maldives. The hawksbill turtle measures between 60 and 100 cm and weighs between 43 and 75 kg, the largest specimen found being 127 cm. Eggs measure between 30 and 45 mm and weigh between 20 and 31.6 g. The hawksbill turtle is a strong swimmer. Scientists have recorded spikes at 24 kilometers per hour for five kilometers.

Figure 17: Hawksbill turtle

Finally, the leatherback turtle is the largest of the seven current species of sea turtles, the largest turtle in general, and the fourth largest reptile after three crocodilians. It does not have keratinized scales on its carapace, but a skin on dermal bones. It is the only contemporary representative of the Dermochelyidae family, the clade of the armoured-backed turtles, also known by various fossil species, some of which are giants such as the archelon. The color of the animal's skin is a very dark blue. It is shiny and smooth, which gives it the appearance of leather. The leatherback turtle weighs an average of 500 kg for a length of about 180 cm. It lays eggs on Maldivian beaches.

The hydrophis platurus, also known as the pelamide or black and yellow sea snake is up to one meter long. It is a venomous and pelagic marine snake. Its body is very flattened laterally (like a fish), with a black back and a bright yellow belly. The tail is generally lighter, with large black dots. The black and yellow snake is not aggressive to humans, and has no reason to attack: in case of encounter it will always prefer to flee rather than fight. Occasionally, after big storms, they are found stranded on the beaches, unable to reach the sea.

In terms of fish, the waters of the Maldives are very rich ranging from multicolored reef fish to sharks, manta rays and myliobatoidei rays.

Maldivian waters are also home to the enormous whale shark, a cartilaginous fish, the only member of the genus rhincodon and the only current species of the rhincodontidae family. This shark can exceptionally reach twenty meters in length, for a mass of 34 tons, and is considered the largest fish currently living on Earth. However, its observable size is in practice generally between four and fourteen meters. Massive, moving quite slowly and devoid of aggressiveness, this shark is perfectly harmless to humans. Like the blue whale, its equivalent among the mammals of the maritime megafauna, this giant of the seas feeds mainly on plankton, algae and microscopic animals, which it absorbs through its large mouth. Easily recognizable with its checkered livery, the whale shark is found in open seas and warm tropical oceans. Its lifespan is estimated between 100 and 150 years even if the oldest specimen collected was about 70 years old. Although there are no precise data on its total population, the species is considered endangered.

Figure 18: Whale shark and a swimmer

The sea around the Maldives is abundant in biologically and commercially rare species.

In some rare ponds and marshes, freshwater fish such as milk fish or milkfish (chanos chanos) can be found. They can reach 1.8 meters in length, but adults are more generally one meter long. The body is fusiform, elongated, moderately compressed, smooth and slender. The body color is silvery on the belly and the sides fading to olive green or blue on the back. The dorsal, anal and caudal fins are pale or yellowish in color with dark edges.

Tilapia, a freshwater fish, was introduced by a UN agency in the 1970s. It is found in the only two lakes in the Maldives.

Among the marine mammals, in the vicinity of the Maldives, there are whales and dolphins and very occasionally seals.

One of the most emblematic aquatic animals of the Maldives is quite simply, the coral. Corals are immobile animals of the Cnidaria phylum (which also includes jellyfish), characterized by a calcareous skeleton. Corals generally live in colonies of individuals that are superorganisms. The individuals are called polyps. Each polyp secretes its own exoskeleton, near the base, throughout its life; depending on the species, this exoskeleton is either hard, based on calcium carbonate, or soft and proteinaceous. Each colony thus forms a larger and more durable colonial skeleton, whose shape is species-specific, from minerals taken from the ocean. Hard corals, reef builders, have formed by accumulation of these hard-skeleton coral reefs, some of which have become the largest known complex structures created by living organisms: the great barrier reefs.

Corals are responsible for the myriad of colors and shapes that divers around the world wish to admire.

Jellyfish and sea anemones are also found in Maldivian waters.

Between the piles of the villas of the luxury hotels, it is very frequent to see octopus or squid walking around. Shells, clams, mussels, clams are easily found hanging on human settlements or reefs.

Echinoderms such as starfish, sea urchins, sea cucumbers rest at the bottom of the lagoons. They are not very popular with tourists because of their dangerousness and relative ugliness. These species are subject to heavy poaching to be sold on Asian markets.

Finally, there are shrimps and other crustaceans in the Maldives but they are not fished for human consumption.

Malé, the capital

Malé is the capital, the most populous city and one of the administrative divisions of the Republic of Maldives. The city is located on a homonymous island at the very south of the administrative atoll North Malé which is part of the geographical atoll of Kaafu. It is two and a half kilometers long and one kilometer wide.

Administratively, the city of Malé is made up of five districts, four of which are located on the island of Malé. A fifth district is located on another neighboring island.

Figure 19: Malé, viewed from the sky

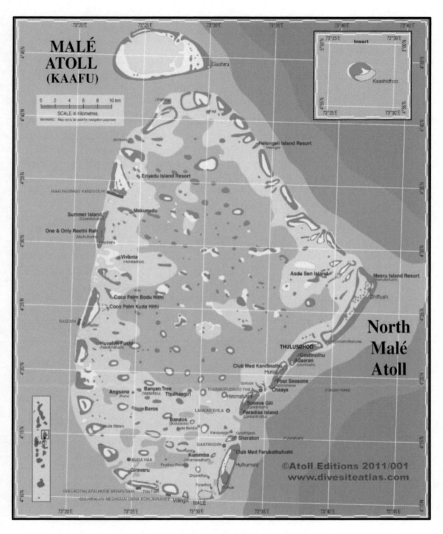

Figure 20: Map of North Malé Atoll

History of Malé

Malé was and still is the center of the trade of coconut, coconut fiber, copra, and cowry shells (or cauri). The cauri (monetaria moneta or cypraea moneta) is a variety of shells found in the Maldives and the Soulou Islands (between the Philippines and Borneo) but present in a large part of the Western Indo-Pacific. Historically used as currency during the Zhou Dynasty (800-300 BC), they continue today to be used as jewelry or decoration and by mediums as divination objects. It is a very small porcelain (three centimeters maximum), irregular and flattened, with a wide, very calloused and roughly subhexagonal rim. The overall coloration is pale (from white to dirty beige), but the dorsum seems colored in transparency, greenish gray with yellowish margins, sometimes with darker transverse bands. The opening is wide and white, with pronounced denticules. The mantle of the animal is zebra white. This shell has been used throughout the ages as a pre-monetary circulation instrument. Traces of its use can be found in China as early as the Shang Dynasty (1600-1046 BC).

Figure 21: Curries

54

Spread by Arab and European sailors from the 10th century, these shells were used as currency in a large part of Africa and the Indian Ocean: the main supplier was the Maldives.

Current Malé

Traditional seat of power and palace of the kings of the ancient dynasties, the intense urbanization under the regime of President Ibrahim Nasir, on such a limited territory, has placed the city far from the postcard image generally conveyed by this archipelago very popular with tourists. Malé is the political, cultural, economic and financial center of the country. The main island has more than 100,000 inhabitants and a large number of visitors from other islands to benefit from the services (shops, health, education) that make Malé a pole of attraction.

With its maximum altitude of two meters, Malé looks like a pizza overhung by modern buildings.

The hotels are mostly located in the southwest of the island because of the proximity to the airport.

Despite the small size of the island, cars - an outward sign of wealth - and especially two-wheelers are legion, causing regular traffic jams.

Against all odds, the inhabitants of Malé, and Maldivians in general despise the bicycle. This means of transport suffers from an image as an outward sign of poverty. When President Nasheed wanted to equip the Maldivian police with bicycles, the police, outraged, never wanted to use them and public opinion did not understand this archaic proposal.

Since there are no open plots of land nearby, all infrastructure is located in the city itself. The central road, Majeedhee Magu, is the main commercial artery of the city.

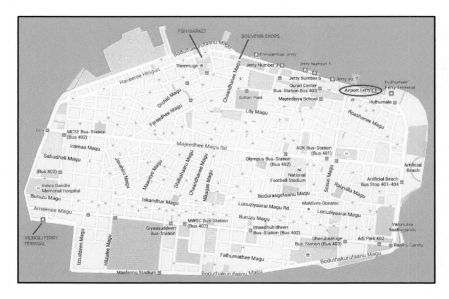

Figure 22: Map of Malé

Drinking water is supplied from water pumped 50 or 60 meters below the city. It is desalinated by reverse osmosis but tends to run out because of excessive consumption.

The waste water from Malé is, unfortunately, discharged into the sea.

Solid waste is transported to neighboring islands, including Thilafushi.

Most of the electricity in the city is produced by oil-powered generators. They produce 84 MWh (megawatt-hour) of power. A few solar panels contribute up to 6 small MWh. In 2011, the World Bank has launched the financing of a project capable of simultaneously meeting the growing need for electricity and garbage on Thilafushi: before 2030 it will be necessary to build a huge power plant of 200 MWh on Thilafushi and supply Malé with electricity via a six-kilometer high-voltage submarine cable. Part of the energy will be derived from burning garbage.

Living conditions in Malé are not paradisiacal. It is a very urbanized capital, bigger than one can imagine. It has hundreds of narrow streets crisscrossed by thousands of helpless motorcyclists. The city center is very congested, overcrowded, humid, dirty. People spit in the streets and passersby bump into each other.

It takes 50 minutes on foot to walk around this world's densest capital. This tour is the only way to do a little jogging, early in the morning, because walking in Malé at any other time of the day is a torture. The polluted air attacks the respiratory voices and the humid heat gives the impression that one has just come out of the shower all the time. In addition, there is almost never a sidewalk.

The concrete jungle allows 25-storey buildings to extend the city in the only possible direction: height.

Figure 23: Photo of a street in Malé

Traditionally, Malé is not an island for tourists. The seaside has always been used as a toilet and public dump. Nowadays, they are covered with plastic garbage. There is no trash can anywhere. It's not uncommon to see parents saying to their children "when you're done drinking your juice, throw the package into the sea".

On the beach of Malé, there is no cultural tourist exception: as the country is strictly Muslim, it is not allowed for women to swim in bathing suits. In Malé, most women wear the veil.

In the absence of real entertainment in Malé, cafes are an essential social place. One can drink tea, coffee, sodas but not alcohol. They often serve as restaurants as well, offering mainly fried food or hot dogs. Sometimes there is music in the background but if someone feels like dancing, the bar manager or the police will quickly call the offender to order.

On September 11, 2018, Malé is finally connected to the international airport: The China-Maldives Friendship Bridge (or Sinamalé Bridge) is open to traffic. This building, two kilometers long, 20 meters wide and 20 meters above sea level, connects the capital of Malé to the island of Hulhulé, on which the international airport is located. This bridge, inaugurated on Thursday, August 30, 2018 by President Abdulla Yameen, is one of China's emblematic projects in the Maldives, as part of China's New Silk Roads strategy. It cost US$300 million in total and was financed mainly by China (US$170 million in concessional loans and US$100 million in grants). Construction started in 2015 and was carried out by the Chinese company Second Harbour Engineering, belonging to the China Communications Construction Co Ltd (CCCC) group.

Figure 24: Synthesis image of the Sinamalé Bridge

This bridge is of no use to international tourists usually residing in resorts far from Malé.

Addu city, new city

It is the second largest city in the Maldives. Located very far from Malé, 535 kilometers from the capital, it is home to 32,000 Maldivians in the southern hemisphere.

The city of Addu consists of six localities: Hithadhoo, Maradhoo-Feydhoo, Maradhoo, Feydhoo, Hulhudhoo and Meedhoo. Other islands are part of the same atoll, Addu Atoll, but are not administratively included in the city of Addu, such as Gan for example.

A sixteen-kilometer suspended highway, the Addu Link Road is the second longest road in the Maldives. It connects Hithadhoo, Maradhoo, Maradhoo-feydhoo, Feydhoo, and Gan. However, Hulhudhoo and Meedhoo are not physically connected to the rest of the city. In fact, the two localities named Hulhudhoo and Meedhoo are on the same island known as Hulhumeedhoo. In order to connect it to the rest of the city, another 15-kilometer bridge would have to be built over the lagoon.

History of Addu city

The city of Addu is very young: it was during the mandate of President Mohamed Nasheed, that the decision to group all these islands in one city was taken in order to decentralize the country. In 2010, a referendum was then held on the six islands in order to obtain the consent of the population. Of the 26,676 voters, 16,695 voted in favor of city status. The inhabitants voting against were mainly those of Feydhoo and Meedhoo: they were afraid of losing their identity.

The city's first mayor is Abdulla Sodiq (MDP party), elected in February 2011 and re-elected in February 2014.

The language of the inhabitants is significantly different from that of other Maldivians. While the Divehi language spoken in Malé, Divehi-Malé is the official language of the whole country, the inhabitants of Addu speak Divehi-low. It slightly resembles the language of the inhabitants of Fuvahmulah, the lower mulaku.

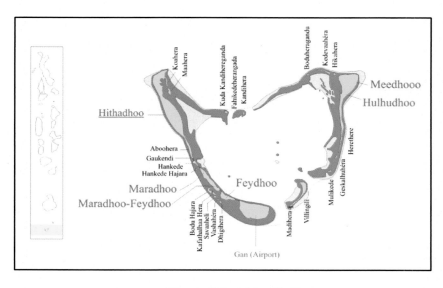

Figure 25: Addu Atoll

From a tourist point of view, Addu is atypical because the city does not hesitate to mix inhabitants and foreign tourists. The city benefits from a law of former president Nasheed which authorizes and encourages the opening of inns and small hotels on islands inhabited by Maldivians. The first hostel, Stellar Maradhoo opened in 2013.

The international airport of Gan allows Addu to be connected to the world without the intermediary of its rival Malé.

In November 2011, the city of Addu acquired a convention center, the Equatorial Convention Center (ECC), which contains a 3,000-seat amphitheater.

Figure 26: Equatorial Convention Center

Other notable islands

Fuvahmulah

Populated by 12,000 inhabitants, Fuvahmulah is an isolated island since it is not located in an atoll. Its current name and its former name (Fua Mulaku) mean the island with the arec nut, also called betel nut, which is the tree on which the arec nut grows.

More than 494 kilometers away from Malé, Fuvahmulah is rich in a history, geology, geography, fauna and flora totally different from the rest of the country. Fuvahmulah has, for example, lakes and forests, ecosystems almost non-existent on the other islands.

Historically and religiously, Fuvahmulah is one of the few islands containing traces of the country's Buddhist past in the form of a ruined stupa: the Fua Mulaku Havitta. A little further, the Gen Miskit (or Gemmiskiy) is a small coral house which would be the oldest mosque of the island. Finally, Fuvahmulah was one of the islands of the separatist movement of the Suvadives and as such retains a history of latent conflict with the capital, Malé.

Villingili

Situated in the immediate vicinity of Malé, the island of Villingili is the only district of the capital that is not on the island of Malé. A ferry runs 24 hours a day for the two kilometers that separate the two islands.

Its surface area is 0.27 km² for 6,956 inhabitants. It is therefore an extremely high population density: 25,800 inhabitants/km².

Originally, Villingili was a resort island. It is even the second island to have been developed for tourism. But afterwards, it became a residential island to absorb the overpopulation of Malé.

It attracts tourists but not foreigners: it is the inhabitants of Malé who go there to relax or practice water sports. There was a detoxification center there between 2010 and 2016.

Figure 27: Villingili (left) and Malé (right)

Hulhumalé

Hulhumalé is the result of the expansion on the sea of a small original island as part of a vast real estate project aimed at providing a solution to the overpopulation of the island and city of Malé, the capital of the country located not far to the southwest. The island was inaugurated on May 12, 2004 by President Maumoon Abdul Gayoom.

The island currently has 30,000 inhabitants. Hulhumalé wants to be modern, airy and pleasant to live in contrast to its big sister Malé.

Other future projects will push the population of Hulhumalé to 240,000. The inspiration of its town planners undoubtedly comes from famous seaside cities such as Miami, Dubai, Monaco, ...

Figure 28: Futuristic Vision of Hulhumalé (1)

The quantity of equipment, the modern infrastructure and the proximity of the island to the international airport predestine Hulhumalé to a wealthy, international, young and dynamic population.

Figure 29: Futuristic Vision of Hulhumalé (2)

Figure 30: Hulhumalé's Future Vision (3)

Ancient history

First settlement

Little is known about the ancient history of the Maldives. The first Maldivians did not leave many archaeological remains. Their constructions were probably made of wood, palm branches and other perishable materials that quickly degraded with salt and wind. Tribal chiefs did not reside in sophisticated stone palaces. Nor did their religion of the time require the construction of large temples.

The first evidence of settlements dates back to the 4th and 5th centuries B.C. but various legends and scientific theories, partly supported by archaeological remains, put forward the hypothesis that the islands may have been inhabited a millennium earlier. There are reliable written accounts of the islands left in the first century by Ptolemy (who counted 1378 islands), in the fourth century by Pappus of Alexandria and Scholastica of Thebes, and in the sixth century by another Alexandrian, Constantine of Antioch.

Various studies on the oral, linguistic, cultural traditions of the Maldives indicate that the first humans settled there were descendants of Tamils from Tamilakam (this is the geographical region that currently corresponds in India to Tamil Nadu, Kerala, Pondicherry and the southern parts of Andhra Pradesh and Karnataka). They arrived during the Sangam period, i.e. years -300 to 300, and were probably fishermen from the coasts of southern India or the northern coast of Sri Lanka. Among these people are the Giraavaru. They are mentioned in ancient legends and local folklore as the origin of the settlement of Malé. The accounts describing the Giraavaru bear witness to a matriarchal society where each atoll was ruled by a queen or, according to other sources, by a kind of priests called sawamias practicing heliolatry (the deity is the sun), selenolatry (the deity is the moon) or astrolatry (the deity is one or more stars). Many travelers of the time, mainly Arabs, wrote that the Maldives was ruled by a queen, Queen Damahaar. Little is known about her. The exact dates of her reign are not known. The Maapanansa, i.e. the copper plates on which the history of her dynasty is written, have all been lost.

But the writings are contradictory. For some sources, the written history of the Maldives begins with the arrival of the Sinhalese. Prince Vijaya of Sri Lanka (reign from -543 to -505) and several hundreds of Sinhalese reached the Maldives around 543/483 BC. One of the ships carrying Prince Vijaya was heading towards Sri Lanka in the year -500 BC, but it drifted and ran aground on an unknown island they called Mahiladvipika. The settlement of the Sinhalese in Sri Lanka and the Maldives marks a significant change in the demography and development of the Divehi language which is very similar in grammar, phonetics and structure to Sinhalese. As a reminder, Sinhala is the official language of Sri Lanka, spoken by 70% of Sri Lankans.

Philostorge, an ecclesiastical historian born in 370 in Cappadocia, writes the story of a prisoner held on an island called "Diva" who could be Divehi, that is to say the Maldives. This prisoner, Theophilus the Indian, bishop and Christian missionary of the 4th century, would have been sent there in 350 to convert the population to Christianity.

It is almost impossible to find writings testifying to the beginning of Buddhism in the Maldives. The man who has most investigated this question is HCP Bell (Harry Charles Purvis Bell). Bell, a British man born in India in 1851, was shipwrecked in the Maldives in 1879 and returned there many times to learn about the Maldives' Buddhist past. According to him, the ancient Maldivians followed the Theravada current, an ancient branch of Buddhism hīnayāna from the school Sthaviravāda. Relatively conservative, it is also closer to early Buddhism than other existing Buddhist traditions. This is consistent because it is also the current followed at the time by the Sinhalese.

Buddhism probably spread to the Maldives in the 3rd century BC. Almost all the archaeological remains that have been found in the Maldives are monasteries or stupas, a Buddhist and Jain architectural structure found in the Indian subcontinent, where it originated, but also in the rest of Asia, where it followed the expansion of Buddhism. It is both a non-iconic representation of the Buddha and a monument commemorating his death. All of the excavated artifacts display characteristics of Buddhist iconography.

Figure 31: Buddhist Ruin on Fuvahmulah, 1922

According to Maldivian legend, an Indian prince named Koimala stranded with his young wife in a lagoon in the Maldives and settled there, becoming the first sultan in the 12th century. Concerning Koimala, the borders between mythology and history are fine. There is no written record. Koimala Siri Mahaabarana Mahaa Radun would be a medieval prince coming from Sri Lanka. He would have sailed to Rasgetheemu Island in the Maalhosmadulu atoll and from there, he would have gone to Malé to establish a kingdom. This does not agree with another writing which indicates that Koimala's father would have been the previous king of the Maldives: King Bovana Aananda (duration of reign unknown). Koimala, great traveler conqueror or little heir prince? Which of these writings is true?

It is possible that the Maldives was ruled by two dynasties, one on the southern atolls and one on the northern atolls. In both cases, the common point is that it is known with near certainty that the two founding kings of these dynasties were Indian princes in exile, originating from the Kalinga (a historical region roughly corresponding to the present Odisha). They are kings Balaadeettiya and Soorudasaruna-Adeettiya, both having lived well before Koimala. The latter is probably simply the unifier of the country and to carry out his task used boats, hence his reputation as a navigator.

Still, at his death in 1141, the Maldives was unified into a single kingdom of Buddhist faith. He is replaced on the throne by his nephew, Dhovemi.

Dhovemi is the second king of the Maldives from 1141 to 1166 or 1176 depending on how one reads the rare writings found on brass plates: lōmāfānu. Dhovemi was the son of Henevi Maavaa Kilage, Koimala's sister. As a Buddhist, he ruled the country for twelve years.

Malé, the king's island, being a convenient stopover, it was very early known to Arab merchants and according to sources, the Maghrebian traveler Abu Barakaat Yusuf al-Barbari or Sheikh Yusuf Shamsuddin, a scholar from Tabriz, are credited with being at the origin of Dhovemi's conversion. But which of the two frequented Dhovemi? Abu Al Barakaat Yusuf Al Barbari was a Moroccan Berber adventurer who settled in the Maldives in the 12th century. While Sheikh Yusuf Shamsuddin (1349 - 1408) whose other name was Mulla Muhammad Shirin Maghribi was an influential Sufi poet as well as a great traveler and disciple of the great philosopher of Sufism, Ibn Arabi. The word Maghribi in his name refers to the northwestern region of Africa, probably Morocco, but he was actually born in Persia (Iran). Some sources report that he was born in Tabriz (currently the capital of the province of Eastern Azerbaijan) but other sources refer to the village of Ammand near Lake Ummia or Orumieh, a salted lake in northwestern Iran. He himself chose his nickname of Maghribi because he is famous for having visited the Maghreb at a time when people travelled little. Shamsuddin is said to have received enlightenment during the arba'een (religious celebration known by the French term arbaïn) under the aegis of his spiritual sheikh. It is very difficult to know whether one or both of these men played a role in Dhovemi's conversion. Some even raise the possibility that it may have been the same person. However, the Maldivians officially remember only one: Abu Barakaat Yusuf al-Barbari is the only one, so the body lies in a mausoleum in Malé. Nowadays, one can visit his tomb only with permission from the Islamic Center of Malé. The inhabitants have great respect for him.

Figure 32: Mausoleum of Abu Barakaat Yusuf Al-Barbari

Increasingly close cultural and commercial ties with the Arab world resulted in the establishment of a sultanate on July 7, 1153.

Thus converted, Dhovemi became the first sultan of the country during thirteen years of reign. He sent emissaries to the various atolls to convert his people to Islam. The king even took the initiative to take his boat to convert some islands himself, such as Nilandhoo Island on Nilande Atoll. He even had a mosque built.

However, it will still take several centuries before Islam becomes preponderant on the many islands and in the whole Maldivian society.

The first mosques in Malé were built by order of the king by al-Wazir Shanivirazaa or by the hands of King Dhovemi himself. Vigorous measures were then taken by the sultans to suppress non-Muslim beliefs and practices, measures that went as far as rewriting history and disavowing the pre-Islamic heritage of the islands. Nevertheless, the sultans continued to use ancient titles in Sanskrit until the middle of the 20th century.

Dhovemi's death is not precisely written but he is said to have disappeared in 1166 during a pilgrimage to Mecca. A document recounts "The Sultan, after performing the Jumu'ah, Friday prayer, at the mosque, rushed to the port to board his ship without crew or food. The ship went over the horizon as fast as lightning and no one ever saw it again. It is said of this sultan that he was just, impartial, pious, secular and loved by his subjects for his wisdom, kindness and generosity."

During a long period, difficult to date, the Maldives served as a bank for all the countries of the Indian Ocean using the cauri (shells of the mollusc monetaria moneta) as currency, still today symbol of the Maldivian Rufiyaa. It was not until the arrival of the Portuguese in the 16th century and the arrival of metal coins that this use fell into disuse. The Maldives was then a crossroads of trade. The Maldivians received rice in exchange for the shells of cauri. Rice is still a staple food of the Maldivians although it does not grow on the archipelago. The boats also stopped in the Maldives to buy drinking water, fruits, fish (bonito, to be more precise). Ancient texts describe Maldivians as kind, civilized and hospitable. They produced, at the time, brass utensils, textiles such as turbans. These two industries depended heavily on the import of raw materials.

The other products of the archipelago were coconut fiber ropes.

Over the centuries, the islands have been visited and their development has been influenced by sailors from the countries of the Arabian Sea and the Indian Ocean coast. The Mopla pirates of the Malabar coast - now the state of Kerala in India - made it a theater of their actions.

The Chinese explorer Zheng He, in his expedition of 1413-1415, visited the region during his fourth, fifth, sixth and seventh voyages. Zheng He (1371 - 1433) was a Chinese Muslim eunuch and a famous maritime explorer, whose travels took him as far as the Middle East and East Africa.

The archipelago was first approached by a European in 1506: the Portuguese explorer Lourenço de Almeida.

The Portuguese

In the 16th century, the Portuguese seized the archipelago, built a trading post in Malé and governed it for fifteen years (1558-1573). They appoint a treacherous and catholic Maldivian, Andiri Andirin, as regent under the governance of King Dom Manoel installed in Goa, India. Dom Manoel is, in fact, the Portuguese name of a Maldivian king converted to Christianity, Sultan Hassan IX.

The Portuguese occupation, particularly harsh and violent according to some sources, provoked several attempts at rebellion, which finally succeeded thanks to the heroic deeds of the three Thakurufaan brothers, originally from the island of Utheemu. In the text called "Tarikh el-fettach", the Portuguese occupation is described as "a time when intolerable atrocities were committed by the unfaithful invader, a time when the sea became red with Maldivian blood, a time when people were drowning in despair".

In 1573, the three brothers and other resistant Maldivians, all determined to die for their country and their faith, kill one by one the entire Portuguese garrison and restore independence to the Maldives. Muhammad Thakurufaanu, a completely unknown man at the time, decides to put an end to the presence of the Portuguese by leaving the Maldives with his two brothers, Ali and Hasan to join Minicoy, an Indian island not far from the Maldives. There, the three brothers build a boat, the Kalhuoffummi. It is said that they were able to benefit from the abundant help of another man, Raaveribe living on the island of Maroshi. The work of the latter consists then in repairing and maintaining the Kalhuoffummi (the fighting ship) and providing drinking water to the three brothers each time it lands on Maroshi, an island that will be of major importance in the fight. The sails of the Kalhuoffummi were made on Maroshi.

For several weeks, the three brothers landed on a different island each night, fought the Portuguese and sailed back to the ocean before sunrise. They reach the capital, Malé, the night before the Portuguese plan to convert the country to Christianity. The penalty for the Portuguese for not converting a Maldivian is simply death.

The remaining Portuguese flee and Muhammad Thakurufaanu kills with his own hands Andiri Andirin, the regent under King Dom Manoel.

After this event, the Maldivians stopped recognizing the sovereignty of King Dom Manoel and automatically appointed their hero, Muhammad Thakurufaanu Al Auzam as sultan. He remains in history as a wise, just and attentive sultan, who protected the poor and listened to the interests of the people. In reality during his reign, the situation was legally complex: Muhammad Thakurufaanu Al Auzam was officially only regent (kateeb) under the responsibility of King Dom Manoel. Then at the death of Dom Manoel, officially it is his son, Dom João who takes back the throne (also in exile in Goa) while

Thakurufaanu is co-regent of the Maldives with his brother Hassan. Thakurufaanu dies of natural death on August 26, 1585. His son, Ibrahim becomes sultan or regent (it depends on the point of view) under the aegis of Dom João.

In 1603, Dom Philippe becomes king to succeed his father Dom João. Simultaneously, regents continue to be appointed until the situation becomes clear in 1632 when Muhammad Imaduddin I is finally fully recognized as sultan and completely abolishes the cumbersome principle of regency under a king based in Goa.

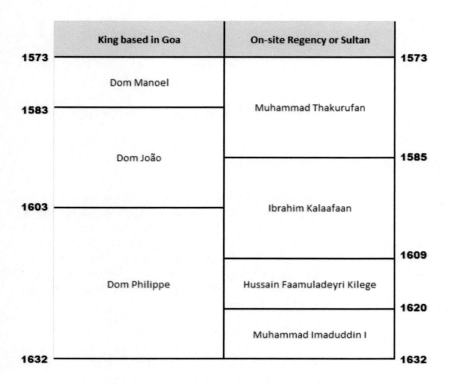

Figure 33: Leaders from 1573 to 1632

In 1751, Louis de Jaucourt is the author of a rather detailed article on the Maldives in the Encyclopedia of Diderot and d'Alembert:

[...] It is certain that the number [of islands] is large, although it decreases every day by the currents & high tides. The whole seems to have once formed a single island, which has been divided into several. The sea is peaceful, and has little depth. Between these islands, there are many uninhabited islands, covered only with large crabs and birds called pinguy. ...] Honey, rice*, & many kinds of roots grow in abundance in the Maldives. Coconut is more common than anywhere else in the world, and bananas are delicious. The religion of the Maldivians is that of Mohammed; the government is monarchic and absolute.

Louis de Jaucourt, 1751

*Author's note: Contrary to this, it is unlikely that rice could have grown in the Maldives.

The Kingdom of Cannanore

The Kingdom of Cannanore, still called the Arakkal Kingdom or Sultanate of the Laquedives and Cannanore, is a small state formed in 1545 on the coast of Malabar and annexed to the British Indies (Provinces of the Indian Empire) in 1819. It was a monarchy led by an Ali Raja and whose territory was composed of the city of Cannanore (nowadays it bears the same name and is in the state of Kerala, India) as well as the Lakedives Islands and the island of Minicoy.

Figure 34: The three parts of the Kingdom of Cannanore

This country can be considered the only state at war with the Maldives in the country's history. Indeed, from 1573 to about 1773, the Kingdom of Cannanore will not cease to attack and occupy the island of Malé in order to integrate the Maldives into its territory. Several Maldivian sultans were taken prisoner. The Malabars manage to take control of the Maldives only from December 20, 1752 to April 7, 1753.

The Dutch

In the middle of the 17th century, the Dutch, who replaced the Portuguese at the head of Sri Lanka, established their hegemony over the Maldivians without getting involved in their local affairs, which are managed by centuries-old Islamic customs.

Although close trade relations were established with the Dutch after they seized Ceylon, the Maldives remained outside the influence of Western powers for another two centuries. Thereafter, the British began to fear that the islands might fall under the influence of another foreign power, such as the Germans and Italians developing their interests on the eastern coast of Africa or the French on the islands off the southeast coast.

The British

Thus, the British expelled the Dutch from Sri Lanka in 1796 and included the Maldives in their Protectorate. England found itself mired with the Maldives when violence broke out during the rivalry between two dominant families: the Athireege and the Kakaage.

The English feed the negative memory of the short Portuguese colonization attempt to their advantage in order to present themselves as a preferable alternative.

On 16 December 1887, the Sultan signed an agreement with the British governor of Ceylon (Sri Lanka) transforming the Maldives into a Protectorate. In fact, the Sultan gave up part of his sovereignty in foreign policy.

During this era, the Maldives continued to be ruled by a succession of sultans. It is a period during which authority and power are increasingly taken over by the Sultan's Prime Minister to the chagrin of the British Governor General, who continues to deal only with the impotent Sultan. As a result, Britain encouraged the country to develop a constitutional monarchy and the country's first constitution was written in 1932. However, these new arrangements favored neither the old Sultan of the day (Sultan Muhammad Shamsuddeen III) nor the Prime Minister, but rather a community of young reformers, educated in the English language. The angry people are rising up against this constitution, which they consider unjust, and want to tear it up in public.

World War II will affect the Maldives in several ways.

On June 9, 1940, an Italian banana transport ship, the Ramb I, was requisitioned by the Royal Italian Navy. The ship was then transformed into a warship by the addition of four 4.7-inch QF Mk I - IV guns and two Breda Model 31 missile launchers. Thus, the Ramb I found itself embarked in the Second World War, mainly to protect the town of Massaoua, Eritrea, from possible aerial bombardments. But around February 1941, it became increasingly clear that Italy was losing ground and was suffering too many setbacks in East Africa to recover. It decided to abandon the area and send several ships to Japan. On 27 February 1941, the Ramb I sailing north of the Arabian Sea came face to face with the HMNZS Leander, a New Zealand warship. The two ships are six miles apart and communicate by radio and visual signals. By cunning, the Ramb I flies the British flag. The HMNZS then requires the password of the Allies to verify the identity of the ship. Unable to respond to this request, Captain Bonezzi concluded that he had no alternative but to fire on the New Zealanders. The Ramb I then lowered its false British flag, raised the Italian flag and opened fire on the HMNZS Leander at a distance of 2,700 meters. The Leander was hit only once and responded with five rounds of missiles. The battle lasted twenty minutes. The Ramb I is severely hit. The Italians lowered their flag. As a result, the Leander ceases firing. While the Leander moves closer to see the damage done by her enemy, Captain Bonezzi gives the order to abandon the ship and then scuttle it.

Figure 35: Scuttling of Ramb I

The Leander rescues the 112 men of Ramb I, one of whom will die of his burns. Then, the explosive charges set by the Italians caused the Ramb I to explode and the Ramb I began to sink at the 01°00′N 68°30′E position, i.e. 534 kilometers west of the Maldives. The crew of Ramb I was then landed on the atoll of Addu where the Italians were taken prisoner and sent to camps in Sri Lanka.

Also, during the Second World War, in 1941, the Royal Navy (British Army) set up a military base on the island of Gan and then in 1942, the Royal Air Force (also British Army) in turn set up a military base on the island of Hithadoo. Both islands belong to the atoll of Addu. The British army builds airstrips on both islands. At the end of the war, it recovers part of the material and abandons the rest.

But the only real impact of the Second World War on the people of the Maldives was the famine caused by the lack of rice supplies. This period of famine is locally called bodu thadhu. This lack of food was an opportunity for the Maldivians to discover the importance of their mangroves. A mangrove is an ecosystem of maritime marshes including a group of specific plants mainly woody, developing only in the tidal sway zone of the low coasts of tropical regions. One of the plant species found there is the bruguiera cylindrica, better known as kandoo in the Maldives. Originally, the dense and sturdy wood of the bruguiera cylindrica is used for construction, including canoe keels. It has also been used for centuries as a fuel for cooking by Maldivians. Propagules, the kind of green beans that grow on the tree, are eaten boiled to remove its strong bitterness. During the Second World War, when most Maldivians starved to death, the people living on Kandoofa Island remained the best fed as they used their abundant supply of kandoo. The dried fruit of the breadfruit tree was also used as a staple food. After the war, the availability of cheap rice decreased the interest in kandoo.

Figure 36: Bruguiera cylindra or kandoo

Upon the death of Sultan Majeed Didi in 1952, members of Parliament elected Muhammad Amin Didi to succeed him. But the latter refused to ascend the throne. Then a referendum was held and following the result of the ballot boxes, the Maldives became a republic. Amin Didi became its first president. He initiated many reforms, notably on education and women's rights.

From the 1950s onwards, the political history of the Maldives was largely influenced by the British military presence on the islands. In 1954, the sultanate was restored. Two years later, the United Kingdom obtained permission to re-establish the military base on the island of Gan (nicknamed RAF Gan), just south of the Addu atoll. The Maldives granted the British a 100-year lease on the island of Gan in exchange for a rent of 2,000 British pounds per year, as well as a 440,000-square-meter square on Hithadoo for their radio installations. These two bases became stopover points for British military flights to

Japan or Australia, replacing the RAF Mauripur base in Pakistan.

In 1957, the new Prime Minister, Ibrahim Nasir, called for a revision of the agreements between the Maldives and the British army. He wanted to reduce the length of the lease and increase the annual rent. In addition, he announced a tax on boats. But Nasir was put in difficulty in 1959 by a secessionist movement in the south of the country that benefited economically from the British presence on the island of Gan. This dissident group cut all ties with the Maldivian government and declared itself an independent state under the name United Suvadive Republic on January 3, 1959.

Figure 37: Flag of the United Suvadive Republic

The United Suvadive Republic

This dissident movement thus became a state in 1959 without being officially recognized by anyone. The Suvadives are simply the southern Maldives: the islands of the southernmost atolls of the country, Addu and Huvadhu plus Fuvahmulah. The etymology of the word suvadive is not clear: this word could well come from the French word sud (south). The navigator François Pyrard would have confused the word sud (south) with the name of the atoll Huvadhu by creating, in spite of himself, the word "Suadou".

At that time and since time immemorial, a cruel lack of communication persists between the capital, Malé and the most distant atolls. For example, the southernmost island of the country, Gan, is 543 km from Malé. Forgotten from the capital, the inhabitants of the southern Maldives do not even have a postal service. The result is a chronic lack of everything on these remote atolls, such as food, clothing and even, in times of epidemics, a lack of medical assistance. Faced with the capital's inability to provide decent public services, southerners are becoming accustomed to fending for themselves. The void is filled by the initiatives taken by wealthy families in the three southern atolls. Using large sailboats, they organize trade with neighboring countries: Sri Lanka and India, without passing through Malé.

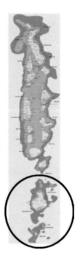

Figure 38: Location of Suvadives

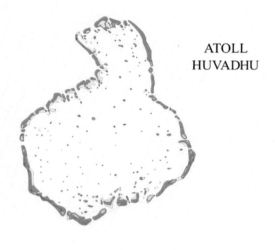

ATOLL
HUVADHU

EQUATEUR ——————————————————————————— 0°

 FUVAMMULAH

ATOLL
ADDU

Figure 39: Map of Suvadives

Paradoxically, it is much easier for the voluminous boats from the southern Maldives to sail in the Indian Ocean to Ceylon or India, protected by the Pax Britannica (a period of peace on the sea routes of the world thanks to British supremacy) than to slalom between the reefs of the atolls to Malé. After all, at the time, Malé was a very small counterpart to Colombo, Cochin or Tuticorin. But this practice meant that the sultan and the government no longer had any control over imports from the southern islands. This did not generate any conflict until the Second World War. When the sultan's government granted Gan and Hithadhoo to the British, they banned all trade between the local people and the British military. Worse, the government began to invent new taxes in order to regulate imports to some extent. The tone gradually increased. The government of Malé decided to position its own militia on the atolls to ensure that no more trade was conducted without informing the government. The arrest of the son of a rich family from a southern atoll triggered a first popular revolt.

The situation softened when Malé, in a new decree, finally authorized the inhabitants to apply for jobs at the two military bases. In doing so, the inhabitants finally have access to high salaries and luxury goods. But a rebellion was organized all the same. It was led by a young, educated and highly respected man named Adbullah Afeef, who worked as a translator for the British. Then he officially becomes a facilitator of communication between the British and the locals.

In December 1958, the government announced a new tax on boats. Immediately, riots broke out throughout the Addu atoll. Government buildings were attacked. Government officials were forced to withdraw their law for the security of British barracks. In fact, the southerners had no intention of ransacking British premises. It must be understood that the British presence is seen as an opportunity for prosperity for the southern islands since it gives them jobs, health facilities, and other supplies that help circumvent the kind of embargo that Malé is imposing on them.

On January 3, 1959, a delegation of the Addu people arrived in Gan and declared independence from the British. The delegation stated that Afeef was their leader. Afeef is chosen as the natural leader of the Suvadives because the British insist that a reliable and trusted person known to the British be chosen. In exchange, the British agree to support the secessionists. The people of Addu are followed by the atolls of Huvadhu and Fuvahmulah. However, the Maldivian government reacted by sending a gunboat towards Huvadhu, commanded by Ibrahim Naser himself, the Prime Minister. Impressed, the people of Huvadhu forget their plans for secession. But on the other hand, Addu, protected by the British, and Fuvahmulah who has no port and therefore is not easily attacked by the gunboat are not afraid of Ibrahim Nasir.

In 1960, the Maldives allowed the United Kingdom to continue using Gan and Hithadoo for another 30 years but in exchange for a rent of 750,000 British pounds to be paid between 1960 and 1965 to allow the Maldives to continue its development. On this occasion, the British gave up the separatist republic. It is a brutal reversal of vest which will be fatal to the United Suvadive Republic. By order of the British government, all commercial vessels belonging to the Suvadives are seized and immobilized. The inhabitants are then served neither by boats from Malé, nor by boats from Ceylon or India. The skyline is scanned for weeks without success.

Initially, this lack of support did not affect the determination of the Suvadives. A second revolt is launched. But once again, the Prime Minister, Nasir takes the matter personally and responds fiercely and ruthlessly. The capital of the United Suvadive Republic, Huvadhu Atoll is attacked. A warship, the Elizabeth Boyer borrowed from Ceylon by Ibrahim Nasir, dropped anchor in Havaru Thinadhoo on February 4, 1962. Without any attempt at dialogue, Maldivian soldiers disembark and embark on a meticulous and systematic destruction of every house in Havaru Thinadhoo. The inhabitants are forced to leave the island to wait in the lagoon during high tide for hours. Drinking water wells are filled with garbage and gravel. Trees are all cut down. The houses are vandalized under the eyes of the inhabitants. Women and some children are raped in front of the rest of their families. Between 200 and 300 prisoners are brought back to Malé, where they are tortured and most of them killed. The population of the island is totally dispersed, going from 4,800 to zero inhabitants. The dead are estimated at 2,400 and are buried in anonymous mass graves. In Maldivian history books, this day is named "Genocide of 1962 in Thinadhoo".

The same boat then heads towards Fuvahmulah and tries to disembark but without success this time. The inhabitants, massed on the beach, send stones at the soldiers who shoot back, killing one man and wounding three others. Noteworthy fact: Fuvahmulah is the birth island of Ibrahim Nasir.

The United Suvadive Republic was unceremoniously dismantled by the British on September 22, 1963. An ultimatum was sent to the inhabitants of Maradhoo with the order to remove the Suvadive flag and to hoist the Maldivian flag. They did so the following day.

Abdullah Afeef is forced to resign from his self-proclaimed mandate as president of the Suvadive government. He is sent into exile in the Seychelles with his family on board the HMS Loch Lomond. On the island of Fuvahmulah, the head of the island carries out the orders: he brings down the Suvadive flag and collects all the official documents of this fallen republic and then goes to bury everything in a large hole on the edge of the island.

The Suvadive territories are then considered part of the Maldives.

The United Suvadive Republic is a dark page in the history of the country. After the military operation of Nasir, it was not until 1966 that people returned to settle on Thinadhoo: 1,800 Maldivians forming 440 households. Nowadays (2018), it is populated by 5,230 inhabitants. The only ceremony commemorating the massacre was held on February 4, 2009, after 47 years.

Independence

On July 26, 1965, the Maldives gained its independence thanks to an agreement signed with the United Kingdom. The British government retains the right to use its facilities on Gan and Hithadoo.

Figure 40: Signing of independence

The independence ceremony takes place at the residence of the British High Commissioner in Colombo. The agreement is signed by the Prime Minister, Ibrahim Nasir and Michael Worker representing the United Kingdom.

The Maldives was admitted to the United Nations a few months later.

Before tourism

In 1970, the Maldives is a country totally unknown on the international scene. The encyclopedia "India, Ceylon, Bhutan, Nepal and The Maldives" published in 1970 tells us that the population of 100,883 speaks a dialect derived from Sinhalese. Hunting and primitive agriculture covers the food needs. Half of the men work in fishing, the others gather coconuts, hunt turtles and look for crustaceans and oysters that they export to Ceylon or India. The capital had 11,560 inhabitants at the time. The book says that the cooking is done outdoors; the people have only the bare minimum to live on. The sense of mutual aid is strong: people come spontaneously to help the fishermen to bring their catch to the shore. The fish is sold immediately to overcome the heat, which quickly degrades the food. While the men repair their nets, the women of the family clean their clothes in the sea by beating them on the sand and then dry them on groves. The general atmosphere is serene and healthy, with no major nuisances. In 1970, there were no traffic jams, no police, no television. Daily life is as calm as the surrounding forests. Only the sultan owns a car and all other land vehicles are bicycles. There is no street cleaning service so garbage is left at the mercy of birds and other animals. The only means of communication with Ceylon is a steamboat which takes several days to cross. Since 1966 there is an airport in the Maldives.

The city of Malé consumed 497,000 kWh of electricity in 1970, i.e. 43 kWh per inhabitant per year. As this figure does not speak much to the layman, it should be noted that in the same year, France consumed 2,623 kWh per inhabitant!

In order to be reassuring, the book wants to specify that this description should not leave the reader thinking of a backward people: only 10% of the population is illiterate in 1970. The piety and the sense of work of the people are striking. In a lighter register, the people love kites and people make very nicely decorated kites that they fly during the monsoons.

Women are known for their beauty and picturesque dresses with high collars, long sleeves and bright colors. They wear beautiful handcrafted jewelry and comb their hair with turtle shell combs.

These islands are described as a treasure of splendid shells.

Finally, the author notes the importance of mysticism and magic in the population. Several Maldivians of the time proclaimed themselves sorcerers or exorcists. All illnesses or pathologies are attributed to some evil spirit called jinn, and are cured with magic. Forty official and recognized magicians take care of the inhabitants' illnesses. Conventional medicine in the Maldives at that time did not have the same prestige as it was given in the West.

Regime timeline

The following timeline represents 1,000 years of Maldivian history between periods of occupation, external attacks on the Kingdom of Cannanore (the Malabars) and political regimes.

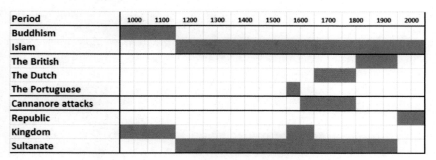

Figure 41: Timeline of the Maldives

Recent history

The transformation into a postcard

The recent history of the Maldives is what makes this tiny country famous. It can be summed up by its transformation into a string of "dream islands" or "paradise islands". The paradise island is a very old concept. In Greek mythology, the Islands of the Blessed are a place in Hell where virtuous souls enjoy perfect rest after their death. They were placed at the western confines of Libya (in the ancient sense, i.e. North-West Africa), thus in the Atlantic Ocean. In the 16th century, Thomas More used the framework of an island to describe an ideal society, Utopia. Later on, novelists will use the island as a setting for their novels so that their Robinson Crusoe will approach and live there in seclusion from society for a certain period of time. This concept of "living like a survivor" has nowadays been taken up by tourism, to make it the privileged place for vacations that change the scenery and catch the eye in advertisements.

Figure 42: Example of Advertising for the Maldives

The country has long been preserved from Western mass tourism because of its remoteness and sprawl. The will to equip itself with an international airport only dates back to 1960. Named in turn Hulhulé Airport, Ibrahim Nasir Airport and finally Velana International Airport of Malé, it is located on the island of Hulhulé in the north of the capital, on the atoll of Malé. On October 19, 1960, for the first time, a plane landed in the Maldives. For comparison, in France, Paris has had an airport since 1909.

On April 10, 1962 at 3:50 p.m., the first commercial flight landing in the Maldives was an Air Ceylon aircraft. The world then discovered the splendor of this country.

It is an Italian who is at the origin of tourism in the Maldives. George Corbin on a trip to Sri Lanka met one day, by chance, Ahmed Naseem (at the time he was nobody but later he became Minister of Foreign Affairs). In 1971, the two men took a freighter to the Maldives, accompanied by an Italian photographer, Francesco Bernini.

The two Italians then discovered what Naseem had promised them: the beauty of a country barely touched by the modernity of the outside world.

Overexcited, they share the idea of developing eco-tourism with two Maldivian partners: Mohamed Umar Manik and Champa Hussein Afeef.

Upon returning to Italy, the photographer published an illustrated book on the Maldives, generating interest in this unknown country. Corbin then became the exclusive tour operator for this destination by chartering Air Ceylon for the first 22 tourists landing at the brand-new Malé airport. On that day, there is not even a customs service yet: the 22 tourists get out of the plane and enter directly on Maldivian soil without showing a passport.

Figure 43: First photo showing tourists in the Maldives

The two Maldivians, Mohamed and Champa serve as innkeepers, restaurateurs and cleaners. We are in 1972 and there is not even a telephone in the Maldives. The two friends communicate by Morse code with Colombo in Sri Lanka to order goods.

The first tourists, only Italians, complained about not finding pasta and eating too spicy food. But today's tourism starts that day: snorkeling, fishing, underwater photos and island walks.

Corbin is delighted: he founds the Agenzia Viaggi Sesto Continente. And on the Maldives side, the two men build coral stone huts on Vihamanaafushi. They add two electric generators and import a large quantity of pasta. Their resort can accommodate 60 vacationers. This is the Kurumba Village. This is the model that will be repeated endlessly on the other islands.

On February 27, 1972, the Maldivian press happily recounts how the country suddenly became a tourist destination.

Figure 44: Maldivian newspaper article from 1972

Then it was not until 1991 that a man, a Dane, Lars Erik Nielsen, on a trip to the Maldives, had a bright idea: to develop a fleet of seaplanes to travel comfortably and quickly from one island to another. Born on January 1, 1951 in Frederiksberg, Denmark, Lars Erik Nielsen is a businessman and racing pilot. He is one of the first tourists of the modern era in the Maldives. During his first stay in the Maldives, he encounters an embarrassing problem: after their arrival on the capital's soil, it is mainly by boat that transport is possible to reach the other islands. The pristine beauty of the country attracts the masses but only the closest islands are accessible. During his crossing to the hotel on the island of Kuredu in 1991, Lars Erik Nielsen remembers the passengers vomiting on their knees. This sad image, which contrasts with the paradisiacal side promised by the advertisements, gave him the idea of a more comfortable means of transport in order to transfer tourists from Malé to the other islands. His love of seaplanes and his sense of entrepreneurship led him to found the Maldivian Air Taxi company in 1993.

In its early days, the company operated only two aircrafts, but still managed to carry 500,000 passengers a year.

Figure 45: Maldivian Air Taxi Seaplane

But before Lars Erik Nielsen's seaplanes, the helicopter was a solution proposed by another company: Trans Maldivian Airways. It had been operating a fleet of helicopters since 1989 under its name at the time, Hummingbird Island. Despite this advance, four years later, the idea of Lars Erik Nielsen's seaplanes turned the market upside down because it won the preference of tourists: it's more comfortable and less dizzying. To adapt to this, in 1997, Hummingbird Island changed its name to Hummingbird Island Airways and added seaplanes to its fleet. In 1999, all the helicopters were even sold or jettisoned in order to focus on a fleet exclusively composed of seaplanes.

In 2000, Hummingbird Island Airways again changed its name to Trans Maldivian Airways (TMA). The company quickly acquired sixteen Twin Otter aircraft. These were small Canadian seaplanes that had been manufactured by Viking since 1965. They cost approximately 6.5 million euros (2017) each and can carry a maximum of 19 passengers.

In 2006 to move up a gear, TMA announces its intention to purchase three ATR 42s. These are not seaplanes but conventional wheeled aircraft manufactured by Airbus. They can embark 40 to 52 passengers but require real airports to land, unlike seaplanes, which can land off any island. There are only ten airports in the Maldives (two international and eight regional). They are located in Malé, Gan, Dharavandhoo, Fuvahmulah, Hanimaadhoo, Kaadedhdhoo, Kadhdhoo, Kooddoo, Maamigili and Thimarafushi. This is a limitation since there are many more islands than that in the territory. Fatally, the company realizes its mistake in 2009 and TMA completely stops operating its flights with wheeled aircraft. The ATR 42s are resold to make up for the financial losses.

Maldivian Air Taxi and TMA have been competitors since 1993, but on February 4, 2013, the American financial group Blackstone announced the purchase and merger of the two companies. The name Trans Maldivian Airways was the only one chosen for the merger. Its fleet reaches 49 aircraft and 63 destinations. It adopts the slogan "Sun, Sand, Sea & Seaplane" (Sun, Sand, Sea and Seaplane) and operates its flights from two hubs: Malé and Gan.

Gan airport is the other international airport of the Maldives. It rises only two meters above the sea on the island of Gan in the atoll of Addu, in the very south of the country. It was built by the Royal Navy during the Second World War and was transformed into a civil airport around 1972. Its adjective "international" is relatively excessive considering the number of foreign companies using it: one. Only SriLanKan Airlines uses this airport in addition to the national airline Maldivian.

Still, the profusion of airplanes over the heads of Maldivians has allowed its tourist boom. Today's tourists can combine comfort, a bird's eye view of the lagoons, and speed to reach their "dream island".

Figure 46: Photo of a resort island taken from a seaplane in flight

The nationality of tourists in the Maldives is modelled on the list of countries that include the rich of this world: South Koreans, Chinese, Russians, Indians, Americans and Europeans.

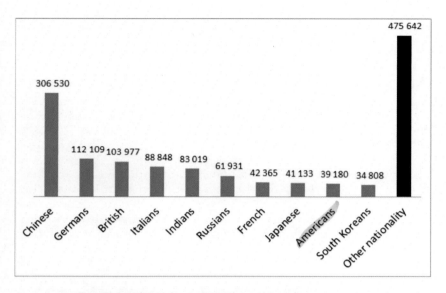

Figure 47: Nationality of tourists in the Maldives in 2017

Americans are not so inclined to come to the Maldives because the place is so far from home. Hawaii and Polynesia are easier for them.

Distance New York - Malé	14,024.90 km
New York / Malé by plane	39h flight + 1 stopover in Shanghai

The French were 42,000 visitors in 2017 but this figure is decreasing. In 2011, there were 60,000 French tourists in the Maldives. This strong decrease is noticed by the Maldivian Ministry of Tourism but has no official explanation. The French may have been sensitized by press articles depicting the darkest parts of the country: problem of democracy, human rights violations, restoration of the death penalty for those over 7 years old, pollution, application of Sharia. This decline in attendance is not observed in countries less concerned about human rights such as China for example.

The resort islands

In this book, the terms island resort, luxury hotel or resort will be used interchangeably to refer to the same thing: an upscale hotel built on an uninhabited island.

A concept invented in the Maldives; the island resort is based on an unsuspected desire: the segregation of populations. The Maldives targets a luxury clientele and has developed the island resort system because it allows to receive tourists from all over the world while preserving the Muslim mores of the locals.

By definition, an island resort is therefore a Maldivian island generally uninhabited before the construction of the said hotel and which respects the doctrine enacted by the Ministry of Tourism, namely "one island = one resort" (with the anecdotal exception of the resorts Niyama and Conrad Rangali Island which each occupy two islands).

There are 127 (in 2016) throughout the territory. The following table gives the complete list of Maldives resort islands ordered by year of opening.

Name of the resort	Atoll	Island(s)	Year
Kurumba	K.	Vihamanaafushi	1972
Bandos	K.	Bandos	1972
Club Farukolhu	K.	Farukolhufushi	1973
Sheraton Full Moon Resort & Spa	K.	Furanafushi	1973
Baros	K.	Baros	1973
Velassaru	K.	Velassaru	1974
Alimatha Aquatic Resort	V.	Alimatha	1975
Banyan Tree Vabbinfaru	K.	Vabbinfaru	1977
Four Seasons Resort at Kuda Huraa	K.	Kuda Huraa	1977

Kuramathi Tourist Resort	A.A.	Kuramathi	1977
Adhaaran Prestige Vaadhu	K.	Vaadhu	1978
Angsana Resort & Spa - Ihuru	K.	Ihuru	1978
Club Med Kanifinolhu	K.	Kanifinolhu	1978
Adhaaran Club Rannaalhi	K.	Rannalhi	1978
Meeru Island Resort	K.	Meerufenfushi	1978
Kuredhdhu Island Resort	Lh.	Kuredhdhu	1978
Emboodhu Village	K.	Emboodhu	1979
Paradise Island Resort & Spa	K.	Lankanfinolhu	1979
Adhaaran Select Hudhuranfushi	K.	Lhohifushi	1979
Huvafenfushi	K.	Nakatchafushi	1979
Coco Palm Boduhithi	K.	Boduhithi	1979
Oblu By Atmosphere at Helengeli	K.	Helengeli	1979
Olhuveli Beach & Spa Resort	K.	Olhuveli	1979
One & Only Reethi Rah	K.	Medhufinolhu	1979
Gili Lankanfushi	K.	Lankanfushi	1980
Thulhaagiri Island Resort	K.	Thulhaagiri	1980
Centara Ras Fushi Resort & Spa	K.	Giraavaru	1980
Club Med Finolhu Villas	K.	Gasfinolhu	1980
Fun Island Resort	K.	Bodufinolhu	1980
Anantara Resort & Spa	K.	Dhigufinolhu	1980
Rihiveli	K.	Mahaanaelhi Huraa	1980
Cinnamon Dhonveli	K.	Kanuoiy Huraa	1981
Fihalhohi Island Resort	K.	Fihaalhohi	1981
Dream Island Villivaru	K.	Villivaru	1981
Cocoa Island	K.	Makunufushi	1981
Asdhu Sun Island	K.	Asdhu	1981
Jumeirah Vittaveli Island Resort	K.	Bolifushi	1982
Biyaadhu Island Resort	K.	Biyaadhoo	1982
Dhiggiri Tourist Resort	V.	Dhiggiri	1982
Vivanta by Taj - Coral Reef	K.	Hembadhoo	1982
Constance Halaveli Resort	A.A.	Halaveli	1982
Eriyadhu Island Resort	K.	Eriyadhu	1982
W. Retreat & Spa	A.A.	Fesdhu	1982
Taj Exotica Resort & Spa	K.	Embudhu Finolhu	1983
Summer Island	K.	Ziyaaraifushi	1983
Makunudhoo Island	K.	Makunudhu	1983
Bathala Island Resort	A.A.	Bathala	1983
Maayafushi Tourist Resort	A.A.	Maayafushi	1983

Nika Island Resort	A.A.	Kudafolhudhu	1983
Soneva Fushi By Six Senses	B.	Kunfunadhoo	1983
Coco Privé Kuda Hithi Island	K.	Kudahithi	1984
Veligandu Island	A.A.	Veligandu	1984
Holiday Inn Resort Kandooma	K.	Kandoomafushi	1985
Ellaidhoo by Cinnamon	A.A.	Ellaidhoo	1985
Naladhu (Palm Tree Island)	K.	Veligandu Huraa	1986
Gangehi Island Resort	A.A.	Gangehi	1987
Lux*	A.Dh.	Dhidhdhufinolhu	1988
Madoogali Resort	A.A.	Madoogali	1989
Velidhoo Island Resort	A.A.	Velidhoo	1989
Angaaga Island Resort	A.Dh.	Angaga	1989
Mirihi Island Resort	A.Dh.	Mirihi	1989
Constance Moofushi Resort	A.Dh.	Moofushi	1990
Thundufushi Island Resort	A.Dh.	Thundufushi	1990
Diamonds Athuruga Beach and Water Villas	A.Dh.	Athurugau	1990
Twin Island Resort	A.Dh.	Maafushivaru	1991
Ranveli Village	A.Dh.	Villingilivaru	1991
Kudarah Island Resort	A.Dh.	Kudarah	1991
Centara Grand Island Resort & Spa	A.Dh.	Machchafushi	1992
Conrad Rangali Island	A.Dh.	Rangalifinolhu and Rangali	1992
Vilamendhoo Island Resort	A.Dh.	Vilamendhoo	1994
Lily Beach Resort	A.Dh.	Huvahendhoo	1994
Vakarufalhi Island Resort	A.Dh.	Vakarufalhi	1994
Holiday Island	A.Dh.	Dhiffushi	1994
Sun Island Resort & Spa	A.Dh.	Nalaguraidhoo	1998
Reethi Beach Resort	B.	Fonimagoodhoo	1998
Coco Palm Dhunikolhu	B.	Dhunikolhu	1998
Angsana Resort and Spa - Velavaru	Dh.	Velavaru	1998
Komandoo Maldives Island Resort	Lh.	Komandoo	1998
Sun Aqua Vilu Reef	Dh.	Meedhuffushi	1998
Kihaad Resort	B.	Kihaadhuffaru	1999
Filitheyo Island Resort	F.	Filitheyo	1999
Kanuhura	Lh.	Kanuhuraa	1999
Cinnamon Hakuraa Huraa	M.	Hakuraa Huraa	1999
Palm Beach Island	Lh.	Madhiriguraidhoo	1999
Medhufushi Island Resort	M.	Medhufushi	2000
Adhaaran Select Meedhupparu	R.	Meedhupparu	2000

Royal Island	B.	Horubadhoo	2001
Hideaway Beach Resort and Spa	H.A.	Dhonakulhi	2005
Four Seasons Resort at Landaa Giraavaru	B.	Landaa Giraavaru	2006
Alidhoo Island Resort	H.A.	Alidhoo	2007
JA Manafaru	H.A	Manafaru	2007
Canareef Resort	S.	Herethere	2007
Roxy Resort	N.	Kudafunafaru	2008
Hilton Irufushi Resort & Spa	N.	Medhafushi	2008
Robinson Club	G.A	Funamauddua	2009
Park Hyatt Hadaha	G.A	Hadahaa	2009
Shangri-La's Villingili Resort & Spa	S.	Villingili	2009
Anantara Kihavah Villas	B.	Kihavah Haruvalhi	2010
Six Senses Laamu	L.	Olhuveli	2011
Jumeirah Dhevanafushi	G.A	Meradhoo	2011
Ayada	G.Dh.	Magudhdhuva	2011
Dusit Thani	B.	Mudhdhoo	2012
Niyama	Dh.	Olhuveli and Embudhufushi	2012
Viceroy	Sh.	Vagaru	2012
The Residence	G.A	Falhumafushi	2012
Safari Island	A.A.	Mushimasmingili	2013
Maalifushi By Como	Th.	Maléfushi	2013
Atmosphere Kanifushi	Lh.	Kanifushi	2013
Cheval Blanc Randheli	N.	Randheli	2013
Velaa Private Island	N.	Fushivelavaru	2013
Kandholhu Island	A.A.	Kandholhudhoo	2014
Loama Resort at Maamigili	R.	Maamigili	2014
Drift Thelu Veliga Retreat	A.Dh.	Theluveliga	2015
AaaVeee Nature's Paradise	Dh.	Dhoores	2015
Amari Havodda	G.Dh.	Havodda	2015
Outrigger Konotta Resort	G.Dh.	Konotta	2015
Malahini Kuda Bandos	K.	Kuda Bandos	2016
Ozen by Atmosphere at Maadhoo	K.	Maadhoo Finolhu	2016
Finolhu Baa Atoll	B.	Kanufushi	2016
Milaidhoo Island	B.	Milaidhoo	2016
The St. Regis Vommuli Resort	D.	Vommuli	2016
Kurumba	Lh.	Ookolhu Finolhu	2016
Bandos	B.	Voavah	2016
Club Farukolhu	Lh.	Hurawalhi	2016

Sheraton Full Moon Resort & Spa	B.	Dhigufaruvinagandu	2016
Baros	R.	Furaveri	2016
Velassaru	N.	Medhufaru	2016

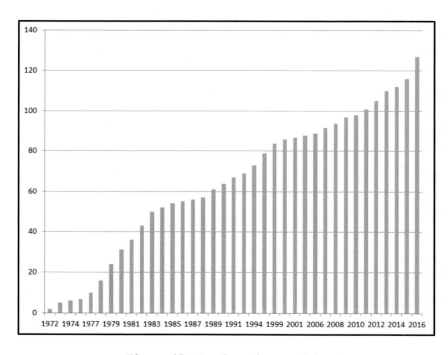

Figure 48: Number of resort islands

With its 14 beds, Coco Privé Kuda Hithi Island is a tiny resort. While the largest resort, the Sun Island Resort offers 852 beds.

With the advent of helicopters and then seaplanes, hotels are gradually moving away from the capital. First there is the construction of the Banyan Tree and the Four Seasons in 1977, about 18 kilometers from the capital. The opening of the Kuramathi Tourist Resort marks the arrival of resorts in the north of the country. The following year, it is again the islands located less than ten to twenty kilometers from Malé that are taken by storm but then a new Maldivian space conquest begins in 1979. Hotels are built at 20, then 23, then 39 and finally at 150 kilometers from the capital. From the year 2007, the opening of the Canareef Resort Maldives marks a period of construction of resort islands very far from Malé: on average, the resorts built between 2007 and 2016 are located 214 km from Malé against 60 km between 1972 and 2006.

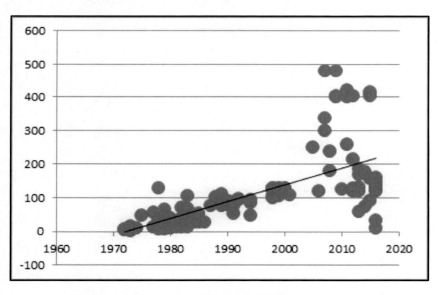

Figure 49: Distances between resorts and Malé (km)

What is astonishing is that the initial capacity of reception, i.e. the number of beds at the inauguration of the resort islands is not proportional to the year of opening nor to the distance from Malé. It remains constant at about 100 beds of initial capacity if we ignore the huge Sun Island Resort & Spa of 700 beds. One could have thought the opposite because moving away from Malé generates a logistical cost that the investors might have wanted to compensate by a large number of clients. But no, the Canareef Resort, for example, located 480 km from Malé, offers only 106 beds.

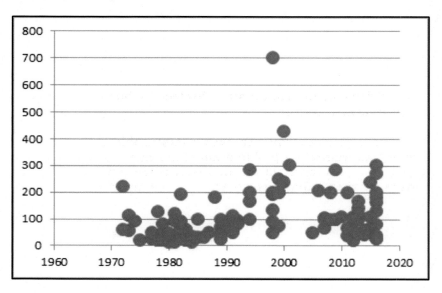

Figure 50: Initial capacities of the resort islands (no. beds)

The buildings located on a typical resort island include villas, restaurants, cafes, stores, lounges, bars, discos, spas and diving schools. Part of the island also contains staff accommodations and services such as restaurants, electricity generation, a laundry and a sewage treatment plant. The stores on the island offer a wide range of products, such as souvenirs, but prices are generally higher than on Malé because of their obvious monopoly position on the island.

Despite the country's religious policy, in order not to disturb or deter tourists, the consumption of alcohol, ham, cold cuts, and bacon for breakfast is fully permitted within the luxury hotels. Similarly, there are no clothing restrictions for female tourists. The copious all-inclusive buffets give the impression of eating all the time. Some tourists sometimes drop a "is it still time to eat?"

The tourist drinks mineral water all day long (while there are no mountains or springs in the Maldives) and can find without raising an eyebrow, famous drinks like Perrier, Evian, Orangina, Coca-Cola and alcohol in bars or in his small hotel room refrigerator while a few kilometers away, the vast majority of Maldivians drink rainwater collected in buckets or used bottles attached to trees.

This need to collect rainwater has a catastrophic impact on the lives of Maldivians: the proliferation of mosquitoes. While these are eradicated every night on the resort islands with a sprayed mixture of diesel and insecticide, on the inhabited islands, mosquitoes swarm by taking birth in the rainwater collection tanks.

On excursions to inhabited islands, tourists are amazed to see how many mosquitoes are circling around them when there are none at their resort.

Figure 51: Contrast between resort island (top) and inhabited island (bottom)

112

To ensure a perfect customer experience, all means are good: mosquito control ensures that no tourist will come across the slightest mosquito during their dream stay. The solution is radical: every night, an opaque pesticide smoke is sprayed into every nook and cranny of the resort islands. No leaves or trees should escape the thick chemical fog. The spraying is carried out at night in order not to scare tourists. However, they have strong risks to breathe this pungent smelling cloud. So pungent that the men who spread it are equipped with a large protective mask and a waterproof suit.

Figure 52: Men Spreading Mosquito Repellent

The product is called Pynosect 10 and is presented by its manufacturer as an effective killer of insects: ants, bedbugs, mosquitoes, silverfish, cockroaches and wasps. It is a Singaporean company, Agro Technic Pte Ltd who markets it, specifying on its official website that this product is extremely dangerous for fish.

Its toxicity is moderate. According to the WHO, it is ranked third out of five on the scale of dangerousness of pesticides. One of its constituents is carcinogenic: permethrin. Like other pyrethroids, permethrin is neurotoxic. Its toxicity in humans has not yet been classified, but it is very harmful to many animals, especially cats and cold-blooded animals such as amphibians or insects. In mammals, skin absorption is very slow compared to the degradation of permethrin in the body, especially by the liver. Similarly, digestive absorption is very low. The toxic risk is therefore minor for mammals under normal dosing conditions, with the exception of cats. It would therefore seem that mosquito control fumes from resort islands are not very toxic, especially if tourists are kept away during the spraying.

The tourist is perfectly enclaved in the dream he has sought: beach, good weather, nature (controlled, as we have seen, with mosquito control), abundant food and Western-style living conditions. An artificial universe is created from scratch for him, a mixture of nature and comfort. The ultimate accommodation sought is the stilted villa or water villa. Symbol of other competing paradise countries such as Bora-Bora in French Polynesia, the villa on piles in the Maldives does not date back to the first resorts installed in 1972. The first two hotels in the Maldives, Kurumba and Bandos did not have water villas on piles and at the time of writing this book still do not offer any. It is the third hotel, opened in 1973, the Laguna Beach which introduces the notion of room above the lagoon.

Then it was advertising that did its work: travel agencies wanted to give a romantic aura to the villas on piles: its isolation predestined it for honeymoons and its exorbitant price restricted it to special occasions.

Figure 53: Villa on piles seen from the outside

The interior of a villa on piles is not at all a fisherman's hut. The tourist would not want it. There are usually barely two rooms: the bedroom and the bathroom, which is usually huge. The bathroom is hidden while the bedroom is more open to the outside of the lagoon to allow the tourist to see the sea 24 hours a day if he wishes.

A clever arrangement prevents neighboring tourists from seeing each other. The room has a king-size bed, air conditioning, a television with international channels such as CNN or TV5Monde, a DVD or Blu-Ray player, a Wifi connection, a coffee maker, a minibar, armchairs, sometimes a coffee table with a glass bottom allowing you to see the fish passing under the villa.

The bathroom usually has a toilet, double washbasin, shower, bathtub, cosmetics, a huge mirror, hair dryer, iron. On the outside terrace of the villa on piles, there are two or three deckchairs and in the fancier cases, swings, slide, swimming pool or jacuzzi.

Figure 54: Piles villa from the inside

Nothing is missing in these ultra-equipped and ultra-connected bungalows. It is under the wooden jetties that electrical cables, pipes and air conditioning systems connect the villa on piles to the rest of humanity. Large PVC pipes carry the wastewater from the villas to the sewage treatment plant. This is not very glamorous and the tourist who swims under the wooden piers will tend to be afraid of getting drops on his head. Fortunately, if there is a drop, it will probably be due to condensation from the air conditioners.

Figure 55: Pipes and cables under wooden walkways

Generally, even without any kitchen, the villas on piles may never be left for the whole stay, since room service is provided. For those who accept to walk, on the other hand, you just have to leave the villa, take the wooden jetties to reach the restaurant(s) built on the island.

Figure 56: Villa on piles and its dream environment

During the days, the particular pleasure of those who have opted for this kind of accommodation will be to go down to the sea without even having to walk on sand or plan to lock your villa. No bags to prepare. No walking to do. Depending on the time of day, the sea can be low or high which will give different types of activities. In the case of high tides, there are many opportunities to meet marine animals, especially if the silence of the lagoon is respected: sharks, turtles, octopus, squid, swordfish.

At low tide, on the other hand, it will be necessary to walk on the coral, which turns out, in fact, rather painful! Bathing shoes are to be provided. But the low tide offers the opportunity to easily move away in the lagoon to take pictures.

Stilted villas are not the only type of accommodation. A more economical range of accommodation exists and is called a beach villa or beach villa. These are simply little houses built on the sand.

The main activity is the absence of activity

Tourist couples, often newlyweds, are not supposed to be short of ideas to keep busy, but this is not strictly speaking an active vacation offer that the Maldives has to offer. The idea is above all to immerse oneself in the life of Robinson Crusoe without any inconvenience. The coupling with the concept of "all-inclusive" is therefore not very obvious. Robinson Crusoe is known to be a hard worker. Yet on these islands, any form of effort is useless. There are no stairs to climb, no means of transportation (except for small golf carts), no meals to prepare, no supermarkets to frequent. Everything is done to stop at least once in one's life from being a slave to subway-work-asleep life. Meals are served almost all day long from 7 am to 11 pm and fruit baskets are laid out in the rooms. In case of heavy rain (which happens almost only at night), the tourist is not supposed to lack anything and can indulge in reading or surfing on his wifi tablet.

On the inhabited islands, the offer of entertainment is very limited. For tourists, the situation is different: the offer of activities abounds and reaches peaks of originality and variety. The specialized site "DreamingOfMaldives.com" states that there are at least 40 things to do in the Maldives.

Here is the complete list:

1. Fly aboard a seaplane and take extraordinary photos. It is a must since the seaplane has become the only means of transport between the capital and the resort islands.
2. Explore the underwater world.
3. Discover each other. This is a very common commercial argument: the Maldives is a great place for honeymooners. Nothing is done to welcome groups or children at most resorts.
4. Live the adventure on a desert island. Thanks to the large number of islands and the high prices of the

stays, the Maldives offers the possibility to be often alone or little disturbed.

5. Get lost on a sandbank in the middle of nowhere. A sandbank is an island without vegetation: it represents isolation from the usual daily life of tourists.

6. Living in a villa on piles. This concept does not only exist in the Maldives but is a great success.

7. Take a cruise on a sailing boat. Of course, we are talking about a sailboat with all the comfort and not a traditional boat conducive to seasickness.

8. Go in search of dolphins.

9. To survey the lanes of Malé. In fact, this activity is not recommended because on the one hand, it requires a return to the classic urban life (pollution, traffic jams, ...) and on the other hand, the political climate pushes the French authorities to post the following notice: "Due to recent political developments in the archipelago and the high risk of violent demonstrations, it is recommended to suspend all non-essential travel in the city of Malé and the villages of the archipelago."

10. Try new water sports on the blue lagoon. Like for example the flyboard: a type of water jetpack connected to a personal watercraft (a jet ski) that supplies it with pressurized water. The pilot stands on a platform connected by a long hose to the boat, his feet are secured by a pair of boots like snowboards. The pressurized water produced by the PWC's water jet is directed to jet nozzles and provides thrust that allows the pilot to climb up to fifteen meters in the air or dive headfirst into the water.

11. Big game fishing. It is the only activity that will give the impression of living like a Maldivian.

12. Party and dance on the sand of a tropical island. This activity is not only inaccessible to Maldivians but is outright forbidden to them.

13. Wake up at dawn to contemplate the sunrise over the archipelago.

14. Swing in a hammock and let your ideas run free.

15. Observe wildlife. The wildlife is mainly underwater but there are also crabs, birds and bats.

Figure 57: Submarine for tourists

16. Visit the island of Utheemu and discover 450 years of Maldivian history. This island was one of the theaters of war between the Maldives and Portugal in 1573. Some of the sultans who ruled the Maldives were originally from Utheemu. Finally, from 1602 to 1607, a Frenchman, François Pyrard de Laval settled there and wrote a work in three volumes considered as the first book of history of the Maldives.
17. Take the time to talk with the locals and discover their lives on the islands. This is an illusion because the language barrier can hardly be lifted by the level of English of the Maldivians.
18. Get healthy by swimming in an infinity pool on the lagoon.
19. Take sublime photos.

20. Spend the evening on the beach for a special dinner. The magic of the moment will be proportional to the amount of mosquito repellent spread by the hotel.
21. See divinely beautiful sunsets.
22. Play and marvel with fluorescent plankton. It's a surreal show: a seashore that sparkles with a thousand lights, not at sunset but at night, in an electric and strange blue like the one we see in Avatar. Present on the surface, these microorganisms that make whales happy (like the one that appears in the movie "Life of Pi") are deposited on the beach with the waves. Their phosphorescence, similar to that of fireflies, is linked to a state of stress: they light up the entire beach, where the waves touch the sand and agitate the small creatures. They also light up under pressure, when people walk on the sand.
23. Go in search of sea turtles and swim with them.
24. Play Robinson on heavenly beaches.
25. Surf on sublime waves.
26. Celebrate your wedding vows or your love for each other on a beach of blond sand. The resort islands of the Maldives gladly offer beach facilities made of white canvas and flower petals to celebrate weddings. In a video broadcast on social networks in 2010, the ceremony turned into a humiliation. The Sun Aqua Vilu Reef Maldives hotel organizes such ceremonies for the modest sum of US$1,300. At that price, a couple of European tourists had no idea they would be discreetly insulted in the Divehi language. The man playing the role of the priest used a solemn tone and religious gestures but, in the end, poured a torrent of hatred on the young couple: "Your marriage is not valid. You are the kind of people who cannot have a real marriage. You are unfaithful. You fornicate and have lots of children. You drink alcohol and eat pork. "People who understand the Maldivian language report that in the rest of the video, the man evokes terms such as bestiality, sexually transmitted diseases and

homosexuality. At the end of the ceremony, unsuspecting tourists are invited to plant a small coconut tree, but the insults still rain down. The man comments on the bride's chest. This video caused a scandal and the hotel had to apologize. The President of the Maldives, Mohamed Nasheed, in a statement condemned the incident as absolutely shameful and even called the couple to apologize on behalf of the Maldivians. Following this incident, the Ministry of Tourism passed a law which obliges the resorts to celebrate the renewal of vows in the language of the spouses. Since marriages of non-Muslims are forbidden in the Maldives, the resorts have opted for the term "renewal of vows".

27. Go to the spa to regenerate.

Figure 58: Massage over water

28. Parachute jumping over islands and blue lagoons.
29. Rent a seaplane for a tour of the islands. Still count between 250 and 450 dollars.
30. Sleep under the stars.
31. Rent a dhoni and sail like the Maldivians. It is the traditional boat of the country. Of a very flared shape, rather comparable to a drakkar, they measure between six and twelve meters, carry a crew of four to eight people and sail.
32. Discover the craft industry of the Maldives.
33. Going to the movies on the beach.

Figure 59: Outdoor cinema for tourists

34. Doing yoga.

35. Get a massage under water. This sentence has two meanings. It is possible to have a massage of the body immersed in water. But beyond that, the Huvafenfushi Hotel has a glass wall spa immersed in the middle of its lagoon.
36. Watch baby sharks learn how to hunt at the shoreline.
37. Tasting Great Wines, with your feet in the lagoon.
38. Slide on the clear waters of a sand bank.
39. Swim with whale sharks.
40. And finally, practice the art of doing nothing!

In addition, there are four golf courses, all reserved for the clients of their respective resorts: Kuredu Resort & Spa, Meeru Island Resort & Spa, Velaa Private Island and Shangri-La Villingili Resort & Spa.

Figure 60: Golf of Shangri-La

Inverted Aquariums

The big luxury hotels are in fierce competition to attract tourists: they must both offer perfect service and distinguish themselves with unique attractions. A race that sometimes comes at the expense of the environmental footprint, even though these islands are one of the most fragile ecosystems in the world.

As such, let's take the example of the restaurant in "inverted aquarium": the Ithaa Undersee Restaurant. It is an eight-million-euro glass dome immersed six meters deep in the lagoon of Rangali Island under which holidaymakers of the Conrad Maldives Rangali can enjoy dishes among the fish.

Ranked "the world's most beautiful restaurant" by the New York Daily in 2014, it offers a 180-degree panoramic view of the coral gardens.

Figure 61: The Conrad Maldives Rangali Island Restaurant

The originality of this construction made this restaurant immediately famous. How not to succumb to the pictures of this romantic glass bubble in the middle of the fish? Culinary luxury is also on the plate: the chef, Bjoern Oever, has no budget limits and offers a top-of-the-range, globalized menu for customers who are not too keen on prices.

195 USD per person at lunch (children's menu at the same price). 320 US dollars per person at dinner (children not accepted in the evening). At this price, the ingredients come from all over the world, regardless of the carbon footprint required to transport them: poached lobster, dried tuna, miso soup with squid ink, crispy tofu, fresh oysters, edamame peas, Bresse chicken, cheesecake, caviar, foie gras, truffle, quail eggs, beef filet, Bolivian chocolate, ...

But tourists don't know everything. The reefs visible from the inside of the glass bubble are a staging: concrete blocks have been submerged and corals uprooted and then replanted. The reason behind this artifice is that at this depth, there are not naturally many coral reefs.

All food is imported from Rungis and received at Malé airport. The restaurant manager does not hide his disinterest in the carbon footprint of such logistics. Potentially, the ingredients contained in the plates therefore travel several thousand kilometers by plane. Tourists thus become "distavores"; a neologism designating a person who eats products from far away. However, this kind of excess is not unique to this particular restaurant.

Aperitif
Oscietra caviar
Served with dill sour cream and lemongrass blinis

Amuse bouche
Foie gras and truffle dumpling
Accompanied with cucumber and green grape consommé

Appetizer
Carabineros prawn tartare
Served with plaintain chips and quail egg gravlax

Entrée
Reef lobster stuffed calamarata pasta
With burrata and lemongrass veloute

Cleanse
Green apple and ginger sorbet

Main
Coconut crusted légine
Served with curry bisque, steamed sea beans and spicy sea snails
Or
Sous vide veal tenderloin
Served with yabby ragout, smoked garlic and celery root purée,
charcoaled kohlrabi and black garlic gnocchi

Dessert
Bolivian cru sauvage chocolate and kaffir lime panna cotta
With coconut sorbet and aerated chocolate

Figure 62: Ithaa Dinner Map

In another hotel, the Niyama Maldives, we find a similar concept. In turn bar, restaurant then nightclub, since August 2012, the Subsix answers to all those who wish to move their body in the middle of the fishes. They must then go to this island of the atoll of Dhaalu, 175 kilometers southwest of Malé.

Figure 63: Brides and grooms in front of the windows of the Subsix

Designed by a Sri Lankan submarine manufacturer, this restaurant protects its guests with 10-centimeter thick glass. The structure had to be manufactured on the surface, then brought by boat to its final site and submerged by pouring concrete for a week. Then, coral reefs were planted all around because otherwise the view would be of no visual interest.

The objective for the hotel is to attract a more party-oriented clientele than the usual tourists who are usually young couples. The irony of this kind of submerged restaurant is cruel: it is estimated that by the year 2100, the entire Maldives will have sunk under the rising oceans.

Socio-economic impact

But who do these big luxury hotels belong to? The resort islands belong to large international groups such as Hilton, Sheraton, Shangri-La. But these companies need a local partner, i.e. a Maldivian who is generally high-ranking and/or very rich in order to obtain the concession on the island. This Maldivian then becomes the only successful national in the business. The management of the resort is always entrusted to Westerners, and the manual work such as cleaning or cooking is entrusted to immigrants who are very hard-working, such as Nepalese or Bangladeshis for example.

There are a few Maldivians in the workforce but it is rare. They suffer real discrimination. Maldivian women are even rarer. They account for 3% of the employees of resort islands for really restricted jobs: sweeper or cook of Maldivian dishes. There is a simple explanation for this absence: we don't want to confront women with the non-Muslim practices of tourists, i.e. we don't want to expose them to the consumption of alcohol, pork or the sight of tiny bikinis. It is the parents of young Maldivian women who are the most vehement. Very possessive, they are afraid that their daughters will be tempted to do "bad things like Europeans" if they work in a hotel.

For the Maldivian population, the effects of mass tourism are therefore ambiguous. Tourism is a gold mine: the budgets allocated to education, health, transport and communications have risen from about 53 million rufiyaa in 1984 to more than 1,330 million in 2000. On a national scale, the main consequence of this has been the uniform equipment of the various atolls, particularly in schools and health structures. There is no difference between the schooling rates of the tourist atolls and those of the other atolls. The observation is the same in the health sector, where the redistribution of the benefits of development has been equitable throughout the country (UNDP-MPND, 2000). In the early 1980s, eight years after the opening of the first resort islands, five regional hospitals were put into service - in addition to the national hospital created in 1960 - for the entire territory on Haa Alifu, Raa, Meemu, Gaafu Dhaalu and Addu. It seems, therefore, that the growth in tourism revenues has made it possible to equip the infrastructure.

At the individual level, the effects are more negative. In 2000, less than 3% of hotel employees were Maldivian, so the effect on employment is not obvious. Wages are modest and transportation between islands is too expensive for employees to use on a daily basis. As a result, they live a long way from their families when they work and sleep on a resort island. They have to sleep on a small part of the island, away from tourists. The area reserved for them is less welcoming than the tourist area: noisy generator, water purification plant, desalination plant, kitchens, compost, temporary dump. These backstage areas are forbidden to tourists. Employees are surrounded by foreigners (other employees and holidaymakers). For the first time in their lives, Maldivians are confronted with non-Muslim practices such as nudity, alcohol and pork products. Such a context upsets the identity and social references of local workers and generates deviant behaviors (homosexuality, alcohol and drug consumption, ...) in relation to Maldivian societal norms. Beyond that, the distance from the father weakens the family structure, even though it is traditionally matriarchal.

On each resort island, a mini feudal system is organized. De facto, the director of the hotel is the mayor of the island. The HRD is the equivalent of the chief of police. Then underneath, several castes stack up. The directors, kitchen brigade chiefs, sommeliers belong to a certain nobility. They are almost always European and don't stay long, but intend to add their Maldivian experience on their CV. The second rank consists of all the small chiefs such as accountants, barmen, human resources who are Sri Lankan, Indian or Maldivian. And then at the very bottom of the ladder, there is the proletariat: waiters, cooks, maintenance staff, receptionists, gardeners. They are Nepalese or Bangladeshis who live crammed into dormitories. They are not allowed to leave the island even outside working hours, are not allowed to enter the management offices and are not allowed to fraternize among themselves or to meet in unions.

In fact, strikes and mini-state coups are legion. It is easy to imagine the working-class rebelling against the ruling class by discovering, for example, the inequalities in the redistribution of the tip pool among the wage earners. As peasants armed with pitchforks and torches, we sometimes find mutinies in the middle of the hotel in the form of ransacking the manager's room or physically attacking the hotel owner. The director of the Kurumba, a Frenchman, had the bitter experience in 2010 when strikers decided to scare off all holidaymakers, forcing the hotel to evacuate them to a competing hotel. The Frenchman found himself chased by his own employees until the police intervened, arriving by boat. The head office of this hotel had to resolve to respond to the grievances of the proletariat: wage increases, renovation of the dormitories.

In August 2011, the deputies with the most financial ties to the resort islands discreetly passed a law that outright forbids strikes.

Religious impact

The country, whose state religion is a rigorous Islam, has organized itself to avoid as much contact as possible between tourists bringing in foreign currency and the inhabitants who reside on separate islands. In addition, customs officials are very careful about the contents of tourists' luggage, which must not contain alcohol or erotic or religious (other than Muslim) objects or books. Books or objects of a Jewish, Christian, Buddhist, or Hindu nature are totally prohibited, even for personal use. It is not allowed to visit by oneself places other than the resort island in which the stay has been booked, nor to come into contact with the population, except hotel staff. That said, excursions to inhabited islands are organized and supervised but not prohibited. The tourist then discovers the enormous difference in treatment and comfort between the resort islands and the inhabited islands.

Segregation is therefore not racial but simply religious and economic. It allows for a sleight of hand: being a strict Muslim country but without denying itself the financial manna of rich tourists.

This religious segregation is not as absolute as one might think. For example, on the island of Maafushi, there is a strange mixture of genres since it is both an island inhabited by Maldivians and an island housing the largest prison in the country and yet it is home to a few hotels of modest size and amenities and souvenir stores. The strict separation between Maldivians and tourists on different islands was an idea of ex-president Gayoom, while ex-president Nasheed found it difficult to live with the idea that only 50 Maldivians were taking advantage of the resort island system. So, he wanted smaller hotels, hostels, to be built directly on islands inhabited by Maldivians to bring them closer to the economic benefits of tourism. But this mixture of genres was perceived as a huge risk of confronting the population with bikinis, beer and bacon. By 2013, nearly 171 hostels located on islands inhabited by Maldivians had opened their doors. Economically speaking, the business is a good idea. On Maafushi, for example, having authorized the construction of hotels and thus the reception of tourists has increased the average income of the inhabitants from $600 to $4,424 per month. It has become one of the islands where Maldivians are the richest.

There is something that must be of concern to anyone interested in the economy of the Maldives: how can a country that is so respectful of Islam and Sharia law allow the consumption of pork and alcohol on its territory? Yet Islamic law is very clear: if alcohol is haram (forbidden by Islam), then all the economic ramifications that flow from it should also be forbidden. In principle, it is even forbidden to use money from the profits from the sale of a haram product. Therefore, in principle, the Maldives should not levy any taxes, nothing, not a penny from the resort islands. The trick used by the Muslim government to hide its face (voluntary pun) is to consider that the resort islands are uninhabited and therefore nothing happens there, either halal or haram. Yet on these so-called uninhabited islands, there are hotel staff including Maldivians. The question regularly rages between the two major political parties of the country. For pork nothing is clearly stated but for alcohol, a license granted to each hotel gives the right to serve only foreigners. For the rest of the country it is absolute prohibition. This prohibition in the name of Islam is fiercely defended by the Maldivian owners of resort islands who, paradoxically, are major importers of alcohol. Indeed, this allows them to be in a monopoly situation.

But Maldivians, no more ascetic than any other people, like to party and like to drink. It is thus a few kilometers away, in Sri Lanka, that one finds the well-off Maldivians, glass in hand in the bars of Colombo. They are not used to drinking alcohol, and generally end up fainting or vomiting everywhere, leaving a catastrophic image of their country to the Sri Lankans.

One would think that the people who own or manage the luxury hotels for tourists are in conflict with the good Muslims of the Maldives. This is not the case. Take the example of Gasim Ibrahim who, in a political meeting, chanted "I have carried out my religious and national obligations courageously thanks to Allah. With Allah's will I was able to succeed. Two years before this sentence was uttered, however, Gasim Ibrahim was already the largest importer of haram products in the Maldives, with his various island hotels importing 121,000 liters of beer, 2,048 liters of whisky, 3,600 liters of vodka and 219 kilos of pork per year.

Ecological impact

The Maldives needs energy to make this dream machine work. A lot of energy.

The archipelago relies essentially on fossil fuels. There is no nuclear power plant in the Maldives.

Energy source	Production (kWh)	Percentage
Oil	876 million	96,2 %
Renewable	34 million	03,8 %
Others	0	0,00 %

The renewable energies exploited in the Maldives are wind, solar, biomass and geothermal. But as the table above shows, this is negligible compared to the use of oil.

The islands are far away from each other and therefore it is impossible to mutualize the means of production: each island must have its own power plant on its soil. In terms of electricity production, the Maldives generates 325 million kWh per year, i.e. about 761 kWh per inhabitant. In France it is 6,519 kWh per person, so treating the Maldives as an electric abyss would be excessive. What is shocking is the source of energy: oil.

It is nevertheless striking: a country located at the equator, therefore flooded with sunshine all year round and yet has virtually no solar panels to produce electricity. This was the observation made by Mike Mason, a British engineer, in 2010 when he became an advisor to President Nasheed. The vast majority of the islands produce their electricity from diesel generators at a particularly poor rate of return. Electricity costs about $0.70 per kWh on the islands and $0.28 per kWh in Malé. For comparison, in France, electricity costs about $0.15 per kWh.

With a clever assembly of solar panels and batteries, Mason predicts that the Maldives will spend only $0.23 per kWh during the day and $0.44 per kWh at night. He then sets up an ambitious project to cover the islands with solar panels in order to produce 90% solar-generated electricity. With his project, Mason easily secured $200 million in foreign investment and promises of future investments of more than $2 billion.

The World Bank is enthusiastic and describes the project as the most "exciting and transformative" of all the issues it is pursuing.

Yes, but here it is, the day planned to materialize the contract is ill-chosen: on February 7, 2012, President Mohamed Nasheed was overthrown by a crowd of rebel police officers. The investors slam the door and Mason takes a plane ticket and leaves the Maldives. Mason will estimate that this event destroyed in one day two to three billion dollars of investment and condemned the country to a complete dependence on diesel.

Air conditioning

The villas need to be air-conditioned abundantly because the average temperature in the Maldives is 30 degrees all year round. Of course, this temperature is what tourists are looking for but they do not accept this stifling heat in closed spaces, nor to sleep. Air conditioning is like everywhere else in the world a greedy technology.

However, one technology, the SWAC (Sea Water Air Conditioning), or in French, Climatisation à l'Eau Naturellement Froide (CENF) allows energy savings in the production of fresh air. The principle of this technology is to pump very cold water from the bottom of the oceans with a long borehole in order to bring it up into the installations and buildings. It promises 90% savings compared to conventional gas-fired air conditioning. The water found at depth in the Maldives can drop as much as 4° to 1,000 meters below sea level. Raising it requires electricity, but not as much as that consumed by a traditional air conditioner. At the surface, a device similar to a radiator exchanges the heat present in the hotel rooms with the cold pumped into the water and then the warm water is discharged into the sea.

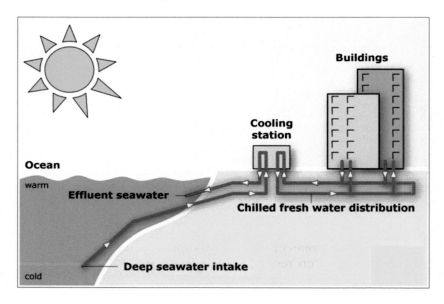

Figure 64: Schematic of the SWAC

Naturally Cold-Water Cooling has several advantages: it is a low cost, renewable energy air conditioning method for residential and commercial buildings in coastal areas. It uses only between 1/10th and 1/5th of the energy required by a conventional system, i.e. using a heat pump.

SWAC systems do not use any ozone-depleting gases. This is an important point for large installations, even if there are other environmentally friendly solutions.

In addition, these systems generate local employment. Indeed, their implementation requires workers and divers. The cost of the system is thus mostly reinjected into the local economy instead of being exported to energy-producing countries (oil, uranium, coal, etc.).

Several disadvantages are notable, however. SWAC systems require the close presence of a relatively large amount of deep water. The installation is expensive and labor-intensive. The system requires many elements for its construction and launching. For example, pipes can be several hundred meters long for large installations.

The major ecological question in this facility is what impact does this fresh water withdrawal and warm water discharge have on the corals? The optimal temperature for the coral is between 25 and 30 °C. If the temperature rises for too long, corals bleach and then die.

Desalination of sea water

As a countermeasure to the absence of watercourses and to avoid rainwater harvesting that favors mosquitoes, the resort islands opt for seawater desalination. There are several methods, all of which require electricity or fuel. The most well-known is of course distillation: sea water is boiled and the unsalted water vapor is condensed against a cold wall in order to return it to a liquid state. The salt remains at the bottom of the initial tank.

But the most modern and most used technique is reverse osmosis. It is a technology that is difficult to explain to the layman but which causes the separation of salt and water through ultrafiltration under pressure through membranes whose pores are holes so small that the mineral salts remain retained. It consumes about 5 kWh to treat one cubic meter of water. Reverse osmosis actually produces two liquids: for 100 liters of seawater, this technology generates 50 liters of very salty water and 50 liters of fresh water. The 50 liters of very salty water are discharged into the sea and the 50 liters of fresh water are piped to the taps.

For the anecdote, the Coca-Cola factory in Malé is the only one in the world that produces the famous soda from (desalinated) sea water.

The waste

Another energy-demanding necessity is the arrival of goods and the departure of waste. Each resort island must arrange to have the many goods that tourists consume (food, toilet paper, sheets, cosmetics, mosquito repellent, etc.) flown in by seaplane or boat and must dispose of the accumulated waste (packaging, uneaten food and even toilet waste) on a daily basis. The task is immense and complex: each hotel must find a way to reprocess its wastewater (especially from the toilets) while avoiding as much as possible the discharge of dirty water into the lagoon in which the holidaymakers splash around.

The trick again comes from electricity: local wastewater treatment plants remove the pathogenic content of the wastewater, then a long underwater pipe carries the remaining water away from the tourists and discharges everything into the sea, preferably further than the reef. Heavy residues are accumulated and leave the island by boat.

However, the dumping of sewage into the Indian Ocean is no more scandalous in the Maldives than in the rest of the world.

On their official website, some hotels even announce that they do not throw anything into the sea. For example, the Kurumba hotel displays "wastewater from toilets, bathrooms and kitchens is treated in a treatment plant where it is naturally purified and then used to water the gardens. Absolutely no impure water reaches the surrounding crystalline waters.

Figure 65: Discharge of Wastewater to Sea

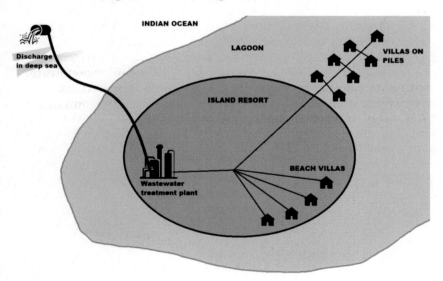

Figure 66: Wastewater management on a resort island

Beyond all the energy considerations, it is worth mentioning the pollution caused by the tourists themselves.

The suntan lotion

The sun hits hard in the Maldives and every good tourist knows that it is necessary to apply sunscreen.

According to an EHP (Environmental Health Perpectives) study conducted by Professor Donovaro, sunscreens used to protect against solar radiation have a negative impact on coral reefs. This is in addition to the many other effects of our society such as global warming, ocean pollution and environmental destruction. Experiments have been conducted in different seas around the globe and have shown that certain UV (ultraviolet) filtering components contained in many sunscreens can stimulate the development of infections that destroy zooxanthellae, a microalga that lives in symbiosis with the coral and is necessary for its development. Thus, the coral bleaches and dies. It is estimated today that more than 50% of the world's coral reefs are in poor health. It is easy to understand what is happening on beaches where many tourists are concentrated near coral reefs as in Thailand, Mexico or the Caribbean. Every year, it is estimated that more than 4,000 tons of sunscreen are found in the world's seas. Already some marine reserves, such as the Tulum Biosphere Reserve in Mexico, prohibit the use of sunscreen creams based on chemical filters. What solutions to protect yourself while respecting the marine environment? There are two types of sun creams. Sun creams with chemical filters that are not biodegradable and that by penetrating the skin can irritate or trigger allergies. It is these creams that once in the water are found in marine animals and threaten coral reefs. Sun creams with mineral filters of zinc or titanium are safe, the minerals do not penetrate the skin and do not cause allergies. They are designed to limit the impact on marine ecosystems. It is advisable for the sunblock to privilege the organic lotions containing mineral filters. But the best solution remains the T-shirt and a cap.

Luxury real estate

In this universe of Robinson Crusoe of the rich, it is not only the resort islands which are proposed to the tourists. Luxury real estate is also on the niche to offer for sale or rent, villas on piles or on the beach. Whoever has the means can then afford a real palace in the middle of the Indian Ocean.

Figure 67: 9-bedroom villa for 12 million euros

Figure 68: Villa on piles at 3 million euros

The site privateislandsonline.com even offers for sale entire uninhabited islands for about six million US dollars.

Figure 69: Sales site of uninhabited islands

The rates can be scary, but in fact, it's very cheap! For comparison, an uninhabited island in Thailand sells for an average of $160 million and an island in Florida for $95 million. Kuramaadhoo, on the illustration above sells for six million dollars or 5.2 million euros. It has the shape of a disk with a radius of 200 meters, so its surface area is 125,000 square meters. Its price per square meter is therefore 42 euros/m². For comparison, the average price of building land in France is 128 euros/m².

Figure 70: Kuramaadhoo Island

The tsunami of December 26, 2004

The December 26, 2004 earthquake in the Indian Ocean is an earthquake that occurred off the Indonesian island of Sumatra with a magnitude of 9.1 to 9.31. The epicenter is located at the border of the Eurasian and Indo-Australian tectonic plates. This earthquake had the third strongest magnitude ever recorded in the world. It lifted a 1,600-kilometer long strip of the ocean floor to a height of six meters.

146

In the minutes and hours following the start of the earthquake, a tsunami, in some places over 30 meters high, struck Indonesia, the coasts of Sri Lanka and southern India, and western Thailand. The death toll is estimated to be at least 250,000 people, including nearly 170,000 in Indonesia, 31,000 in Sri Lanka, 16,400 in India and 5,400 in Thailand, according to official estimates. It is one of the ten deadliest earthquakes and the worst tsunami in history. It has claimed victims all around the Indian Ocean.

At 9:23 a.m., the Maldives are affected.

An inhabitant of Malé speaks about it as follows: "The first thing that made me think that something was happening was when I heard the din in the streets near the sea. There were people walking around Malé with their clothes wet to the chest. We turned on the TV and they were saying that a tsunami had hit the Maldives. The TV presenter started crying and had to stop reading his script. I didn't even know what the word tsunami meant. I learned the word that day."

During the earthquake, 187 of the 200 inhabited islands of the Maldives, with 188,450 inhabitants and about 17,000 tourists at the time of the tragedy, were at least partially invaded by the waters, 29% of them on more than a third of their surface and 35% in their entirety. In total, 57% of the country's inhabited surface area was more or less submerged. There were 82 deaths and 22 missing, 15% of the population was affected by this disaster, mostly outside Malé. 12,802 people had to be displaced. 3,997 of the country's 29,135 buildings, or 14% of the total, were affected by the tsunami, of which 1,850 were completely destroyed. The country lost nearly 60% of its GNP, which depends mainly on fishing and tourism. As of March 2005, 17 resort islands were closed, representing 25% of the accommodation potential (17,618 beds before the tsunami) and at the end of 2005, several establishments had still not reopened.

Figure 71: Seawater in the streets of Malé

Figure 72: 2004 Tsunami Memorial, Malé

In an official document entitled "Maldives: One Year After the Tsunami," the government admits that such a disaster seemed so far away in the minds of many that there were no operational plans or resources to respond.

After the total loss of telecommunications facilities on 182 islands for more than ten hours, it was impossible to immediately measure the extent of the disaster. As contact was established with the distant islands, the extent of the devastation inflicted by the wave became evident. The island ramparts were destroyed on most of the islands causing severe flooding. In some cases, the entire island was submerged. 53 of the 199 inhabited islands were heavily damaged. Of course, the floods destroyed the electricity generating stations and contaminated the drinking water supplies. The essential infrastructure to connect the rest of the world: the landing stages and ports have been severely damaged. The tsunami also destroyed roads, agricultural production and fishing boats.

Figure 73: Building with water on the first floor

The National Security Service (NSS) immediately triggers a series of search and rescue operations and logistical missions. Within three days, the Coast Guard managed to visit all the inhabited islands and set up coordination centers in groups of atolls. From day one, the priority was to re-establish communication with each atoll. The Coast Guard, fishermen and commercial vessels then use radio frequencies to relay information between the islands and the coordination centers.

Several foreign food assistances arrive by boat. The Pakistani army is in charge of recovering all the tourists isolated in the resort islands in order to allow them to reach an international airport. The Bangladeshi army offers to help clean up and evacuate the sick and wounded. The French Navy is also carrying out medical evacuations and assisting with food distribution and the repair of electrical generators. The U.S. Army is providing drinking water. The British army brings landing barges for supply helicopters.

A Maldivian survivor testifies to the situation: "We received food from several sources. People from Malé sent us fresh or canned fish, the government gave us rice, and other groups sent us unusual food from countries I had never heard of in my life.

After this emergency phase comes the delicate problem of housing. The Maldives has no experience in dealing with the displaced, but it does manage to provide decent housing for families.

At the time, the chief of the island of Dhiggaru speaks about it as follows: "People can't wait to have a new home. You can read the discomfort in their eyes. Their lifestyle has deteriorated since the tsunami. People who have lost their homes are tired of living in crowded conditions with friends and family, but everyone is grateful to have someone to take them in. Many people on other islands are not so fortunate."

With the invaluable help of the International Federation of Red Cross and Red Crescent Societies, the Maldives can hastily build transitional shelters made of plywood and zinc roofing. Within six months, each shelter, consisting of two bedrooms, a bathroom with toilet and shower, has electricity, a kitchen and gas cooking facilities. Thus, the number of people living in tents or damaged housing will be greatly reduced by November 2005.

Situation of homeless people	Percentage as of November 2005
Lives in transitional shelter	46,3 %
Hosted with friends	35,0 %
Lives in a damaged house	18,2 %
Lives in a tent	00,5 %

But the hardest part is ahead: 2,879 houses have to be rebuilt and 5,215 repaired. Unfortunately, the Maldives faces more challenges than other countries. For example, simply transporting construction materials to the islands is a problem. Most of the islands no longer have landing stages.

At the same time, the price of diesel is rising to the point where a single boat trip can cost several thousand dollars.

As time passes and the number of houses in need of repair increases, the porous soil on the islands continues to be wet for months after the tsunami: inevitably, houses sink or tip over.

On Kandholhudhoo for example, instead of making repairs, it was decided to find an uninhabited island and to build everything there, ex-nihilo to accommodate 3 600 Maldivians without housing: schools, houses, gymnasiums, town hall, roads, ...

This island, Dhuvaafaru owes its settlement to the 2004 tsunami. It is the emblem of one of the first climatic settlements in history.

Figure 74: Dhuvaafaru

The inhabitants of Kandholhudhoo all moved to the island of Dhuvaafaru in new houses on December 14, 2008, four years after the tsunami.

Finally, the irony in this functioning is that the Maldives has so many uninhabited islands that it becomes a form of natural resource that can serve as a solution to all problems.

In fact, there are clues that there was a human presence on Dhuvaafaru a long time ago. A cemetery, a well, and a stone structure were discovered and protected during the construction of the dwellings. Legends tell that the former inhabitants of the island all left because the island is said to be haunted. It is even possible that the former inhabitants may have left at that time to populate Kandholhudhoo, the island destroyed by the tsunami.

Figure 75: Kandholhudhoo on Google Maps

Kandholhudhoo has become a ghost island. It is possible to visit it virtually with Google Maps. Tourists also come to Kandholhudhoo to get shivers when visiting a gloomy and abandoned place, or to raise awareness about the damage of a tsunami.

On the religious level, the 2004 tsunami had an unexpected impact. The low level of scientific knowledge among Maldivians led the majority of the population to justify the magnitude of the tsunami by the will of God. It is easier to believe that the tsunami was triggered by God to punish Maldivians for their lack of respect for the principles of Islam than to understand the mechanics of plate tectonics. So foreign Arab countries like Saudi Arabia or Pakistan jumped at the opportunity to provide Maldivians with all the help they needed to rebuild the destroyed mosques as well as free stays to go and study in madrasas.

It only took a wave for Maldivians to feel insufficiently Muslim, which had the effect of increasing the breeding ground for fundamentalism.

The attack in Malé in September 2007

On September 29, 2007, the only bomb attack in the history of the Maldives took place in Malé. Around 2:30 pm local time, a bomb explodes in the Sultan Park near the Islamic Center of Malé and wounds twelve foreign tourists: eight Chinese, two British and two Japanese. The bomb is handmade: a gas bottle, a washing machine motor and a cell phone.

Police arrested 12 suspects in 48 hours. Then, on October 3, in a press conference, the police commissioner made public the names of two main suspects: Ahmed Naseer and Moosa Inas, two Maldivians in their twenties. In December 2007, three men were sentenced to fifteen years in prison after confessing to the attack. Mohamed Sobah and Ahmed Naseer were released in August 2010. It is likely that some humanitarian missions following the 2004 tsunami were a pretext for the recruitment and indoctrination of some Maldivians by Pakistani terrorist groups.

The attack in Malé puts the country in turmoil. The country itself and the rest of the world then discovered that Al-Qaeda had managed to infiltrate some of the inhabitants of these paradise islands. The government, for its part, realizes that having so warmed the minds of Maldivians with Islam may have put tourism at risk.

After all, if an attack ever takes place in one of the resorts, not only will the targets (i.e. Western tourists) have no chance of escaping, but the entire tourist industry will be wiped out.

The Maldives is exactly on the border between the two worlds: The Westerners and the religious fundamentalists.

To assuage religious fundamentalists, President Nasheed opted for a strategy of openness, freedom of expression and a return to tradition. According to him, by allowing all Islamic movements to express themselves fully, they will have less need to act violently. He also wants to divert the attention of Maldivians by reminding them of their deep traditions: we now attend official ceremonies to the sound of bodu beru, the national instrument, accompanied by troops of pretty Maldivian dancers in traditional dress, that is to say without veils, wiggling their hips lasciviously. At some meetings, Nasheed does not hesitate to dance, and some CDM deputies sing. The opposition is outraged.

But all this comes too late. The various Islamist factions in the country are already formed. The attempt to diminish the influence of religion will cause many CDM votes to be lost in the parliamentary elections.

Political instability

The Maldives has a political history full of political upheavals and government reversals. The table below lists the endings of reigns or presidential terms of office of heads of state since 1900.

Head of State	End of term	Year
Muhammad Imaaduddeen VI	Reversal	1902
Muhammad Shamsuddeen III	Arrest	1934
Hassan Nooraddeen II	Forced abdication	1943
Abdul Majeed Didi	Natural death	1952
Mohamed Amin Didi	Reversal	1953
Ibrahim Muhammad Didi	Referendum	1954
Muhammad Fareed Didi	Referendum	1968
Ibrahim Nasir	End of term	1978
Maumoon Abdul Gayoom	End of term	2008
Mohamed Nasheed	Forced resignation*	2012
Mohammed Waheed Hassan	End of term	2013

Abdulla Yameen		

Forced resignation*: Mohamed Nasheed resigned at gunpoint to his head during a well-organized mutiny.

The recent political history of the Maldives is also a succession of demonstrations, riots, police violence, political violence, unrest and general social crises detailed in the next chapter. The most significant moments occurred in 2003, 2004, 2005, 2012, 2013, 2015 and 2018.

Policy

The first rulers of the Maldives came from two simultaneous dynasties: one proclaiming itself "of the Moon" and the other "of the Sun".

Solar Dynasty or Kingdom of Adeetta Vansa

Name	Start of reign	End of reign
King Adeettiya	Unknown	Unknown
?	Unknown	Unknown
Queen Damahaar	Unknown	Unknown

It is impossible to find writings testifying to the first king of the Maldives but it is admitted that he is an Indian prince coming from Kalinga (India). He settled in the Maldives and took the name of King Adeettiya. One of his descendants is Queen Damahaar.

Lunar Dynasty or Kingdom of Soma Vansa

Name	Start of reign	End of reign
King Balaadeettiya	Unknown	Unknown
King Loakaabarana	Unknown	Unknown
King Maha Sandura	Unknown	Unknown
King Bovana Aananda	Unknown	Unknown

According to the rare existing texts, on another part of the archipelago, another exiled Indian prince, Balaadeettiya, is installed and ends up marrying Queen Damahaar of the other dynasty. The union of the two monarchs makes automatically disappear the dynasty of the queen. Their son is King Loakaabarana. The latter has a son who becomes king Bovana Aananda. The latter is the father of Koimala.

It is commonly accepted that the politician who united the entire archipelago in 1117 was King Koimala (Mahaabarana Adeettiya). Before him, each atoll or island was governed by a different tribal chief.

Then, it is in 1153 that the Islamic history of the country begins when King Dhovemi, Koimala's successor and nephew, converted to Islam. As a result, he converts the Maldives and changes his title of king to sultan.

The following tables list all Maldivian kings or sultans from Koimala to the first reign of Shamsuddeen III.

Lunar Dynasty or Theemuge

Name	Start of reign	End of reign
King Koimala	1117	1141
King then Sultan Dhovemi	1141	1166 or 1176
Sultan Muthey	1166 or 1176	1185
Sultan Ali I	1185	1193
Sultan Dhinei	1193	1199
Sultan Dhihei	1199	1214
Sultan Wadi	1214	1233
Sultan Valla Dio	1233	1258
Sultan Hudhei	1258	1264
Sultan Aima	1264	1266
Sultan Hali I	1266	1268
Sultan Keimi	1268	1269
Sultan Audha	1269	1278
Sultan Hali II	1278	1288
Sultan Yoosuf I	1288	1294
Sultan Salis	1294	1302
Sultan Davud	1302	1307
Sultan Omar I	1307	1341
Sultan Ahmed Shihabuddine	1341	1347
Sultan Khadijah	1347	1363
Sultan Mohamed el-Jameel	1363	1364
Sultan Khadijah	1364	1374
Sultan Abdullah I	1374	1376
Sultan Khadijah	1376	1380
Sultan Raadhafathi	1380	1380
Sultan Mohamed I	1380	1385
Sultane Dhaain	1385	1388
Sultan Abdullah II	1388	1388
Sultan Osman I	1388	1388

Let us pause for a moment on the life of Sultan Khadijah. She is one of the first women to lead a Muslim nation and the first woman to rule the Maldives after its unification by Koimala. Khadijah was the eldest daughter of Sultan Omar I. Upon the death of her father in 1341, her brother Ahmed Shihabuddine ascended the throne but in 1347 she had him assassinated to reclaim the throne, becoming the first sultan in the history of her dynasty, the Theemuge.

During his visit to the Maldives, Ibn Battûta recounts that during Khadijah's reign, women did not wear the veil as women in other Muslim countries would have done. Sultan Khadijah also did not wear the veil.

In 1363, the woman who did not hesitate to have her brother killed was overthrown by ... her husband. Indeed, Mohamed el-Jameel, vizier (minister) of his wife wanted to be sultan instead of the sultan. He forces his wife to abdicate and obtains the crown.

Only one year passes under the reign of Mohamed el-Jameel and then Khadija uses a method she knows well: she assassinates Mohamed el-Jameel and ascends to the throne for her second reign from 1364 to 1374.

You have to see it to believe it: Khadija's new husband, Abdullah, also a vizier, also forces Khadija to abdicate. He thus became Sultan Abdullah I for two years.

The rest is not even surprising: Khadija murdered Abdullah I while he was asleep, in order to ascend the throne from 1376 to 1380. In 1380, she died and her sister Raadhafathi succeeded her for a few days ... then gave the throne to her husband. (Some sources present Raadhafathi as having ruled from 1380 to 1383).

Sultan Khadija is one of the most popular historical figures in the Maldives. The history of the Maldives is full of stories of heroes like Muhammad Thakurufaanu but the stories of queens are only a few lines in the history books. Queen Khadija is an exception to this. She has been in power for more than 30 years despite the challenges. Her career would be notable even for a man. She has never ceased to be jealous or infantilized by her husbands, two of whom asked her to leave the Maldives throne.

And of course, she had the inordinate ambition to be queen, so much so that she murdered or had a brother and two husbands murdered, and yet she escaped that kind of fate.

Khadija has become a symbol of the courage and autonomy of Maldivian women.

Hilaalee Dynasty

Name	Start of reign	End reign
Sultan Hassan I	1388	1398
Sultan Ibrahim I	1398	1398
Sultan Hussain I	1398	1409
Sultan Nasiruddine	1409	1411
Sultan Hassan II	1411	1411
Sultan Isa	1411	1411
Sultan Ibrahim I	1411	1421
Sultan Osman II	1421	1421
Sultan Danna Mohamed	1421	1421
Sultan Yoosuf II	1421	1443
Sultan Aboobakuru I	1443	1443
Sultan Hasan III	1443	1467
Sultan Sayyid Mohamed	1467	1467
Sultan Hasan III	1467	1468
Sultan Mohamed II	1468	1480
Sultan Hassan IV	1480	1480
Sultan Omar II	1480	1484

Sultan Hassan V	1484	1485
Sultan Hassan IV	1485	1491
Sultan Hassan VI	1491	1492
Sultan Ibrahim II	1492	1492
Sultan Kalu Mohamed	1492	1492
Sultan Yoosuf III	1492	1493
Sultan Ali II	1493	1495
Sultan Kalu Mohamed	1495	1510
Sultan Hassan VII	1510	1511
Sultan Sharif Ahmed	1511	1513
Sultan Ali III	1513	1513
Sultan Kalu Mohamed	1513	1529
Sultan Hassan VIII	1529	1549
Sultan Mohamed III	1549	1551
Sultan Hassan IX	1551	1552
Interregnum	1552	1554
Sultan Aboobakuru II	1554	1557
Sultan Ali IV	1557	1558
King Dom Manoel	1558	1573
Interregnum	1573	1573
King Dom Manoel	1573	1583
King Dom João	1583	1603
King Dom Philippe	1603	1632

The names of the last three kings of this dynasty testify to the Portuguese presence on the island. King Dom Philippe was, moreover, the son of a Maldivian and a Portuguese woman.

Utheemu Dynasty

Name	Start of reign	End of reign
Sultan Muhammad Imaduddin I	1632	1648
Sultan Ibrahim Iskandar I	1648	1687
Sultan Kuda Muhammad	1687	1691
Sultan Muhammad Mohyeddine	1691	1692

Hamawi Dynasty

Name	Start of reign	End of reign
Sultan Muhammad Shamsuddeen I	1692	1692

Shamduddeen I is an Arab and not a Maldivian in the ethnic sense. Few historical texts speak about him. He probably arrived in the Maldives between 1648 and 1687. Mentor of the previous sultan, he acceded to the throne after his death without any blood relationship. Very quickly, he dies poisoned. He is the only monarch of his short dynasty.

Isdhoo Dynasty

Name	Start of reign	End of reign
Sultan Mohamed IV	1692	1701
Sultan Ali V	1701	1701
Sultan Hasan X	1701	1701
Sultan Ibrahim Mudzhiruddine	1701	1704

Dhiyamigili Dynasty

Name	Start of reign	End of reign
Sultan Muhammad Imaduddin II	1704	1720
Sultan Ibrahim Iskandar II	1720	1750
Sultan Muhammad Imaduddin III	1750	1757
Sultane Amina I	1753	1754
Sultane Amina II	1757	1759

This dynasty was disrupted by an invasion followed by a period of occupation: in 1752, the sultan of the time, Sultan Muhammad Imaduddin III was taken prisoner by the Ali Raja (sort of king) of Cannanore, a region of India (now Kerala), and Malé was sacked. During the incarceration of the sultan, the niece of the sultan, Amina I then his daughter Amina II assume the role of sultan. To understand the reasons for this period of occupation, we must go back a long way. In 1573, after the defeat of the Portuguese, the hero Muhammad Thakurufaanu Al Auzam assassinates Andiri Andirin with his own hands. After this heroic but nevertheless illegal act, Thakurufaanu finds refuge with the head of state of Cannanore, the Ali Raja. At the time, the Kingdom of Cannanore, still called the Arakkal Kingdom, is a small country located on the Malabar coast in the southwest of the Indian peninsula. In exchange for the protection of the Ali Raja, Thakurufaanu promised him that he could annex the Maldives. But Thakurufaanu does not keep his promise. From this moment on, the "Malabars" (it is the name of the inhabitants of Cannanore) will keep the idea in mind to get their hands on the Maldives.

First, in 1609, the Malabars arrive in Malé and kill the regent Kalaafan but they are repulsed. Then, in 1650, it is the opposite: the Maldives attack Cannanore and take prisoners whom they release in exchange for the promise that Cannanore will no longer disturb the Maldives. However, the Malabars reattacked the Maldives in 1690 and again in 1752. In 1753, after 17 weeks of occupation by the Malabars, Malé is released but not the sultan. He dies then in captivity in 1759.

During the next attack on the Maldives by the Malabars, Dhon Hassan Manikufaan took on the task of duplicating them by disguising several Maldivian fighters as Malabar soldiers in order to better destroy the invading fleet of Cannanore. Crowned of success, Dhon Hassan takes the head of the country, is called sultan Hasan 'Izz ud-din and founds a new dynasty: Huraa. Amina II thus leaves the throne.

Huraa Dynasty

Name	Start of reign	End of reign
Sultan Hasan 'Izz ud-din	1759	1766

In 1763, the Malabars are still back, led by Ali Raja Kunhi Amsa II. They occupy the Maldives and capture Sultan Hasan 'Izz ud-din and bring him back to India.

It is the Sultan of Mysore, Hyder Ali Khan, shocked by the violence of the attack and the treatment reserved for the captured sultan, who puts an end to the reign of Ali Raja Kunhi Amsa II. Hasan 'Izz ud-din is then escorted to the Maldives.

Dhiyamigili Dynasty (restoration)

Name	Start of reign	End of reign
Sultan Muhammed Ghiya'as ud-din	1766	1774

At the death of his predecessor, Muhammed Ghiya'as ud-din is designated sultan although he belongs to a different dynasty, which causes the discontent of the family of the previous sultan. The two dynasties, the Huraa and the Dhiyamigili will dispute the throne during all the reign of Muhammed Ghiya'as ud-din.

His reign was also marked by numerous military attacks from the Kingdom of Cannanore (the Malabars), at the end of which the Maldives emerged victorious. He even took part in some battles in person and succeeded in putting an end to 200 years of conflict with this enemy country.

In 1774, he lost his throne during his absence from the country to make his pilgrimage to Mecca. In total political chaos, several people from the opposite dynasty (the Huraa) ascended the throne in his absence. On his return, he was tied to weights and thrown into the sea, then drowned on October 8, 1774. He is commonly referred to as the "Martyr Sultan.

Huraa Dynasty (1st restoration)

Name	Start of reign	End of reign
Sultan Muhammad Shamsuddeen II	1774	1774
Sultan Muhammad Mu'iz ud-din	1774	1779
Sultan Hassan Nooraddeen I	1779	1799
Sultan Muhammad Mueenuddeen I	1799	1835
Sultan Muhammad Imaaduddeen IV	1835	1882
Sultan Ibrahim Nooraddeen	1882	1886
Sultan Muhammad Mueenuddeen II	1886	1888
Sultan Ibrahim Nooraddeen	1888	1892
Sultan Muhammad Imaaduddeen V	1892	1893
Sultan Muhammad Shamsuddeen III	1893	1893

Secondly, the political life of the Maldives is marked by strong regime instability. Republics and monarchies are intermingled in a way that recalls the history of France from 1789 to 1878.

Nearly all the following Maldivian heads of state ended their term of office abruptly or unexpectedly.

Muhammad Imaaduddeen VI (1893-1902)

Figure 76: Muhammad Imaaduddeen VI

From 1893, the history of the country brings us to Sultan Haji Muhammad Imaaduddeen VI Iskandar Sri Kula Sundara Kattiri Buwana Maha Radun born on October 25, 1868 in Malé. He belongs to the Huraa dynasty. His accession to the throne of the Maldives was made on July 20, 1893. He does not speak Maldivian but rather Urdu and Arabic. In 1902, by leaving the country for a few days to marry Sharifaa Hanim in Egypt, the Maldivian people took the opportunity to oust him from the throne. He then chose to stay in Egypt and died there on September 30, 1932.

His successor and predecessor are the same man.

Muhammad Shamsuddeen III (1902-1934)

Figure 77: Muhammad Shamsuddeen III

Muhammad Shamsuddeen Iskander III (Huraa dynasty) born on October 20, 1879 and died on March 12, 1935 was Sultan of the Maldives for a handful of weeks in 1893 following the popular discontent provoked by his predecessor and half-brother, Muhammad Imaaduddeen V, an incompetent eight-year-old sultan! Indeed, when their father, Sultan Ibrahim Nooraddeen, died in 1892, it was surprisingly the youngest of the brothers who ascended to the throne despite the rule of royal succession in the Maldives. Shamsuddeen's mother managed to change the decision and put her son on the throne in 1893. But he is only fourteen years old and is therefore scorned by the ruling class: the council of ministers of the time encourages the nephew of Sultan Nooraddeen to take the throne. Thus, Shamsuddeen loses his seat in favor of Muhammad Imaaduddeen VI, 25 years old.

During the absence of Muhammad Imaaduddeen VI gone to marry in Egypt, the small island of Malé is shaken by a popular revolution. Shamsuddeen, his predecessor, this time 23 years old, then takes advantage of this revolution to regain power in 1902. The coronation ceremony took place on July 27, 1905. Among the witnesses were Sir John Keene sent to represent Edward VII (King of the United Kingdom and the Dominions, Emperor of India at the time) and the governors (katheeb) of the northern and southern atolls. He is remembered as the first to endow the Maldives with a constitution on 22 December 1932.

He was arrested on 2 October 1934 and sent into exile on Fuvahmulah. He died at the Moonimaage residence in Malé. The reason for his arrest is not very clear. His son is also arrested and dies in captivity.

Hassan Nooraddeen II (1935-1943)

Figure 78: Hassan Nooraddeen II

Sultan Hassan Nooraddeen was born on 21 April 1887 in Malé. He is a son of Sultan Muhammad Mueenuddeen II. He belongs to the Huraa dynasty.

He acceded to the Maldivian throne on February 22, 1935, although the coronation ceremony did not take place until August 20, 1938. He abdicated under duress on 8 April 1943 but was offered the leadership of the Regency Council proposed by the British. He died in Malé six days before his 80th birthday.

Abdul Majeed Didi (1944-1952)

Figure 79: Abdul Majeed Didi

Al Ameeru Abdul Majeed Rannabandeyri Kilegefaanu was born on 29 August 1873 in Malé and died on 21 February 1952 in Colombo on Ceylon. He was Sultan of the Maldives from 1944 to 1952 during a period of British protectorate. He belongs to the Huraa dynasty. He speaks fluent Divehi, Urdu, English and Sinhalese. He spent most of his life in Egypt. He was "elected sultan" in 1944 but refused the throne and never decided to move to the Maldives, preferring to live in Sri Lanka. Despite this, Didi is recognized as a reformist sultan and is remembered as the father of the modern Maldives. After his death, the Maldives proclaimed its first (very short) republic under President Mohamed Amin Didi.

Mohamed Amin Didi (1953-1953)

Figure 80: Mohamed Amin Didi

Al Ameer Mohamed Ameen Dhoshimeynaa Kilegefaanu born on 20 July 1910 in Athireege in the Maldives was, for a handful of months (from 1st January to 21 August 1953), the first President of the Maldives. Before that he was the first secretary of the very first political party of the Maldives, the Rayyithunge Muthagaddim party. He is recognized for the efforts he made to modernize the country, particularly on the schooling of girls, the nationalization of the fishing industry and his unpopular fight against smoking.

Son of Athireegey Ahmed Dhoshimeynaa Kilegefaan and Roanugey Aishath Didi, he is a descendant of a famous Maldivian dynasty: the Huraas. In 1920, he left to study at St. Joseph's College in nearby Sri Lanka. In 1928, he went to India to further his studies and returned to the Maldives a year later. Upon his return, he held various government positions such as Chief Customs Officer, Director of the Postal Service, Minister of Commerce and even Member of the first Maldivian Parliament.

With the help of the people, he succeeded in abolishing the sultanate regime that had been in force for 812 years and at the same time became the first President of the Maldives.

Upon the death of the deposed Sultan Abdul Majeed Didi and Prince Hassan Fareed Didi, members of Parliament elected Amin Didi as the Sultan's successor. But Didi angrily replied, "For the sake of the Maldivian people, I will not accept a crown or throne!" Consequently, a referendum is organized and leads to the proclamation of the republic. But the latter is short-lived.

Amin Didi suffered from diabetes: in the summer of 1953, he flew to Colombo, Sri Lanka to undergo a battery of medical examinations. A popular revolution broke out in Malé in his absence. On August 21, 1953, the people put an end to his mandate because of his absence.

On September 2, 1953, the people of Malé appointed Velaanaagey Ibraahim Didi (also known as Ibrahim Muhammad Didi), Amin Didi's vice-president as head of government. Amin Didi then had no idea what was happening during his absence and returned to the Maldives unaware of the situation. Upon his return, to ensure his safety, he is taken directly to exile on the island of Dhoonidhoo and is held under police supervision, but treated with the respect of a head of state. On Dhoonidhoo he discreetly organizes the fall of this revolutionary movement and tries to re-establish the monarchy by secretly contacting Ibrahim Hilmy, an aristocrat from a powerful Maldivian family. The pact provides for Hilmy to become king and Didi his prime minister.

On the night of December 31, 1953, Amin Didi went to Malé and tried to take control of the city but he provoked a strong response from the inhabitants and was almost beaten to death.

He is then thrown unceremoniously into a small boat (bohkuraa) near Malé. Mohamed Amin Didi, Ibrahim Hilmy, and others were condemned to exile.

The health of the former president deteriorated and he died on the island of Vihamanaafushi (the current Kurumbaa village, a resort island) on 19 January 1954. A modest funeral ceremony is organized on the island.

In spite of such a poorly finished term, today this man is honored by the current inhabitants of the Maldives as the first President of the country and remains renowned as the first to establish democracy.

As an assiduous historian and writer, it is ironic that Mohamed Amin Didi studied and documented the fall of Sultan Shamsuddeen III at length in his youth.

Ibrahim Muhammad Didi (1953-1954)

Figure 81: Ibrahim Muhammad Didi

Born on 20 March 1902 and died on 6 October 1981, Ibrahim Muhammad Didi was the first vice-president of the Maldives from [1] January 1953 to 2 September 1953, i.e. during the presidential term of his cousin, Mohamed Amin Didi.

He is considered by various sources to be the instigator of the coup that overthrew Mohamed Amin Didi. From September 2, 1953 he held the role of interim president.

But on March 7, 1954 he was forced to resign as the people demanded, by referendum, the restoration of the monarchy.

Muhammad Fareed Didi (1954-1968)

Figure 82: Muhammad Fareed Didi

King Muhammad Fareed Didi, born on January 11, 1901 and died on May 27, 1969, was the son of Sultan Adbul Majeed Didi. He is the last king in the history of the Maldives. His accession to the throne marks the second restoration of the Huraa dynasty.

After the fall of President Mohamed Amin Didi, a referendum is held and highlights the fact that 98% of the people vote in favor of returning to the monarchy. The country is thus again declared under the regime of the sultanate. In a secret vote organized by the "Majlis" (an Islamic term used to describe various types of formal legislative assemblies in countries with a linguistic or cultural connection with Islamic countries), Muhammad Fareed Didi was elected 84th sultan of the country on March 7, 1954. He then opted for the title of king rather than sultan.

In December 1957, he appointed Ibrahim Nasir as Prime Minister.

Under his reign, the separatist United Suvadive Republic was born and then disappeared (1959 - 1963).

Then the political whirlwind continued and on November 15, 1967, a vote was held in Parliament to decide whether the Maldives should continue as a constitutional monarchy or become a republic. Of the 44 members of Parliament, 40 voted in favour of a republic. Thus, on 15 March 1968, a national referendum was again held and 81% of the votes cast were in favour of a republic. The republic, the second thus, was declared on November 11, 1968, this time putting an end to 853 years of monarchy.

After this date, the king peacefully left the royal palace and withdrew from public life in his own residence: Maabagychaage, whose building now houses the Parliament of the Maldives.

He died on 27 May 1969 and was buried with honours in the Galolhu cemetery.

Ibrahim Nasir (1968-1978)

Figure 83: Ibrahim Nasir

For precisely ten years, the Maldives was ruled by Ibrahim Nasir. Born in Fuvahmulah on 2 September 1926 and died on 22 November 2008 in Singapore, he was a Maldivian statesman, Prime Minister under the Sultanate from 1957 to 1968. After the deposition of Muhammad Fareed Didi, he naturally became President of the Maldives from November 11, 1968 to November 11, 1978.

The Maldives became a republic on November 11, 1968 following a popular referendum on March 15 in which 81% of the participants voted in favor of establishing a republic. Ibrahim Nasir, the former Prime Minister, becomes President. The king died six months later. However, the new regime retained monarchist tendencies, and the new president was from a noble family.

Nasir remains in history as the president who modernized the very archaic Maldives and opened it to the rest of the world.

His major accomplishments include the country's accession to the United Nations despite opposition from other countries that considered the membership of such a small state unnecessary. He laid the foundations of the nation by modernizing the fishing industry with the addition of motorized boats and kick-started the tourism industry. Even in 2018, the country still relies heavily on these two industries as a source of income and as the engine of the economy.

On the educational front, it has led to improvements such as basing instruction on English in public schools. He brought television and radio to the country with the founding of the companies Television Maldives and Voice of Maldives.

He abolished the Vaaru tax, a tax that only applied to people living outside Malé, and other import taxes, although some have since been reinstated.

When Nasir stepped down as president, the Maldives had no external debt and corruption was under control. The Maldives was an example of success in South Asia with a commercial fleet of 40 ships. Nasir is therefore still considered the hero of the Maldives today. He is also the one who signed the independence of the Maldives on July 26, 1965 and thus the exit of the British protectorate.

Among the positive actions of this president, we can also mention:

- Use of English in school in 1961,
- Establishment of an "A-level" in education in 1976,
- Creation of the Atoll Education Project in 1977,
- Women's right to vote in 1964,
- Creation of a training course for nurses in 1963,
- Opening of health centers on all the atolls in 1965,
- Opening of the first hospital in the country in 1967,
- Construction of Malé International Airport in 1966,

- Opened to tourism in 1972,
- First motorized boat for fishing in 1964,

For such politically effective men, the flip side of the coin is often brutality. Nasir's methods are considered authoritarian. He is criticized for his violence when dealing with demonstrations such as the insurgency of the inhabitants of Thinadhoo, Addu and Huvadu.

In 1976, Nasir forced the country to abandon the Maldivian alphabet, the thaana, and adopt the Latin alphabet in order to allow the use of telex (the ancestor of computers) in the administration. Clarence Maloney, an anthropologist expressed his dismay at the inconsistency of the transcription of the thaana into Latin letters. After the introduction of the Latin alphabet, many people became illiterate overnight. Officials were relieved when the next president, Gayoom, re-introduced thaana in 1978.

Ibrahim Nasir appointed Ahmed Zaki as Prime Minister in 1972. In 1973, Nasir was re-elected for a second term and Zaki was confirmed as Prime Minister by the People's Council. In March 1975, Zaki was arrested in a bloodless coup and banished to an isolated atoll. Observers at the time speculated that Zaki was becoming too popular and posed a threat to Nasir's faction. The popularity of the Nasir government was also suffering from a commercial decline due to the British withdrawal that same year from the Gan International Airport, which they had until then reserved for themselves.

Towards the end of his term in 1978, it became apparent that Ibrahim Nasir did not wish to be re-elected. Parliament decided to nominate candidates to succeed him. The deputies express themselves: Nasir obtains the majority with 45 ballots whereas he does not want to be re-elected. The three remaining ballots are in favor of Abdul Gayoom. Another vote is held in Parliament and this time Abdul Gayoom is nominated as the sole candidate for the 1978 presidential election.

On November 11, 1978, Nasir stepped down on his normal retirement date and handed over to Gayoom.

In December 1978, Nasir fled to Singapore for reasons still unknown today. A later investigation claimed that he fled with millions of dollars from the public treasury. However, there has been no evidence so far, and this accusation passes for an act of propaganda by the new government in order to gain popularity and support from the citizens.

His successor, Gayoom, sentenced him in absentia to a prison term on the grounds of corruption and attempted coup d'état. Thereafter, Gayoom will not cease to criticize and insult Nasir in his absence, going so far as to organize meetings to tell a huge crowd how Nasir was a traitor and a thief of public funds. In 1990, Gayoom pardoned him but still refused to let him return to the Maldives.

On November 22, 2008, Ibrahim Nasir died of kidney problems at Mount Elizabeth Hospital in Singapore. His body was transported to the Maldives and exhibited at the Theemuge Palace. He is buried in the cemetery adjacent to the Friday Mosque in Malé.

Maumoon Abdul Gayoom (1978-2008)

Figure 84: Maumoon Abdul Gayoom

Maumoon Abdul Gayoom is a Maldivian politician born on December 29, 1937 in Malé. He is the 11th child of a polygamous family of 25 children born to eight women. His intelligence is such that he is the youngest Maldivian to receive a government scholarship to study abroad at the age of just ten.

He spent most of his youth in Egypt.

His confrontation with Ibrahim Nasir began on March 12, 1973: he was arrested for calling President Ibrahim Nasir's policies anti-human rights. He was tried in court and sentenced to exile for four years on 14 May 1973. On 21 May he was taken to the island of Makunudhoo. But he is already released on 13 October after serving only five months following a general presidential pardon due to Nasir's re-election.

In 1974, he was appointed Deputy Director of Telecommunications. He was quickly promoted to Director. During this time, he was also a part-time teacher in private schools where he taught English, Arabic and Islam.

On June 28, 1974, he was again arrested for criticizing Nasir. This time he was kept in solitary confinement in a prison in Malé which has been called "the Chinese garden" since Chinese fishermen were detained there in the past. After 50 days in prison, he was released. Later, during his presidency, this prison will be destroyed and an Islamic center will be built in its place.

Six weeks after his release from prison, he became deputy in the office of Prime Minister Ahmed Zaki. When Ahmed Zaki was sentenced to exile on 6 March 1975, Gayoom's position as deputy also disappeared. Instead, he was appointed Deputy Ambassador of the Maldives to Sri Lanka. He was then sent to the United Nations headquarters for two months as representative of the Maldives. Nine weeks later, he was appointed Deputy to the Minister of Transport. One year later, he returned to the UN again from September 1976 to January 1977. On March 29, 1977 Gayoom became Minister of Transport and thus took a seat in President Nasir's cabinet: the same man who had made him sleep in prison or in exile twice for criticizing him.

On November 11, 1978, Gayoom won the presidential election with 92.96% of the vote. Then, this man will follow a succession of mandates for which he will be elected against no other candidate.

In 1983, a referendum was held and allowed him to be re-elected to the same position with 95.6% of the votes.

In 1988, he was re-elected with 96.4% of the votes.

On October [1,] 1993, he was re-elected with 92.76% of the votes.

On 16 October 1998, as usual, he was re-elected for a fifth term as President of the Maldives, but this time with a score down: 90.9%.

Finally, in October 2003, he was re-elected for the last time with 90.28% of the votes.

During Abdul Gayoom's numerous presidential terms, three coups d'état against him were organized but failed. Although the 1980 and 1983 coup attempts were minor, the 1988 coup attracted international attention: a Maldivian group led by a man named Abdullah Luthfi accompanied by a Tamil militia from Sri Lanka (the People's Liberation Organization of Tamil Eelam) planned to overthrow Gayoom's government. It is the intervention of the Indian army that prevents this coup: 19 people lose their lives in the confrontation. It is the only foreign military intervention on Maldives soil in the history of the Maldives.

Crisis of 2003: the death of Evan Naseem

On September 19, 2003, Hassan Evan Naseem, a 19-year-old man serving a prison sentence on the island of Maafushi for drug use, was beaten by prison staff in an isolation cell. He died the next day from deep lung injuries.

Upon learning of his death, around 11:00 a.m. on September 20, Naseem's cell mates asked to meet with a security officer from the prison administration. Despite repeated requests, they received no response. Some prisoners refused to eat lunch to reflect their dismay at the death of Evan Naseem.

Evan Naseem's cell mates are reciting funeral prayers, when suddenly a tumult is heard from Block C, the wing where Naseem's cell was located. Two inmates jumped out of their cells after smashing corrugated iron plates. Other prisoners follow them and begin to attack the guards. The guards try to calm the prisoners at first, but then disperse to protect themselves as the prisoners refuse to stop. Prisoners from block C help prisoners from the other blocks to get out.

Captain Adam Mohamed, in charge of prison security, is informed of the events. He gives instructions to block all access. On this advice, the guards put on their riot gear. The prisoners being almost all on the run, and far more numerous than the guards, the latter quickly retreat.

The rioters then attacked Captain Adam Mohamed directly. Mohamed Faseeh, a prisoner, begins to question the captain about Evan Naseem's death but refuses to explain himself. Sergeant Shahid Ali Manik fired a shot in the air at 12:30 p.m., then turned to Mohamed Faseeh and shot him without warning. Agents Hassan Rifaau, Ahmed Mujuthaba Hussain and Mohamed Jinaah also shoot prisoners. Some were shot from behind, others from the front. Twelve firearms were used during the battle.

A total of twenty people including a security officer were killed during the incident. 15 of the 20 were shot above the knees and nine of the 20 dead were shot in the back. Abdualla Ameed was shot in the head.

Several people attend Evan Naseem's funeral. During the funeral, news of the events from the prison begins to spread. From this point on, the crisis begins in Malé: several police stations are burned, government buildings are attacked, and state vehicles are burned or otherwise destroyed by the angry crowd. The hottest places are the electoral building, the Parliament and the High Court.

Tear gas spreads in all the streets of Malé during the evening. As the Shaheed Hussain Adam Building approached, police began to use serious force against the rioters.

Figure 85: Arson in Malé

At 11:00 pm, several people were arrested. President Maumoon Abdul Gayoom addressed the nation and ordered an investigation to shed light on the death of young Evan Naseem.

The investigation will take investigators to the main scene of the events: Maafushi prison but also to every hospital housing survivors of the prison attack including as far as Sri Lanka.

It would appear that Evan Naseem's solitary confinement was due to an error: a list of troublemakers had been drawn up. The prisoners on this list were all to be placed in solitary confinement and handcuffed. Evan Naseem was not on the list but was in the same cell as those on the list. Probably feeling innocent, Evan Naseem protested violently not to go to solitary confinement by shouting "don't touch me!" It was at this point that the guard began beating Naseem: a police blunder that will put the entire capital on fire and blood.

Following these events, Gayoom called upon a famous public relations firm in 2003 to restore its image: Hill+Knowlton. The firm will play a decisive role in Maldivian politics. As an outside firm, paid 1.7 million US dollars, H+K is listened to carefully by Gayoom. In order to improve the reputation of the president, their proposals are, all in all: to allow the existence of other political parties, to financially support the Maldives Commission for Human Rights (HRCM), to reform the justice system, to end the punishment by flogging, to introduce freedom of worship in the country. Of course, not everything was listened to and implemented by the Gayoom government, but it is to this cabinet that the Maldives owes its existing multiparty system. As soon as the presidential elections of 2008, one candidate will take advantage of it: Mohamed Nasheed.

2004 Crisis: Black Friday

August 13, 2004 is nicknamed "Black Friday" in the Maldives. It all began the day before: the police summoned a man named Mr. Mohamed Yusuf, which provoked the gathering of a small group of reformist activists worried about his conditions of detention. What began as a calm march near Republican Square in Malé gradually turned into a democratic demonstration demanding reforms. Soon, the crowd grew and the clamor for the release of Mr. Mohamed Yusuf became loud: he was finally released in the afternoon. However, the crowd then demanded the release of four other reformists detained in Dhoonidhoo prison.

Figure 86: Dhoonidhoo Prison

In the early morning of August 13, 2004, a large crowd gathered near the Place de la République. Initially, the National Security Service and Minister Iliyas Ibrahim failed to win the confidence of the angry crowd by speaking through a megaphone. The crowd lists its grievances and passes them on to Ibrahim Ismail, a member of the pro-reform Maldivian Democratic Party (MDP). The grievances are:

- Immediate release of the locked-up reformists,
- Immediate release of Sandhaanu magazine employees,
- Immediate release of the artist Naushad Waheed,
- Resignation of President Maumoon Abdul Gayoom,
- Resignation of the President's brother, Minister of Commerce,
- Resignation of the president's brother, minister of the atolls.

Indeed, the reformists are released in the morning. They are transported from the prison of Dhoonidhoo to the Republic Square, barely two kilometers away as the crow flies. Once there, the ex-detainees addressed the crowd, criticized Maumoon Abdul Gayoom and called for his resignation. They took advantage of the occasion to demand that the entire demonstration be filmed and broadcast live on radio and television. However, at this stage, not a single line of events appears in the media and newspapers. The crowd continues to grow and "take its life in its own hands," says Ibrahim Ismail.

At 7:00 a.m., the Maafushi prison was stormed by inmates who believed that the government had indeed been overthrown. The escaped inmates took two dhoni to reach Malé by sea over a distance of 29 kilometers. The National Security Service (NSS) and the coast guard stopped them at sea, sank one dhoni, and pepper sprayed the crew with the other.

As the crowd shouts louder and louder that it wants Gayoom to resign, a handful of pro-government demonstrators also gather near Republic Square.

Figure 87: Republican square

According to the reformists, they were sent as a provocation, to raise the level of violence and thus be able to justify the use of force. Now international journalists are filming: the NSS needs a valid reason to use force to disperse the crowd. On several occasions, pro-government people try to provoke violence. But the reformists do not fall for it and peacefully ignore them.

At 8:30 a.m., a person named Hussain Yoosuf stabbed two policemen. After this incident, a fire broke out near the Huravee building, an administration office building. The NSS accused the crowd of starting the fire. At the same time, people were sending bottles and other objects to the police station. Demonstrators tried to stop them, but to no avail. At 2:30 p.m., the NSS issued a final warning to the crowd, but no one left the square. Believing that the peaceful discussion had gone on long enough, the police began to use their truncheons and to beat the demonstrators brutally. Some arrests were made. Women were beaten with truncheons. Several ambulances made the round trip. At 3:00 p.m. tear gas bombs began to fall on the crowd. Maldivian Democratic Party member Muad Mohamed Zaki was violently beaten with wooden planks by seven NSS officers and then sent to NSS headquarters.

Thousands of demonstrators are gagged, blindfolded, handcuffed and beaten on a day when law and order seem to have disappeared.

President Maumoon Abdul Gayoom declares a state of emergency in Malé and nearby islands. A curfew is instituted. Roads are blocked and checkpoints are set up.

During the whole day, the telecom operators Dhiraagu and Focus Infocom receive the order to cut off the Internet and SMS/MMS to prevent the propagation of videos, photos or information about these events. Television Maldives and Voice of Maldives, the public television and radio services minimise events throughout the day, referring to a "small crowd", "an illegal demonstration" or "a gang of thugs".

Crisis of 2005: the anniversary of Black Friday

On August 12, 2005, to mark the anniversary of "Black Friday," members of the Maldivian Democratic Party (MDP) and pro-reformists began meeting near Republic Square. Despite the large police presence and the presence of the NSS, at 4:30 pm, Mohamed Nasheed and other members of the party decided to join them. The general security in Malé has been very high for the last two days precisely in order to prevent this kind of anniversary event.

Figure 88: Mohamed Nasheed sitting in the center of the square

Mohamed Nasheed decides to sit right in the center of the square with his colleagues. A few minutes later, he is approached by a brigade of the municipal police of Malé. They simply say to him, "Get out!" Nasheed retorts that he does not see why he would leave when he is not doing anything illegal. The head of the brigade informs him that this kind of gathering is forbidden and that he will have to eject him by force if he does not obey within five minutes. To this ultimatum, Nasheed replied, "You give us five minutes. And then what? You beat us to death?" Nasheed, a pacifist, even proposed that the police join them in the movement. The policemen move away.

Later, history repeats itself: the riot police arrive at the Republic Square. Very quickly, they surround Mohamed Nasheed and other party members present with him. But they still refuse to leave the square. The members of the anti-riot unit then decide to grab Nasheed and his acolytes and take them to the NSS headquarters. Further arrests were made.

Prior to Nasheed's arrest, several members of the Maldivian Democratic Party (MDP) went to the Dhunfini Haruge, a large tent under which the party used to gather for various events. The news of Nasheed's arrest was instantly relayed to those present at the marquee. They begin to call for the resignation of the President and the immediate release of Nasheed and then deliver a speech to mark the anniversary of Black Friday. Two hours after his arrest, Nasheed's supporters disperse in the streets of Malé to chant anti-government songs. Around 9:30 pm, they gather behind the Parliament with banners calling for the release of those arrested that day, while under the tent Dhunfini Haruge, the crowd refuses to leave until Nasheed is released.

August 13, 2005 is as violent as August 13, 2004: in the early morning hours, the police storm the Maldivian Democratic Party (MDP) tent and totally demolish the stage, microphones and electrical equipment on the grounds that they found weapons (metal stakes) in the tent. The police locked up several streets in Malé around the NSS headquarters, the Shaheed Ali Building (the central police station), Republican Square (Republic Square), the Majlis (the Parliament), and the MDP headquarters. To avoid further turmoil, the police arrested key figures: Shuaib Ali, a Democratic politician, Ali Shiyam, hotel manager, and Mohamed Ziyad, a senior party official.

At 3 p.m., MDP supporters begin to mass outside the MDP party headquarters, an area cordoned off by the police. At 7:00

p.m., the crowd becomes more demonstrative. The police took out pepper spray canisters to disperse the crowd.

At 7:45 pm the crowd is back but this time in the main avenue of Malé, Majeedhee Magu and still demands the immediate release of the first secretary of the party, Mohamed Nasheed. The riot police also arrived on the scene and began to disperse the demonstrators but they held firm and also demanded the resignation of President Maumoon Abdul Gayoom. The police use various methods on the crowd throughout the night: batons, tear gas, pepper spray, water cannons. The police still arrest demonstrators who, around 11:00 pm, started throwing stones at them. The crowd also became extremely violent. Injured people were injured on both sides.

On August 14, 2005, a curfew is declared from midnight to 4:30 a.m. in Malé, but this does not change anything: the people refuse to go home. The police vaguely control the situation until 1:00 am, making countless arrests. At sunrise, the arrests continue: there is even a chemistry teacher from Malé high school, Imad Solih. The clashes continued all day on August 14.

On the evening of August 14th, after the 5th prayer, the demonstrations resume in Malé, around 7:30 pm near the Athamaa Palace, a hotel. There, begins the most violent night of the crisis. An angry crowd fearlessly confronts the riot police with tennis balls soaked in burning gasoline, bricks, stones and other objects. The tumult was finally brought under control at 1:30 a.m. on August 15, 2005. That night resulted in 160 arrests and transfers to the island of Feydhoofinolhu and to Girifushi, a military barracks.

The NSS and police are accused of verbally abusing the crowd throughout the crisis, which increased the level of violence. One of the incidents described accused them of storming a mosque and insulting people who were praying. Another reported incident indicated that a pregnant woman, Aminath

Massha, was beaten by an NSS police officer. The NSS denied all charges on a public television set.

The opposition criticized the government for provoking the public and taking advantage of the crisis to imprison opposition figures to suppress the CDM.

Outside of Malé, the crisis is also affecting the atolls of Gaafu Dhaalu and Addu.

On August 22, 2005, for sitting in the middle of Republic Square, Mohamed Nasheed was charged with terrorism.

In August 2007, by referendum, Maldivians opted for a direct presidential system where the president is truly elected by the people and not pre-selected by Parliament. Even Gayoom favoured this because the opposite outcome would have been to introduce a parliamentary system of government like India or Germany, countries in which the president has little power.

On January 8, 2008, Abdul Gayoom escaped an assassination attempt by Mohamed Murshid, a twenty-year-old from Hoarafushi. He attempted to stab the President with a knife hidden in a Maldivian flag. It was a sixteen-year-old scout who neutralized Murshid.

In October 2008, the presidential election was the first in which Maumoon Abdul Gayoom faced another candidate. He lost with 45.75%.

The record of Maumoon Abdul Gayoom is a succession of human rights violations, methods worthy of a terrorist towards his opponents, arbitrary arrests, detention without trial, torture, extorted confessions, corruption, ...

When he left power, Gayoom made sure he had completely emptied the country's coffers. It is said that Gayoom owned a palace in Malé with gold toilets, Italian furniture, a swimming pool, 55 cars, ...

Under Gayoom, working in the public service is a non-negligible opportunity. Chic clothes, flat screens, cell phone, job guarantee, all without the big private sector or tourism hours. Gayoom distributes jobs in the public service so easily that there are almost 12% of the active population in the public sector. A world record. Worse, the salary increases for civil servants sometimes reach 66%!

When his successor takes over the reins of the country, he finds that only 1 out of 10 civil servants is really useful! The IMF is quick to hold Mohamed Nasheed's new government to account.

Mohamed Nasheed (2008-2012)

Figure 89: Mohamed Nasheed

Mohamed Nasheed was born on May 17, 1967 in Malé into a middle-class family. He attended the Majeediyya School between 1971 and 1981. He continued his studies in Sri Lanka and the United Kingdom.

Like many people who dare to speak their minds about the Maldives, he was detained in prison in 1991 for writing an article in which he claimed that the 1989 parliamentary elections were rigged. He says he was tortured in detention, including being tied to a chair outside for twelve days and forced to eat food mixed with crushed glass.

His troubles continued in 1992. He is accused by the Gayoom government of withholding information about a planned bombing. On April 8, 1992, he was sentenced to three years in prison. He was released in June 1993, and then regularly re-arrested in 1994, 1995 and 1996. In 1996, he was sentenced to two years in prison for writing an article about the 1993 and

1996 elections. He was named in Amnesty International's sad list of Prisoners of Conscience.

In total, Mohamed Nasheed was arrested 20 times during President Gayoom's term of office. A lost time that makes him miss the births of his two daughters. In prison, he takes the time to study and write three history books on the Maldives.

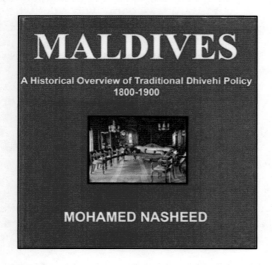

Figure 90: Cover of a book by Mohamed Nasheed

On 28 October 2008, Maumoon Abdul Gayoom was finally defeated in the second round of the presidential election by his opponent, Mohamed Nasheed: an opponent who had been imprisoned many times became President of the Maldives. The latter becomes President of the Maldives following the first multiparty elections in the country's history. This former human rights activist, a champion of environmental protection, overthrows Maumoon Abdul Gayoom, who ruled with authority over the archipelago for thirty years.

That night, the two men, Gayoom the loser and Nasheed the winner, congratulate each other and pose for the photographers. The whole country and the international community celebrate. Malé in particular is celebrating like never before. The state of mind of the people regarding the victory of Mohamed Nasheed is comparable to the election of Barack Obama in the United States on November 4, 2008 (a few days later).

Yet the election of Nasheed is not a cataclysm for Gayoom, who retains much of his relations in Parliament. Before leaving power, he placed his old guard in the administration, notably in the police and the Supreme Court.

Figure 91: Gayoom (left) and Nasheed (right)

In May 2009, former President Gayoom managed to re-enter Maldivian politics by allowing his party, the DRP, to win a majority of seats in Parliament, making him a strong opponent and even saboteur.

Because Maldivians' political education is so poor, Gayoom could offer refrigerators, televisions, travel, or cash to voters to get their votes in parliamentary elections. From then on, sabotage was intense. President Nasheed is unable to pass any laws or austerity measures. The IMF and the World Bank begin to see Nasheed as an angry and incompetent man.

However, the year 2009 sees the rise of Mohamed Nasheed on the international scene. He then surfed on a wave of worldwide attention and popularity. Young, impulsive, reformist, dynamic, his charm fits well with the image of "good-looking" heads of state such as Barack Obama or Justin Trudeau.

First of all, on October 17, 2009, the government of the Maldives is holding a ministerial meeting under water! This is a world first. Objective: to draw attention to the effects of global warming threatening this Indian Ocean archipelago. Protocol obliges, President Mohamed Nasheed dived first, followed by his ministers, in suits and bottles. A dozen ministers take their seats at a depth of six meters around a horseshoe-shaped table. Very symbolically, they adopted a resolution calling for global action to reduce CO_2 emissions.

Figure 92: Council of Ministers underwater in 2009

For this dive organized near Girifushi Island, 25 minutes by boat from Malé, the ministers, who had been training for two months, were accompanied by their instructors.

Then, in December, at the COP15 (2009 Copenhagen Conference on Climate Change), the statesman intends to make his country's ecological cause one of the biggest in the world. Nasheed's intelligence and courage are remarkable: lost in the middle of a huge conference with the likes of Barack Obama, Nicolas Sarkozy, Gordon Brown, Angela Merkel, this president of a small country does not allow himself to be dismayed and seeks to meet and convince the international community, which is generally still reluctant to reach any agreement on climate change. At the 2009 Copenhagen climate conference, Nasheed has the idea of giving journalists the status of members of the official Maldivian delegation, so that they can enter with their cameras behind closed doors and reveal to the world what is being said and what is happening there. With his strong Divehi accent, Nasheed gave the following vibrant speech:

Your Excellencies, Ladies and Gentlemen

In 1999, I was stripped of my mandate as a parliamentarian. I was expelled from Parliament and thrown in jail. Imprisoned without having committed any wrongdoing. Imprisoned for defending what I believed in: democracy, good governance and the rule of law.

At that time, I was little known and had few friends, especially abroad, willing and able to help me. But the IPU (Inter-Parliamentary Union, a world organization of parliaments of sovereign states) was a friend. The IPU fought for me. The IPU used its good offices to obtain my release. For this, I would like to say thank you.

In fact, I believe my case is still pending at the ISU. They are formally continuing their investigation to ensure that I am not being persecuted. Certainly, as president, you face a lot of criticism. But I don't think I can still claim the status of a political prisoner today!

In recent years, the Maldives has experienced a political revolution. Before that, citizens did not dare to talk about politics. Today, we have succeeded in mobilizing them for political action. Yesterday, political parties were banned, and today political parties are flourishing. Yesterday, the media was muzzled.

Today they are free. We have a new Constitution, enshrining fundamental freedoms. We have a new government, democratically elected. And we have a new Parliament, elected no less democratically.

We still have a lot to do. Our parliament has problems getting started. No doubt it has the capacity to overcome them.

Overall, I am pleased to announce that the Maldives is ready to take its place in the concert of new democracies. Issues of good governance are at the heart of democracy. And I believe that issues of good governance are also at the heart of climate change. I believe that without good governance, there will be no successful adaptation.

Let me mention an example from the Maldives. The previous regime launched a multi-million dollar adaptation program. But a few years later, most of the projects were stopped or failed. These adaptation initiatives failed because contracts were awarded to the wrong people. Ports and dikes were built in the wrong places. Residents were not consulted on the solutions best suited to their communities. For me, without democracy and good governance, there will be no successful adaptation to climate change.

Yes, funding is important for adaptation. Yes, it is imperative to choose the right technology. But without good governance and without democracy, in my experience, things don't work.

Ladies and Gentlemen,

We are not here to bring democracy to the Maldives. This battle has been won. We are gathered in Copenhagen to resolve one of the most serious problems facing humanity. And I believe that, in the face of this great challenge of our time, the IPU and parliamentarians around the world have a crucial role to play.

Climate change is faster and more radical than any forecast. Warming of less than one degree since the industrial revolution has resulted in unforeseen and unprecedented changes.

Over the last two decades, a quarter of the North Pole has melted. Coral reefs around the world are in imminent danger of collapse. Greenland is beginning to thaw. Australia is being hit hard by near-chronic, deadly droughts. And between New York and Miami, coastal erosion threatens to destroy all beaches.

All of these changes occur with less than one degree of global warming. For countries with low-lying lands, such as the Maldives, these changes are particularly alarming. No area of the country is more than two meters above sea level. For the Maldives, climate change is not a vague or abstract threat but an immediate danger to our survival.

Not far from here, in the Bella Centre, some major emitting countries are making a commitment to keep the temperature rise to two degrees. In reality, the measures they are proposing will result in an increase of nearly four degrees. So, faced with the devastation caused by warming of less than one degree, why on Earth are we aiming for two degrees, or even four?

Two degrees of warming means the death of the Maldives and of a billion people living in low-lying areas. Four degrees will lead to the near total elimination of the human race. These are the stakes that will be decided in Copenhagen.

Ladies and Gentlemen,

In my opinion, whatever direction is chosen, it will have to be based on the latest recommendations of climate specialists. It is sometimes tempting to think that climate change is an international issue like any other. One can imagine that the *problem will be solved by some kind of ill-conceived political compromise between powerful states. But the reality is that the laws of physics cannot be compromised. You can't make a deal with Mother Nature. We must learn to live within the limits that nature has set on the planet. And it is becoming increasingly clear that we are living far beyond the planet's means. I am not a scientist. But I do know that one of the laws of physics is that you don't compromise with the laws of physics. And the science is clear. If we want to stop climate change and avoid the deadly tipping point that would lead to a runaway global warming, we need to limit warming to 1.5 degrees. Carbon pollution in the atmosphere must be reduced to 350 ppm. Fortunately, some countries are proposing reasonable measures to curb climate change. AOSIS and the Least Developed Countries have proposed measures to limit temperature increases to 1.5 degrees and carbon pollution to 350 ppm. More than 100 countries want to stick to these targets. Our task is to convince the large emitting countries to join them.*

Ladies and Gentlemen,

We cannot dismiss scientific data because it is politically embarrassing. And we don't intend to. That's why, in March, the Maldives announced its intention to become the world's first carbon-neutral country.

The country intends to become carbon neutral within ten years. We are going to move from oil to 100% renewable energies. And we are going to neutralize air transport pollution until a solution is found to "decarbonize" air transport as well.

For us, going towards carbon neutrality is not only the right choice to make. We believe it is also in our economic interest. Countries that have the foresight to "green" their economies today will be the winners tomorrow. They will be the winners of the 21st century.

These pioneer countries will free themselves from the instability of imported oil prices. They will benefit from the new green economy of tomorrow. And they will strengthen their moral stature by acquiring greater political influence on the world stage. In the Maldives, we have given up our aspiration for high carbon growth. After all, it's not carbon that we need, it's development. It's not coal we want, but electricity. It's not oil that we want, but transportation. There are low-carbon technologies today that can bring us all the products and services we need. Let's set our sights on using them.

Ladies and Gentlemen,

Since the announcement of their carbon neutral policy in March of this year, the Maldives has experienced a kind of environmental revelation. We have signed two agreements with international energy companies to build wind farms; investors are offering to turn our waste into "green" electricity; and some of our famous luxury resorts have committed to achieving carbon neutrality.

The people of the Maldives have mobilized, with various islands setting carbon-neutral targets themselves; "green" investors and entrepreneurs are flocking to the Maldives, and it is now clear that power generation facilities using renewable energy will provide cheaper electricity than existing diesel generators.

Many of these changes were not envisaged when we committed to achieving carbon neutrality. So many pleasant surprises. The lesson from the Maldives can be summed up as follows: when leaders set clear directions, individuals, investors and entrepreneurs follow. This creates a virtuous circle of positive change. We need to create this dynamic on a global scale.

Ladies and Gentlemen,

Climate change threatens not only the Maldives but also humanity. And all of us here in this room have a duty to press *for an agreement to save the planet. Parliamentarians, in particular, have a compelling obligation to lead the way. Don't fall into the trap of believing that heads of state can solve all problems. On defense and foreign policy issues, heads of state are on the move.*

But on the climate aspects of energy policy, transport and waste management, parliaments are often more powerful.

If we do not act today, the climate crisis will turn into a catastrophe, threatening the very existence of human civilization. But if we all show historical leadership (each in his or her own capacity) we can avoid the crisis. And we can build a world that is greener, richer and more exuberant than the one we inherited.

Mohamed Nasheed, 16 December 2009

On September 1st, 2011, a documentary, "The Island President" tells the story of President Mohamed Nasheed, a man faced with a bigger problem than all the other statesmen have encountered: the rise of the sea level and consequently the survival of his country with all the Maldivians inside. Having established democracy in his country, Nasheed is confronted with the problem of the "low countries", i.e., all those for whom it will only take a few centimeters of rising water to engulf their entire territory.

Despite the smallness of his country, Mohamed Nasheed has managed to gain recognition from the international community. Time magazine described him in 2009 as one of the "environmental heroes" and a "visionary". Foreign Policy ranks him 37th on its list of the 100 great thinkers of the year 2010. The same year, Newsweek described him as one of the world's ten most respected national leaders.

The organized fall of President Nasheed begins on December 23, 2011 with a demonstration in the streets of Malé. The demonstration is called "Defend Islam". This choice of pretext to demonstrate is an easy plan. The opposition, i.e. the party of the previous president, Gayoom, is playing the only card it has left: to make Nasheed look like an anti-Islamic president. We are then witnessing this kind of demonstration to rewrite history as other countries have experienced. The opposition begins to debunk statues not related to Islam, to reduce to dust the statues of Buddha present in the collections of the Museum of Malé and to demand Nasheed's resignation. This opposition took advantage of the occasion to demand the closure of the spas and massage rooms in Malé, establishments that barely masked their vocation as brothels.

But to fight back, Nasheed pushes where it hurts. Knowing full well that most opposition members are luxury hotel owners, Nasheed asks the Supreme Court whether it is normal for a Muslim country to have bikinis, bacon and alcohol as its economic lung. The judges are cornered: either they respect the country's constitution and put an end to lucrative tourism or they announce that the constitution needs to be rewritten. They refuse to make a decision. Nasheed won that part. The rest of this political battle will take place in 2012.

Crisis of 2012: Nasheed's resignation

At the beginning of 2012, he has to face demonstrations by conservative Muslims who accuse him of being too liberal, and even "anti-Islamic". At the same time, rising prices are undermining the president's popularity, which he is accused of having provoked by his policies of fighting the budget deficit. Last but not least, in January he orders the army to arrest Abdulla Mohamed, president of the Criminal Court, accusing him of protecting members of the former regime. Opposition parties and the Supreme Court denounced the arrest as unconstitutional; demonstrators described Nasheed as a dictator. On February 6, police officers attack a headquarters of the MDP (the president's party). On February 7, the army disperses a demonstration by police and other demonstrators with tear gas; the army then advises Nasheed to resign at gunpoint. Nasheed resigned the same day, explaining that he wanted to avoid violent outbursts. Vice President Mohammed Waheed Hassan replaced him and ordered the release of Abdulla Mohamed. Shortly thereafter, Nasheed stated that he resigned under duress: armed soldiers reportedly surrounded him "and told me they would not hesitate to use them if I did not resign. Waheed denies this version of events. Nasheed denounces an "Islamist coup d'état.

The day after his resignation, Nasheed published an article in the New York Times accusing the judges chosen by Gayoom of "protecting the former president, his family members and his political allies, many of whom are accused of corruption, embezzlement and human rights abuses. He added that the freedom of expression he (Nasheed) had established had been abused by "extremist Islamists. Ministers of the former president have hurled anti-Semitic and anti-Christian slurs against my government, accusing all those who sought to defend our country's liberal Islamic traditions of apostasy, and claiming that democracy gives them and their allies the right to call for violent jihad and utter words of hatred. Regarding the arrest of Abdulla Mohamed, he wrote: "It seems to me that I had no choice but to do what I did.

The mutiny of February 7 leaves a bitter taste in the mouth of the Maldivian population. The next day, the party of former president Nasheed called on the Maldivians to march on Malé to express their consternation. After all, Nasheed had been chosen democratically. 10,000 people gather in the Republic Square for a peaceful march. Notably, women, children and the elderly make the march, which testifies both to the importance of the march and its non-violent vocation. The procession approaches the central bank and falls in front of a line of riot police equipped with shields and tear gas grenades. But Republic Square is a mousetrap: it runs along the sea and thus prevents escape. A second group of policemen, identified as former President Gayoom's former guard, suddenly begins to charge the demonstrators. Trapped between the water, the riot police and the Gayoom police, the crowd begins to panic. The carnage begins. The police are happy to use tear gas and truncheon blows in a sordid violence. The whole thing is filmed by Al Jazeera. Dozens of cell phones film women and elderly people being dragged along the floor in a hair-raising drag-out. Men, women, children, the elderly are treated without distinction. It is said that a young woman is admitted to hospital with a bloody head. During her x-ray examination, her skull was still bleeding.

Despite a crowd full of women and children, at no time did the police warn that they would attack. People had come for a peaceful protest march.

And Nasheed in all this? He was part of the procession and had managed to hide in a store. A video taken by smartphone, shows him when he is discovered and dragged out of his hiding place by the police. He sustained head injuries. The (false) rumor of Nasheed's death is spreading throughout the archipelago. This news, although not verified, puts the country to fire and blood. Chaos spreads throughout the country: on some islands the police barricade themselves to avoid being taken to task, on other islands the police jump into a boat to hide at sea, police stations and courts are set on fire.

At the end of the day on February 8, a police spokesman said that the police found many bottles of alcohol in the garbage of the presidential residence. Since alcohol consumption is illegal outside the tourist resorts, proceedings are envisaged against Nasheed, who could face up to three years in prison, or internal exile on an island far from the capital.

Mohamed Nasheed would later say, "It is very easy to repress a coup. I could have done it. But there would have been blood everywhere. I didn't want that. I didn't want that. I really didn't. The best thing to do was to resign.

In saying this Nasheed surely remembers the bloodbath that ended the United Suvadive Republic. In another register, Nasheed also remembered the fate of the first president of the Maldives, Mohamed Amin Didi, who was beaten and left for dead in 1953. By cooperating quickly, Nasheed avoided being injured and hurting his people.

It is desperate to see how quickly the international community recognized this new government, which was put in place after an armed mutiny. It is likely that the low profile of the Maldives on the international scene has helped to dispel this issue.

On October 7, the former president was arrested by police for refusing to appear in court. He was accused of abuse of power, and a hearing was finally held on November 4, 2012. Nasheed himself no longer even understands the reason for his arrest. At the time, he says "one time they say it's for terrorism, another time they say it's because I acted against the Constitution, and another time they said it was alcohol". A succession of detentions and releases later, Nasheed intends to run for president in 2013. He was again arrested in March 2013 for abuse of power but was released the next day. Nasheed returned to politics in the 2013 presidential election. On 7 September, he came out ahead in the first round with 45.45% of the vote, ahead of Abdulla Yameen Abdul Gayoom (25.35%), half-brother of Maumoon Abdul Gayoom, Gasim Ibrahim (24.07%), a businessman in the tourism sector and Mohammed Waheed (5.13%), the outgoing president. The second round, scheduled for September 28, is postponed by the Supreme Court, a decision that has provoked many international reactions including that of the UN Secretary General, Ban Ki-moon. On October 7, the Supreme Court decided to annul the results of the first round and ordered that it be held again on October 19. However, police intervened on election day to prevent voters from casting their ballots.

Finally, on November 9, the first round of voting was held again, again with Nasheed leading with 46.93 per cent of the vote. Despite this gap, he recorded a defeat against Abdulla Yameen, who won the election on November 16 with 51.3% of the votes.

On February 22, 2015, Nasheed was arrested for terrorism, and the next day, the courts refused his parole. On March 13, 2015, he was finally sentenced to thirteen years in prison. He was defended by the lawyer Amal Clooney. According to Amnesty International, the UN denounced an arbitrary trial.

Figure 93: Arrest of Mohamed Nasheed in February 2015

On January 16, 2016, he is allowed to temporarily leave prison and travel to the United Kingdom for spinal medical care. The Maldivian Foreign Ministry made it clear that "Nasheed is allowed to leave the country on condition that he returns to the Maldives to serve the remainder of his sentence immediately after completing his surgery. Obviously, Mohamed Nasheed remains in the United Kingdom after his operation.

On May 21, 2016, the United Kingdom finally granted him political asylum. He then set up a coalition with several parties, including an Islamist formation.

In February 2018, Mohamed Nasheed in exile in Sri Lanka announces his firm intention to run for the Maldivian presidential elections of September 23, 2018. He plans to run under the banner of the Maldivian Democratic Party (MDP), although the electoral code prohibits people with a criminal record from running. Omar Razak, an MDP official based in Colombo, said that "Mr. Nasheed plans to campaign through social networks, as he cannot return to his country.

On June 29, 2018, he renounced his candidacy for the 2018 Maldivian presidential election after the electoral commission refused to validate his candidacy. Ibrahim Mohamed Solih was chosen in his place. Solih is a Maldivian politician who has been a member of Parliament since 1994, representing the island of Hinnavaru from which he originates. He is one of Mohamed Nasheed's closest friends.

Mohammed Waheed Hassan (2012-2013)

Figure 94: Mohammed Waheed Hassan

Born on January 3, 1953 in Malé, Waheed is an incredibly calm and zen man. Educated at the prestigious Stanford University in California, he is the first Maldivian to receive a doctorate. He is known for his very liberal vision of religion, especially concerning women's rights. He has often expressed his belief that there is common ground between human rights, democracy and Islam. He has three children, all U.S. citizens, with his wife Ilham Hussein.

In 1978, he was the first person to appear live on Maldivian television. The same year he left to resume his studies at Stanford University in the United States, where he obtained a master's degree in educational planning. Back in the Maldives, he worked in the Ministry of Education, preparing curricula and textbooks. He returned to Stanford where he earned a Master's degree in Political Science in 1985 and a PhD in International Educational Development in 1987, becoming the first Maldivian to earn a PhD.

Upon his return to the Maldives, he was appointed Director of Education Services at the Ministry of Education, and then headed the Ministry on an interim basis for a few months.

Candidate in the legislative elections of 1989, he was elected deputy of the capital, Malé. He introduced a bill to guarantee civil and political rights, which received the support of Parliament, but the Speaker of Parliament, Abdullah Hameed, brother of President Maumoon Abdul Gayoom, did not allow it to pass.

In 2003, President Maumoon Abdul Gayoom included Waheed in the Constituent Assembly to draft the country's new constitution. When Waheed realized that the members of parliament would not be able to carry out major reforms, he gave up and moved to Stanford in the United States, where he studied and received several degrees.

In 2006, he joined the recently formed political party MDP, but in June 2008 he left it and formed his own party. His followers in this new party were not loyal to him and quickly returned to the MDP. In the months that followed, Waheed was in demand from all sides: the Gaumee Itthihaad Party (GIP) proposed him as its candidate for the 2008 presidential election and two other parties asked him to be the running mate (future vice-president) of their respective candidates. He finally chose to be running mate for Mohamed Nasheed of the MDP.

Nasheed was elected President of the Maldives on October 28, 2008 and Waheed became its Vice President. The two men took office on November 11, 2008, and together they carried out numerous reforms. It was from April 2010 that tensions emerged. Nasheed did not leave enough room for his vice-president, who then told the press: "I do not feel that I can contribute or that I am being consulted. The people of the Maldives did not elect me to sleep for five years. I believe that I am part of the executive of this country and that it is necessary that I am involved" (interview given to the Minivan News in April 2010).

But Nasheed as president follows a doctrine that is very insulting to his cabinet: "Follow me or get out!" Even in TV shows, Waheed complains about the lack of listening to his president. The effects are predictable: the two men sulk. President Nasheed regularly ridicules Waheed and isolates him from the rest of the cabinet. The relationship between the two is definitively broken the day when Nasheed suddenly decides to dismiss all the ministers of the GIP party, Waheed's party.

J.J. Robinson, a journalist, writes in his book on the Maldives that on the evening of January 30, 2012, a week before the overthrow of the government, Waheed receives three members of the opposition in his own home. Yet officially, the two camps do not speak to each other.

Waheed would have liked this meeting to be secret but the smallness of Malé makes this kind of fraternization with the enemy very visible. In fact, the very next day, the opposition organized a press conference and declared "we asked the vice-president to save the nation. We ask the security forces to recognize that if the president is no longer able to carry out his mandate, the vice-president Mohammed Waheed Hassan Manik should assume the role of president". The man uttering this sentence is Ibrahim Shareef, vice-president of the DRP party (former political party of former President Gayoom).

Yet Waheed will never cease to deny his active involvement in the mutiny of February 7, 2012.

In his defense, Waheed can be metaphorically viewed as an actor hired to act in the film written by the opposition. The title of this film: "Islamic Symposium" (a symposium is a meeting, a colloquium, a congress). A document attests to the preparation of the overthrow of Nasheed since December 29, 2011. The scenario signed by the hands of the main leaders of the opposition parties (DQP, PPM, AP, DRP, PA) initially foresees an action on February 24, 2012. The plan is as follows: gradual escalation of civil disobedience of the police force, followed by the escort of President Nasheed out of Malé. Then Gayoom's friend and lawyer at the Supreme Court would declare Nasheed unfit to continue as president. The plan even calls for the media to be manipulated to create enough of a furore that people would take to the streets and force the military to lay down their arms.

The complete organizational chart is drawn: Waheed is to take the position of president and dissolve the firm, then appoint each script writer to a future senior position.

Like any scenario, this project even has a budget and funding. It is estimated at $2.8 million, including the cost of greasing several legs. The financing is taken care of by the opposition parties as well as interested businessmen.

Still, on February 7, and not on the 24th, a reversal very similar to what is marked in this document, alas not authenticated, takes place. On February 7, 2012, Waheed succeeded President Nasheed following an army mutiny. This mutiny is due to an alliance between the security forces and the Islamist party Adhaalath, which supports the new president. This formation had already made a name for itself by briefly obtaining the closure of spas in hotels, supposedly places of debauchery. As soon as President Mohamed Nasheed resigns, men want to signify the advent of a new era. They burst into the National Museum and destroyed priceless limestone and coral Buddhas, the only witnesses to the archipelago's Buddhist past.

Figure 95: The National Museum's storage room

The Islamist party condemns the sacking, but at the same time refuses the gift of three Buddhist works (offered to the country in November 2011) by India, Sri Lanka and Pakistan. This fury represents a new victory for the most extreme current of Islamism, that of the Taliban or the Saudi militants.

Mohammed Waheed Hassan Manik is a bit of a symbol of the easy coup. The one who comes to power without looking like one. On the evening of February 7, Waheed speaks on television and announces "during this dangerous situation facing the nation, it is my duty to say a few words. I support the many Maldivians who are making peaceful efforts to protect the country's constitution and religion. Waheed is reasonable and unambitious. His lack of charisma is blatant. When he goes on stage to speak, some people sneer.

Upon his controversial accession to the post of president, diplomats around the world discovered a man who was soothing after the tumultuous, angry, dynamic, impulsive Mohamed Nasheed.

If Nasheed or the CDM were expecting an outraged reaction from the international community, they must have been disappointed. The standard diplomatic procedure of democratic nations is to issue a welcome message to each new head of state and acknowledge the legitimate transfer of power. In the event that victory is disputed, the decision whether or not to recognize the new government can have a significant impact in the country concerned. In the case of the Maldives, not really knowing what is happening, Western countries simply turned to one of the few diplomats from a large country based in the Maldives: the Indian ambassador. This one was present in Malé at the time of the forced resignation of Nasheed on February 7, 2012 but in surprising company: Gayoom's half-brother, Abdulla Yameen. The reason for the presence of a member of the opposition in a diplomat's office is complex and confusing. The Indian ambassador was trying to calm spirits and save time by talking to the opposition, but he can be criticized for not having made direct inquiries to Nasheed's government. Worse, the ambassador knew and apparently had some admiration for Waheed. Thus, India began to recognize the transfer of power from Nasheed to Waheed.

The United States followed suit. It was not until February 9 and the release of the images of the new government's violence against the protesters that the Americans began to back-pedal: "The United States will work with the new government of the Maldives, but believes that the circumstances surrounding the transfer of power need to be clarified and suggest that both sides agree.

But it is too late: the new government has formed and appointed the entire family of former President Gayoom to the various ministries. So, the "new" government is, in reality, an old government.

Waheed in his new role as president is even more useless than before. As a puppet of the Gayoom clan, Waheed hasn't even moved into the presidential palace. He is still a tenant of the vice-president's palace: the Hileaage. His entourage even confides that he is "the weakest person politically speaking, in the Maldives".

Finally, on February 23rd, the Commonwealth Ministerial Action Group, the organization that oversees the application of human rights and democracy in the former British protectorates, began to investigate. The organization hardened its tone and demanded that former President Nasheed and current President Waheed open a dialogue and agree on a date for early elections. CMAG's authority is real. Fiji knows this: it was ejected from the Commonwealth in 2009 after the military took power without holding an election. This kind of ejection from the Commonwealth is guaranteed to drive away all Western financial aid, impacting tourism and foreign investment. A few days later, the European Union joined CMAG in its demands.

But the gesticulations of NGOs and various international organizations such as CMAG and the EU are annoying the Waheed/Gayoom government. Dunya Maumoon, the daughter of former President Gayoom and Foreign Minister, predicts a real civil war if early elections are held. On August 30, a commission led by several Maldivian political party leaders, including a representative of Nasheed's MDP party, submits a report to CMAG. The document is supposed to shed light on the events of February 7. The day before its delivery, Nasheed's representative leaves the commission denouncing its lack of credibility and integrity.

What does the report say? That Nasheed did not resign by force and that there was no coup or mutiny. All this is astonishing given the number of photos and videos showing the contrary.

Despite this, CMAG and the international community welcomed the report, abandoned their demands for early elections and closed the case.

Lying to the world was indeed Gayoom's business. It had, moreover, actively contributed to propagating an image of a tropical paradise and apolitical place since the 1970s when the country is one of the strictest Islamic countries in the world.

The political instability of 2012 leaves its mark: tourism in the Maldives will eventually decline under the weight of warning messages issued by the Ministries of Foreign Affairs, which advise European nationals against venturing into such a politically unstable country. Foreign investment is also declining.

At the end of 2012, the country is almost bankrupt. After only a few months in office, Waheed is running a budget deficit of 27 percent of GDP. By October, the government of the Maldives stopped paying its bills and owed $10 million to the power company.

Crisis of 2013: the presidential election

On July 18, 2013, the electoral commission formally accepted Nasheed's candidacy for the presidential elections. This news puts an end to months of speculation and represents the triumph of democracy and diplomacy.

Nasheed thinks that if he wins, he would be back in the position he was forced to leave violently in February 2012. He says, "The slope was soapy and we've come a long way. In spite of all the barriers and obstacles that were put in our way, we never gave up. We are confident that we will win this election in the first round with an insolent majority.

Three other parties present their candidates: Gayoom's PPM supports Abdulla Yameen (Gayoom's half-brother). Gasim

Ibrahim, a businessman with several resort islands, is the candidate of his party, the Jumhoree Party (JP). The current president, Waheed is also an independent candidate.

The local and international press is boiling. The election date is set for September 7, 2013.

The whole country is excited and a festive atmosphere ignites the streets. Election posters are stuck everywhere. The CDM promises jobs, education, and social benefits. The PPM promises reforms for youth, the creation of a new youth-oriented city and an amusement park: there are none in the Maldives at the time.

Nasheed, for his part, performs a typical small-country exercise: he signs 239,593 letters one by one with his own hand and sends them to all the voters. He describes his campaign as "very personal. He says, "I don't think sending printed versions of my signature would be appropriate. Still bitter about the unanimous recognition of Waheed's seizure of power by the international community in February 2012, Nasheed is motivated and galvanized.

In the Maldives, voter corruption is an open secret. A survey of the phenomenon showed that in the Kaashidhoo municipal election in April 2012, each voter received an average of US$230. Bribes are paid in cash or in kind: just ask the candidate what you need, such as a refrigerator or a TV. Or even a bottle of alcohol. On the other hand, the candidate requires assurance that the voter will vote for him or her. There are two methods: either make him swear on the Koran, or ask him to take a picture of the ballot in the voting booth. Proof that Maldivians have no political conscience, they are even paid to paint election posters on city walls. The painters do not hesitate to paint the posters of all the candidates without distinction in order to earn as much money as possible. Others deface the posters in the middle of the night so that their friends can be paid to come and paint them the next day.

On September 7, the vote took place in an orderly and calm manner. The abstention rate was low: 88.44% of those registered voted. The next day, the electoral commission announced the results:

- Mohamed Nasheed: 45.45%.
- Abdulla Yameen: 25.35%.
- Gasim Ibrahim: 24.07%.
- Mohammed Waheed: 5.14%! This is the lowest election score obtained by an incumbent president in any country in the world. Waheed is humiliated. The score of the outgoing president is laughable and astonishes the international community.

For his part, Gasim Ibrahim is furious: he received only 50,000 votes instead of the 70,000 he had "bought by corruption". He does not publicly utter the word corruption but is certain that he should have had 70,000 ballots. He bemoans the electoral commission, which he calls criminal. Not digesting his defeat, Gasim Ibrahim and his party, the JP, are the only ones to contest the result before the Maldivian justice system.

Accordingly, the Supreme Court suspends the organization of the second round until further notice. The international press went wild. President Waheed gets carried away and asks foreigners to stop commenting and speculating on the Maldivian elections.

On the evening of September 27, the electoral commission announced that the second round would be held the next day as required by the constitution.

From that moment on, the Maldives becomes the Maldives again: this country always ready to rebel and fight. The Special Operations Police (affiliated to the Gayoom clan) is sent to the headquarters of the electoral commission in Malé by order of the Supreme Court. In fact, the Supreme Court has still not authorized the holding of elections.

Prevented from carrying out its mission, the electoral commission makes a speech indicating that the conditions are not in place to carry out a second round. The chief commissioner of the electoral commission leaves his post, deputized.

On October 8, the Supreme Court abruptly announced that the results of the first round were annulled. It specified that a new vote must be held before October 20 and a second round on November 3.

The tension is palpable. Each candidate begins to ask for a right to look at the electoral roll and wants to read the electoral register page by page, line by line, to verify that no one appears in duplicate, or that no one has died among the registered voters. Some candidates take their case to the Supreme Court in the middle of the night. Others demand the withdrawal of Mohamed Nasheed's ballots on the pretext that he is irreligious.

On October 18, the PPM and the JP announced that they would refuse to sign the electoral register until each registered voter is fingerprinted. The verification process could take months. The problem is that until they sign the register, the election cannot begin.

However, on October 19, the second first round was held. This time the atmosphere is not festive. At 3:30 a.m., the Electoral Commission announced that the elections would take place even without the signatures of the two PPM and JP candidates, Abdulla Yameen and Gasim Ibrahim.

But the Supreme Court has not said its last word: it formally prohibits an election in which all four candidates have not signed the register. At 5:30 a.m., they sent the police to besiege the electoral commission, those people who have been working 15 hours a day for weeks to help the Maldivian people express themselves at the ballot box.

International opinion and international organizations are beginning to feel that democracy in the Maldives is a distant memory and that there may never be elections.

The country is in a lamentable state. People are demonstrating in the streets. The studios of the TV channel Raajje (rather affiliated with the CDM) are burned down.

At the end of October 2013, the country is resigned. The festive atmosphere has disappeared. The electoral posters and pennants have lost their colors.

The notion of early presidential elections is becoming less and less meaningful as November 11, the date of the elections in the normal electoral calendar, approaches.

A new election attempt is announced for November 9.

On Saturday, November 9, 2013, the fourth attempt at the first round took place and the results are so similar to those of the first round that one wonders what this electoral masquerade was for. The outgoing president, Waheed is too humiliated to try again. He withdraws before the election.

Nasheed received 46.93% of the votes. Yameen obtains 29.72%. And Gasim Ibrahim makes 23.34%.

The result is, this time, accepted by all. But the score of Gayoom's half-brother, 29.72% is astonishing: 30% of Maldivians are ready to be led by the clan that was in power from 1978 to 2008! This 30% represents a vote of stability, a conservative vote, a vote of nostalgia.

The second round thus sees the confrontation of Yameen's dictatorial conservatism against Nasheed's modern democracy.

The problem is that November 11th is, according to the Maldives Constitution, the last day of Waheed's presidential term. Either the country is able to hold the second round on November 10 (only a few hours after the first round) or the constitution has to be rewritten.

This new purely constitutional problem will plunge the Maldives into crisis again.

Parliament decides to let Waheed end his presidential term on the evening of November 10 and appoints the Speaker of Parliament, Abdulla Shahid, as head of the transitional government as of November 11. But this is highly displeasing to the PPM because Mr. Shahid is a supporter of Nasheed's CDM. Immediately, the PPM took the matter to the Supreme Court and asked that Waheed's mandate be extended. The Supreme Court agreed. Waheed also agrees to remain in office until November 16.

This puts the Maldives in an unusual case: the country ends up with two heads of state. On one side Waheed who follows the request of the Supreme Court. On the other, Shahid, the president of the parliament.

The international community is absolutely furious and directs its anger solely at President Waheed, who is accused of remaining in office beyond the date mentioned in the constitution.

Unloved, annoyed and manipulated, Waheed discreetly leaves the country two days before the second round and takes refuge in Singapore, leaving behind a letter in which he exposes his bitterness towards Nasheed.

Gasim Ibrahim, the big loser in the first round, decided to give instructions to vote Yameen in order to "defend Islam".

Yameen, brother of former dictator Maumoon Gayoom who ruled the Maldives for 30 years, was elected president with 51.39% of the votes. Nasheed loses with 6,022 votes.

Abdulla Yameen Abdul Gayoom (2013-2018)

Figure 96: Abdulla Yameen Abdul Gayoom

Abdulla Yameen Abdul Gayoom, born May 21, 1959, is a discreet politician who began his career in July 1978. After studying geometry in Beirut, Lebanon, he returned to the Maldives and became secretary of the finance department in 1982 as well as a researcher at the country's financial market authority. He then spent two years of service at the Ministry of Trade and Industry. He held several positions there: foreign trade development officer, deputy, assistant director, deputy director, director and then director general. Finally, he reached the level of Minister of Trade and Industry on November 11, 1993.

In this position, he modernizes the commercial sector by expanding the economy and attracting more investors. He played a major role in the country's development when he enabled it to join MIGA (Multilateral Investment Guarantee Agency). The Multilateral Investment Guarantee Agency (MIGA), a subsidiary of the World Bank Group, is an international agency whose mission is to promote foreign direct investment (FDI) in developing countries in order to foster economic growth, reduce poverty, and improve people's living conditions. The agency is based in Washington and was founded in 1988.

Subsequently, Yameen became Minister of Higher Education, Employment and Social Security from July 2005 to April 2007, then Minister of Tourism and Civil Aviation from September 2008 to November 2008 only, under the presidency of his half-brother.

His personality is a clever mix of shyness and aggressive determination. "Yameen is a very clever manipulator and an extremely intelligent person, but unfortunately he has a criminal mind," describes Ahmed Naseem, former minister of affairs and opposition member. "He is not a charismatic figure. Even when he tries to carry a baby, he looks like he's holding a fish," he adds.

On November 16, 2013, and after several postponements, presidential elections were held. They bring to power Abdulla Yameen, the half-brother of former president Maumoon Abdul Gayoom. He became the sixth president of the Maldives.

Despite this, the MDP and the Maldivian people in general accepted the vote, and there was no overwhelming response.

From that moment on, Abdulla Yameen Abdul Gayoom will lead a fierce repression against any form of opposition or dissent. His goal is to eliminate all other potential candidates for the next presidential election.

Just before the parliamentary elections of March 2014, the Supreme Court took care to dismiss and condemn to exile all the members of the electoral commission. In the parliamentary election, President Yameen's party, the PPM, won a majority of 54 seats. The Gayoom family at that time is thus in possession of the three powers of the country: the old-style dictatorial Maldives are back.

Gradually during his term of office, the Gayoom family plunged into paranoia and had a staggering number of people fired or convicted, starting with Gasim Ibrahim, an unfortunate former candidate in the first rounds, and Mohamed Nasheed.

Crisis of 2015: the arrest of Mohamed Nasheed

On February 22, 2015, Nasheed was arrested for terrorism. In March he was sentenced to thirteen years in prison.

The sentence leads to the largest popular demonstration in the history of the Maldives: 20,000 people gather in the main street of Malé to protest against the arrest of the former president. 200 demonstrators are arrested.

The case becomes international: Nasheed is defended by Amal Clooney (George Clooney's wife). The government is defended by Cherie Blair (Tony Blair's wife). The fight explodes between these two British women with famous husbands.

Figure 97: Lawyers Cherie Blair and Amal Clooney

In October 2015, the UN declared Nasheed's arrest arbitrary and demanded his immediate release. It highlighted the Maldives' systemic tendency to imprison opposition leaders. However, Nasheed was not released.

On July 22, 2015, the vice president accused of plotting against President Yameen, Jameel Ahmed, was dismissed by Parliament for high treason. While fleeing to the United Kingdom, Ahmed Adeeb Abdul Ghafoor was appointed in his place.

Since the beginning of his mandate, Yameen has received numerous death threats. On September 28, 2015, an explosion exploded on board the presidential yacht that was taking him back to Malé, as he was returning from the hajj. He escaped unharmed, but his wife and two other people were injured. His wife suffered a back injury and remained in hospital for several months. On October 14, the Minister of Defense, Moosa Ali Jaleel, is dismissed from office as a result of this affair. On

October 24, Vice President Ahmed Adeeb Abdul Ghafoor is arrested. The local investigation concluded that the Vice President, some government officials, and soldiers were all implicated in the attack. They were all convicted and sentenced for high treason and terrorism and sent to prison. It was reported that the vice president illegally possessed firearms, allegedly fomented the bombing, and bribed some soldiers to install an improvised explosive device. However, according to the FBI investigation, the explosion left no evidence of a bomb.

On November 4, the president declared a state of emergency for one month. The following day, Ahmed Adeeb was removed from office by Parliament and the state of emergency was finally lifted on November 10.

On October 14, 2016, the Maldives announced its withdrawal from the Commonwealth due to the organization's considerations of the territory's position on human rights.

On October 17, 2016, during a press conference held by Gayoom, the Maldivian people understand that Gayoom and his half-brother Yameen no longer get along at all. At that time, the two men had not spoken to each other for more than a year. After losing all political role in their party, the PPM, Gayoom finds his half-brother ungrateful after all he feels he has done for him. So Gayoom decides to wage a political war against his younger brother, starting by not supporting him in the 2018 election campaign.

On March 26, 2017, former President Nasheed forms an unusual alliance with his predecessor Maumoon Abdul Gayoom. The alliance also includes two other leaders: Qasim Ibrahim and Sheikh Imran Abdulla to "restore democracy to the Maldives, ensure free and fair elections in 2018 and protect the constitution. This new opposition is absolutely incredible: it shows hand in hand President Yameen's half-brother and his arch-enemy, Nasheed.

2018 Crisis: The Supreme Court Decision

On February 1st, 2018, the Supreme Court of the Maldives handed down an unusual ruling: it ordered the immediate release of nine political prisoners and the rehabilitation of twelve members of parliament. These twelve deputies all belonged to the opposition, of course.

President Yameen saw this court decision as a preliminary to a coup d'état against him.

To prevent the spread of the news, the president locks up the press and claims that the Supreme Court's announcement is a fake news (disinformation) posted on the Supreme Court's website by hackers. He dismisses the chief of police to prevent him from following the Supreme Court's order.

On February 2, the CDM and the opposition in general met from 2 a.m. to celebrate the Supreme Court's decision. The police act as usual and send tear gas and pepper spray to disperse the crowd.

On February 3, the opening of the parliament is cancelled to avoid overflow. President Yameen dismissed the replacement for the police chief he had appointed the day before.

On February 5, Abdulla Yameen Abdul Gayoom refused to implement the decision despite the UN's request and pointed out that in his view, the Supreme Court "is not above the law". In one evening, he besieged the offices of the Supreme Court, accusing it of trying to remove him from office, suspended the parliament in which he had just lost his majority, dismissed the chief of police, arrested former President Maumoon Abdul Gayoom, who had joined the opposition in 2017, and declared a state of emergency.

On February 6, after several intrusion attempts, special military forces climbed onto the roof of the building and broke a window, then grabbed the head of justice, Abdulla Saeed. Other opponents and their families are arrested. Yameen justifies this as a "conspiracy" and a "coup". Nasheed then called on India and the United States to intervene. In the end, the three remaining Supreme Court justices decided to overturn the decision. The UN then denounced an "attack on democracy".

In June 2018, the Maldivian judiciary sentenced former Maldivian President Maumoon Abdul Gayoom to 19 months in prison for obstructing the investigation into the alleged plot to overthrow President Abdulla Yameen.

The two allies Gayoom and Nasheed have in common that they are both former presidents of the Maldives who were sentenced to prison after their term of office. Except that Nasheed is not serving his sentence since he is a fugitive and lives in Sri Lanka. According to the Maldivian Democracy Network, Gayoom would be tortured for lack of medical care.

For the 2018 presidential elections, Nasheed is only eligible to vote if he returns to prison in the Maldives. He has no right to be a candidate, of course.

Despite all this political brutality typical of the Maldives, Yameen's record shows some notable developments. He initiated the construction of a huge bridge between Malé and Hulhulé. Yameen directly supervises the development of the artificial island Hulhumalé. And under his mandate, the Malé International Airport will be expanded in 2018 to accommodate a greater number of passengers and aircraft, including the Airbus A380 from September 22, 2018. The goal is to see eight million passengers per year instead of the current 1.5 million.

Again in 2018, the Maldives will hold its twelfth presidential elections. There are initially three candidates:

- Abdulla Yameen is a candidate for his own succession and still represents the PPM.
- The MDP is represented by Ibrahim Mohamed Solih, who heads a heterogeneous opposition coalition that includes the MDP, the pro-Gayoom faction of the PPM, the Jumhooree Party and the Adalat Party.
- A former interior minister, Umar Naseer, is an independent candidate. He is a business leader who has legal problems related to one of his companies. He is known for his firmness towards criminals and his severity in general. During his tenure as Interior Minister, he banned public demonstrations in the streets. In addition, he is a strong advocate of Sharia law and the death penalty.

On August 10, 2018, Umar Naseer threw in the towel and withdrew from the presidential race, severely criticizing all parties in the country. He accused the parties MDP, JP, AP and PPM of working only for their own interests and denounced the destruction of the Constitution by Abdulla Yameen. The number of candidates fell to its lowest level since the country held multiparty presidential elections.

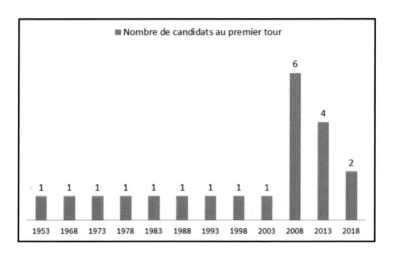

Figure 98: Number of Candidates in Presidential Elections

A few weeks before the election, the international community began to worry about the conditions in which the election would be held. According to the think-tank South Asia Democratic Forum (SADF), evidence that the election promises to be rigged is accumulating: manipulation, intimidation of voters, duplicate voter registration. President Yameen is suspected of using every possible means to stay in office. The means at his disposal are his financial strength, the support of the business world and his knowledge of the police, the army and the justice system.

The local media did not cover Solih's election campaign for fear of government reprisals. This is a far cry from the rules of speaking time or airtime that apply, for example, in France during election campaigns.

Maldivian authorities denied several applications for visas for international media to cover the elections. In particular, foreign journalists are required to name a local sponsor, who will be held responsible if editorial coverage is disagreeable.

During the week preceding the election, the Western media, particularly the French, were pessimistic about the outcome of the election. Some newspapers wrote "The Maldivians are preparing to re-elect Abdulla Yameen" or "he is sure to get a new mandate".

Maldives. Un simulacre de présidentielle pour réélire Abdulla Yameen

Le président sortant des Maldives, le très répressif Abdulla Yameen, a voté ce dimanche. Il est assuré de décrocher un nouveau mandat. | AFP

Figure 99: Article from a major French newspaper saying "a sham presidential election for re-elect Abdulla Yameen"

On the eve of the vote, police raided the MDP campaign headquarters in Malé and searched the premises, but no arrests were made.

On September 23, 2018, more than 262,000 registered voters will go to 472 polling stations to choose their future: the illustrious unknown but nevertheless democratic Ibrahim Mohamed Solih or the aggressive outgoing president Abdulla Yameen.

Figure 100: 2018 Presidential Elections. Counting.

At the closing of the polls, what neither the Maldivians nor the international community had been waiting for happens: the outgoing president Yameen is defeated in the first round!

Solih won 58.13% of the vote against 41.87% for Yameen.

"It's a moment of joy, a moment of hope. It is a journey that ends in the ballot box because the people wanted it that way," Ibrahim Mohamed Solih said to the press in Malé on the evening of his victory. "The message is strong and clear: the people of the Maldives want change, peace and justice. I would like to call on President Yameen to accept the will of the people and begin a smooth transition of power as provided for in the constitution," he added.

Yameen's defeat and Solih's victory can be explained by the excessive repression applied by Yameen during his term of office. It is possible that the scale of his action to improve the lives of Maldivians did not counterbalance his brutality.

On the morning of September 24, the man whom the international press described as a patent electoral fraudster, publicly admitted his defeat, announced that he had met and congratulated his rival and promised to ensure a smooth transition. At the time of writing, there is no evidence that the 2018 election was flawed. This election result raises questions about the impartiality of the international press when trying to predict the results of elections in foreign countries. It is reminiscent of the surprise of the French media when Donald Trump won the U.S. presidential election.

The date for the transfer of power is set for November 17, 2018.

From the evening of Monday, September 24, 2018, the justice system reopens several files. For example, the opposition leader of the Jumhooree Party, Abdulla Riyaz, imprisoned since the state of emergency of February 2018, is released. Other important prisoners, such as Maumoon Abdul Gayoom, were transferred to the court in Malé to be heard again by the justice system. Then, during the night of September 24-25, the justice system began to release one by one Yameen's opponents who had been unjustly imprisoned for months or years.

In the streets, a few voices demand Gayoom's release and Yameen's arrest. On September 30, 2018, former president Maumoon Abdul Gayoom was released in exchange for bail of 60,000 rufiyaa (3,357 euros).

Ibrahim Mohamed Solih (2018-...)

Figure 101: Ibrahim Mohamed Solih

Ibrahim Mohamed Solih, more commonly known as Ibu, is a politician affiliated with the Maldivian Democratic Party (MDP), which he helped to create.

Solih was born on March 1, 1962 on the island of Hinnavaru but spent most of his life in Malé with his 12 brothers and sisters.

Like many former presidents, he is an alumnus of the Majeediyya School. During his studies, he was a popular student and involved in many activities, especially sports.

In 1994, at the age of thirty, he became deputy of the atoll where he was born, Lhaviyani.

In 2001, Ibrahim Solih was one of 42 people who attempted to form an opposition party, but the government refused to do so.

Finally, in 2004, he succeeded in founding the CDM with his friend Nasheed.

He is known as someone who knows how to listen and communicate with people. Even his opponents call him calm and imperturbable. His temperament gives him the advantage in situations of commitment and negotiation.

Discreet, until his election as president of the Maldives in 2018, he did everything he could to avoid appearing too much in the media. On the evening of his victory in the presidential election, he is so little known to the public and the international community that the exact date of his birth is unknown: on his Wikipedia page, he is marked "Date of birth: 1964 (age 53 or 54)".

Government

Executive

Officially, the country's current political regime (2018) is a "representative presidential democratic republic". It is like in France except that there is no longer any notion of Prime Minister since 1975.

Executive power is exercised by the government. The head of government is the president.

The President works and lives in the Presidential Palace, the Muliaage, a building built between 1914 and 1919, except for Maumoon Abdul Gayoom who preferred a much more recent building during his term of office: the Theemuge.

Mohamed Nasheed, a much simpler man in his way of life, refused to live in the former presidential palace of Gayoom, the Theemuge, preferring the Muliaage residence from which he walked to the presidential office every morning.

Under Gayoom, the operating budget for the presidential palace was $150 million a year compared to $4 million for Nasheed. As if to humiliate his predecessor, in 2009, Nasheed had the Theemuge Palace opened to Maldivians and the press so that they could see for themselves where their money went under Gayoom's mandates. Then he put many of the former president's luxury items on sale and used the precious Italian furniture to replace the missing furniture in the administrative offices. Finally, the Theemuge was entrusted to the Supreme Court.

The following timeline lists the Presidents of the Maldives.

Mohamed Amin Didi	Ibrahim Muhammad Didi	Ibrahim Nasir	Maumoon Abdul Gayoom
1953 - 1953	1953 - 1954	1968 - 1978	1978 - 2008
1 mandate	1 mandate	2 mandates	6 mandates

1st Republic	2nd **Republic**

Mohamed Nasheed	Mohammed Waheed Hassan	Abdulla Yameen	Ibrahim Mohamed Solih
2008 - 2012	2012 - 2013	2013 - 2018	2018 - ...
1 mandate	1 mandate	1 mandate	

2nd Republic

Figure 102: Current Presidential Palace, the Muliaage

Figure 103: The Theemuge houses the Supreme Court

The President appoints the rest of his cabinet. Unlike France, in the Maldives, the Cabinet is exactly the same as the government: it is the list of ministers + the Vice-President + the President. Its composition in 2018 is:

- The President,
- The Vice President,
- The Minister of Defense and National Security,
- The Minister of Tourism,
- The Minister of Foreign Affairs,
- The Minister of Economic Development,
- The Minister of Fisheries and Agriculture,
- The Attorney General (Justice),
- The Minister of Education,
- The Minister of Youth and Sports,
- The Minister of the Environment and Energy,
- The Minister of Gender and Family,
- The Minister of Housing and Infrastructure,
- The Minister of Islamic Affairs,
- The Minister of Finance and Treasury,
- The Minister of Health,
- The Minister of the Interior.

The astonishing Ministry of Gender and Family claims to work for the protection and promotion of the rights of "vulnerable groups" in the Maldives, i.e. its work is to ensure:

- Women's rights and empowerment,
- Gender equality,
- Children's rights and family welfare,
- The rights of seniors,
- The rights of the disabled.

Parliament

The Parliament of the Maldives consists of only one legislative chamber called the People's Majlis or People's Council. The Majlis is the authority responsible for enacting, amending and revising all laws except the Constitution of the Maldives. It consists of 85 members. The President is present only once a year, on the last Thursday of February when he opens the session by presenting his political vision and the actions of his government.

The two largest political parties in the Maldives are the PPM (Progressive Party of Maldives) and the MDP (Maldivian Democratic Party).

Figure 104: Interior of Parliament

Founded in 2011, the PPM is a right-wing party whose ideology is based on nationalism and Islamic democracy. The PPM is a fairly young party in the history of the Maldives: it was founded by former President Gayoom in 2011 and then he was ousted from his own party by his half-brother Abdulla Yameen on October 16, 2016 in a manner reminiscent of the internal struggles of the National Front in France. It is the largest party in terms of membership (49,416). The party's objective is to lead the Maldives towards an "independent, safe, secure, rich, developed democracy with a robust and diversified economy while preserving the nation's Islamic heritage".

The country's second party is the CDM, founded in 2003. Until 2018 it represents the opposition. It has 29,277 members. Its stated objective is to promote human rights and democracy. Its ideology is liberal-democratic or center-right.

Forensic

The system of justice is based on Sharia (Islamic law) to which are added appendices from the Common Law (British law) for trade. The Maldives does not recognize any international court decisions such as the International Court of Justice.

Since 2014, the death penalty is back in the judicial arsenal after a moratorium that lasted 60 years. In 2014, referring to the Sharia, Abdulla Yameen Abdul Gayoom, the Maldivian president, proclaims loud and clear: "Murder must be punished by murder!" He then buried the 1954 moratorium by reintroducing capital punishment for criminals. It could theoretically apply to those convicted of murder, terrorism, national treason, adultery and apostasy. It is applicable to all individuals aged at least... 7 years old!

Since the end of the moratorium, there are between 17 and 20 people on death row. The modus operandi that awaits them is lethal injection. In 2016, the murderer Hussain Humaam Ahmed narrowly escaped the death penalty: the execution was postponed after repeated calls from the international community.

No future execution date is officially mentioned. It is likely that the government of the Maldives is trying to avoid the bad reputation that the news of an execution would cause and fears its impact on the tourism industry. There have been no executions in the Maldives since 1953.

The Maldivian population

The Maldivians are a people of just over 500,000 inhabitants spread over 202 tiny islands. The main cities are Malé (103,000 inhabitants) and Addu City (32,000 inhabitants).

This people isolated from the world speaks a little-known language: the divehi (or dhivehi). But due to its past British colonization, English is well mastered. And a third language penetrates well the Maldivian population: Arabic.

Distribution

According to the official statistics of 2012, the population of the Maldives is distributed mainly in the 10 localities below. The term "locality" is generic: in this table, some localities are islands, others are cities. There are only three cities in the Maldives: Malé, Fuvahmulah and Addu.

Rank	Location	Population
1	Malé	103 693
2	Addu City	31 999
3	Fuvahmulah	11 857
4	Kulhudhuffushi	8 974
5	Thinadhoo	7 108
6	Naifaru	5 133
7	Hinnavaru	4 676
8	Gan	4 385
9	Dhuvaafaru	4 368
10	Dhidhdhoo	3 848

Composition

In 2014, the population of the Maldives consisted of precisely 402,071 people: 338,434 Maldivians and 63,637 permanent resident foreigners. Immigrants were thus 15.82% of the population.

In 2018, this population is revised upwards: 512,038 inhabitants are estimated with a large male/female imbalance. 192,375 women and 319,663 men were counted in the census. This is mainly due to the contribution of foreign male workers.

The most numerous foreigners (except tourists) in the archipelago are Bengalis, Indians and Sri Lankans.

5,589 Maldivians (people with a Maldivian passport) live outside the Maldives, making it a very small diaspora.

Ethnically, the most represented group is the Dhivehis, the historical ethnic group of the Maldives, Minicoy Island and Lakshadweep, two overseas regions of India bordering the Maldives. Anthropological studies attest that the Dhivehis share common genes with the Sinhalese of Sri Lanka as well as with other populations of northern India such as the Marathis,

Konkanis or Gujaratis to which are added genetic traces of Arabs, Malaysians, South Indians and Africans.

It is easy to believe that the ethnic origins of the Maldivians come essentially from India, 620 km away, or Sri Lanka, 770 km from Malé. In addition, the nearest Arab country is Oman, located 2,500 km away. Finally, the African continent is about 2,600 km from the Maldives. On the other hand, there are very few East Asian origins (Japan, China) in the chromosomes of Maldivians. Their eyes are not slanted.

Figure 105: Maldivian Youth

Moreover, in the past, there was a different ethnic group: the Giraavaru of Kaafu Atoll. The Giraavaru are descendants of Tamils from the southwest coast of India who probably settled on Kaafu in -300. They are the ones who founded the capital, Malé. Until the 20th century, the Giraavaru were physically, linguistically and culturally very different from the inhabitants of the other islands of the country. Their culture and language were clearly a derivative of Tamil/Malayalam.

The Giraavaru were strictly monogamous and prohibited divorce. Their music was very distinctly different from that of the Divehi. Their clothes and jewelry were also distinctive: blue beads and necklaces that no other Maldivian was wearing.

History tells us that the Giraavaru people were always led by a woman, the foolhuma-dhaitha, representing the authority of the Sultan of the Maldives on the island of Giraavaru. The sultans also recognized the cultural exception of the Giraavaru and their autonomy: they did not enforce the laws of the kingdom on the Giraavaru.

In 1932, things changed: The Constitution of the Maldives was adopted and the customary rights that the Giraavaru enjoyed were no longer recognized at all. Any derogations granted by the sultans were cancelled.

Figure 106: Centara Ras Fushi Resort and Spa on Giraavaru

In 1968, due to the rapid erosion of the island, the Giraavaru community was reduced to a handful of members. They are forced to abandon the island because of an Islamic rule that stipulates that no island populated by less than 40 males is allowed in the Maldives. This rule is based on the minimum number of men required for Friday prayers.

Figure 107: Giraavaru women in traditional costume

It is by ferry that the remaining inhabitants are deported to the island of Hulhulé, 12.9 kilometers away. Hulhulé is the current island of the international airport of Malé.

Since then, the culture and ethnic characteristics of the Giraavaru have been assimilated into the wider Maldivian society. From marriage to marriage, it is certain that there is no longer a person with a "pure blood" giraavaru. In any case, this community, due to its millennial isolation had ended up being highly inbred and developing genetic problems. This inbreeding had already been fought in the 1940s by forcing the Giraavaru to mix with the rest of the country.

As for the island, after having lost a considerable amount of land, it has been taken over by the hotel industry. The Centara Ras Fushi Resort & Spa hotel is built on it. One population drove out another: Islamic law said it was uninhabitable; the law of capitalism found a way to populate it with 280 vacationers.

Human Development Index

The Human Development Index (HDI) is a composite statistical index to assess the human development rate of the world's countries. The HDI is a dimensionless, composite index ranging from 0 (terrible) to 1 (excellent). It is calculated by the average of three indices quantifying respectively:

- health / longevity (measured by life expectancy at birth), which indirectly measures the satisfaction of essential material needs such as access to healthy food, drinking water, decent housing, good hygiene and medical care;
- knowledge or level of education. It is measured by the average length of schooling for adults over 25 years of age and the expected length of schooling for school-age children. It reflects the satisfaction of intangible needs such as the ability to participate in decision-making in the workplace or in society;
- Standard of living (logarithm of gross income per capita in purchasing power parity), to encompass elements of quality of life not described by the first two indices such as mobility or access to culture.

As such, the Maldives score 0.712 points in 2018 and ranks 101st out of 189 countries.

The following is a comparative extract of the HDIs in 2018.

1st	24th	101st	123rd	189th
Norway	France	Maldives	Morocco	Niger
0,953	0,901	0,712	0,667	0,354

Divehi language

Maldivian, divehi, dhivehi, or locally called ދިވެހިބަސް (divehi-low), is an Indo-Aryan language spoken by about 340,000 speakers, mainly in the Maldives, of which it is the official language, as well as in Lakshadweep, another archipelago with the status of territory of the Indian Union (in the form of the Mahl or Mahal dialect). This language has been influenced by many others throughout its history, including Arabic. Other influences include Sinhala, Malayalam, Hindi, French, Persian, Portuguese and English. Divehi is thought to have common origins with Sinhala. The language from which these two idioms are said to have originated became extinct around the year 500 BC.

After the arrival of Islam, Arabic had a significant impact on the language. It began to borrow many Persian or Arabic words such as

- namādu - " prayer " (from Persian namāz)
- rōda - "young" (from Persian rōzā)
- kāfaru - "non-believer" (from Arabic kāfir)
- taareekh - "date" or "history" (from Arabic tarikh)
- zaraafaa - "giraffe" (from Arabic zarafah)

Of the colonial Portuguese presence, there are very few words left in the vocabulary:

- lonsi - "hunting spear" (from Portuguese lança)
- mēzu - "table" (from Portuguese mesa).

Due to the dispersion of the islands of the archipelago, variations have appeared in pronunciation and vocabulary, mainly between the northern and southern atolls. Thus, the inhabitants of Malé do not understand the dialect of Addu.

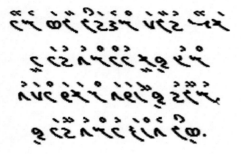

Figure 108: Love poem in Divehi

Divehi is currently written using a specific Semitic consonant (abjad) alphabet: the thaana, which is written from right to left.

But in the past, the divehi was written with the dhives akuru alphabet, from left to right. This writing was used throughout the archipelago until the 17th century, that is to say until the introduction of Islam, and continued to be used until the beginning of the 20th century for the writing of official texts. Its use was still frequent in the very isolated islands and by some rural communities until the 1960s. Since the death of the last user at the end of the last century, this writing is no longer taught to Maldivians, except for historical purposes.

The literacy rate in the Maldives is very high (98%) compared to other Southeast Asian countries. Since the 1960s, English has become the language of education in most schools, although there are still classes in Divehi. English is used throughout the administration.

The introduction of English into the educational system poses a threat to the Divehi language. English has a level of linguistic sophistication that relegates the Divehi language to linguists alone.

Divehi	Translation
Haalu kihineh?	How are you doing?
Shukuriyaa (Hindi word)	Thank you
Kon nameh tha kiyanee?	What is your name?
Kohfa members	Please.
Aan	Yes
Noon	No
Baajjaveri hendhuneh	Hello
Ahannakah neyngunu	I do not understand
Kobaa?	Where?
Ekeh	A
Dehyh	Two

Maldivian speakers abroad live mainly in Sri Lanka (20,000), India (10,000), Malaysia (1,500), the United Kingdom (1,000), Singapore (1,000), Pakistan (450), Australia (450) and Egypt (150).

The first Westerner who took the initiative to study the Divehi language academically was the linguist Christopher Reynolds (1922 - 2015). Reynolds' work is considerable: after living in Malé for four months in 1967, this Oxford graduate tirelessly studied Divehi until 2003, when his English/Divehi dictionary was published. It is a 432-page book that sweeps through 5,000 words. It costs the trifle of 150 euros on Amazon.

In 2005, a second English/divehi dictionary was published. Its authors are a Maldivian and an Australian: F. Abdulla and M.

O'Shea. It is sold in electronic format only, 8.99 euros on Google Play.

Family

The legal age of marriage is 18, but in practice about half of all women marry at about age 15. Marriages are not arranged. Under Islamic law a man may have up to four wives provided he can support them financially. However, polygamy is rare today. Sex before marriage is a crime. Marriages can only be performed between two Muslims. Needless to say, the Maldives allows only heterosexual marriages.

The country holds the world record for the divorce rate. A study published in 1977 showed that one in two women in their thirties had been married four or more times.

Country	Number of divorces per year per 1,000 inhabitants
Maldives	10,97
Russia	4,50
Aruba	4,40
Belarus	4,10
United States	3,60

It is extremely interesting to find out why the Maldives holds this divorce record. The answer lies in three principles.

On Earth, about 23,000 years ago, humans began to grow food by inventing agriculture. Then the invention of the plough 4,000 years ago led to an increase in production but also to an efficient division of labor between men and women. Because men were physically stronger and less tied to their children (we are only talking about pregnancy and breastfeeding), agriculture laid the foundation for the notion of family: men stayed on to work the land and women took care of the children and a myriad of other domestic tasks. From this organization, the concept of marriage was born to unite two people in the eyes of the community. Agriculture united people to their plot of land and men and women together so that after three, four years of effort neither man nor woman would be tempted to go elsewhere. Staying together made it possible to consume together the food that was grown and to take care of the children that were raised.

But in the Maldives, the situation was not at all like that since agriculture was embryonic for centuries. It was the lack of importance of agriculture that caused the lack of importance given to marriage.

The second reason is the half-nomadic, half-sedentary life of men. This string of islands, sometimes separated by just one kilometer of lagoon, has allowed the population to be very mobile. The men in particular were able to have any leisure to change islands for any pretext, by taking to sea in fishing boats. This is the concept of "the woman in every port": it was enough to bring back fish and the woman was seduced, whatever the island.

There is a third reason: it is the prohibition of fornication, in other words, sexual relations outside of marriage. Maldivian men and women know that to avoid being whipped in public for fornication, it is enough to get married before having intimate relations with a new partner and then, if necessary, to divorce. This is called temporary marriage (mut'a in Arabic).

Generally speaking, weddings are so unimportant in the Maldives that by arriving, for example, two minutes late to a wedding, a guest may miss the entire ceremony! There is rarely a party in the evening.

Conversely, divorce is not a disgrace. It is even well seen to have often divorced: it is a sign of sexual maturity.

258

Contrary to other Muslim countries, Maldivian homes are quite small, i.e. like in Europe: one father, one mother, two children. (Fertility rate = 2.09 children per woman in 2015). Families are matriarchal.

Because of the small size of the population, the communities outside of Malé are married groups with a high risk of consanguinity.

Until a few years ago, it was rare to call a person by his or her real first name. Instead, people were called by "alternative names" such as Dohuttu, Lahuttu, Tutteedi, Kudamaniku or Don Goma. The rationale behind this strange practice is that if the evil spirits do not know a person's real name, the person is not likely to be subjected to spells. However, Maldivians have many first and last names: usually three words. The first name, followed by the father's first name, followed by the last name. This is taken from Maldivian and Arabic names. Common Maldivian surnames are Bee, Beefan, Boo, Didi, Fan, Fulhu, Kader, Kalaminja, Kalinga, Kalo, Kavah, Kavya, Koi, Koya, Manik, Manika, Manike, Manikfan, Naha, Raha, Rana, Tarkan, Thakhan, Thakur, Thakurfan, Veer.

Human relations and character

One of the striking aspects of the character of Maldivians is their obvious lack of emotions. They are calm and not very expressive. Children are taught to keep their thoughts to themselves, even at home. People do not seem close to each other. In particular, there is a great emotional distance between the children and their father. When Maldivians meet friends, they don't seem happier than that. There isn't even a word divehi to say "hi! (informal greeting) and the word "thank you" must have been borrowed from the Hindi language. There is little expression of compassionate emotions. It takes a long time for a Maldivian to become friends with a foreigner, despite his courtesy. One can try to explain this stoic attitude with a theory that this people, surrounded by water, knows that they are at the mercy of the elements and take nothing for granted.

Habitat

The traditional Maldivian house is the bodruge: a shed made of woven coconut leaves and a thatched roof. The kitchen was historically separated from the rest of the house and made of wood branches other than coconut. The mild weather conditions explain the absence of complex thermal insulation elements.

Figure 109: Traditional Coconut House

Later, the Maldivians used a more solid material: stone, but at first only for tombs and mosques. This stone is, in fact, the corpse of an animal: the coral. The coral reefs that helped build the country played a vital role in the economy and the well-being of the inhabitants. Coral has become the main material for the construction of buildings and roadways. Coral blocks are extracted in shallow water at a depth of one or two meters, sometimes with the help of an iron bar to break off pieces of coral, sometimes alive. Being the only accessible stone, for many years, coral has been largely removed. The most coveted species of coral is porite, a kind of coral producing large balls of limestone.

Figure 110: Porite coral

Over the years, Maldivians stopped using coconut palm branches and turned to coral stone because owning a coral house was considered prestigious and a sign of a certain lifestyle. The other use of coral as a building material is lime: to make lime one simply collects and crushes coral debris (there is plenty on the ground in the Maldives), puts it in a crucible and heats it. The powder obtained can be used as cement to glue the coral bricks. Nowadays, the preservation of the country's underwater heritage makes it totally forbidden to extract coral, dead or alive.

Figure 111: Coral house

Except in Malé, there is no concept of apartment. Maldivians are used to live in individual houses. In 2000, for example, there were 43,556 dwellings in the Maldives of which only 324 were apartments.

The average size of the homes ranges from three to six rooms. 68% of the inhabitants rely on rainwater as their primary source of water. Only 43% have a septic tank. They rarely have a garage because the vast majority of residents do not have a car. 99% of people have access to drinking water and 98% have sanitary facilities.

On the rural islands, it is the government that historically allocated each family's land: a piece of land about 15 meters by 30 meters. The house is in the center of the rectangle and is only used for sleeping. The kitchen and bathroom are separate constructions. The bathroom traditionally had no roof.

In Malé, most of the inhabitants live in apartments. The architectural style of the capital is inspired by Colombo in Sri Lanka.

Across the country, imported materials such as concrete and metal are now being used in existing buildings.

Figure 112: Apartments buildings in Malé

Religion

Islam is the state religion of the Maldives. However, due to its isolation from the historical centers of Islam in Asia and the Middle East, pre-Islamic beliefs have persisted. Clarence Maloney, an anthropologist, studied the Maldives in the 1970s. An imam explained to him that for many Maldivians, Islam consisted of observing ablutions, fasting, and reciting formulas that were incomprehensible in Arabic. Nevertheless, the situation has changed since the turn of the Iranian Revolution. In 1991, the Maldives had a total of 725 mosques and 266 women's mosques.

Figure 113: Hulhumalé ultramodern mosque

The conversion of the Maldives to Islam is rather late compared to other parts of South Asia. Arab merchants had converted the people of the Malabar coast to Islam as early as the seventh century. The conqueror Muhammad ibn al-Qasim had subjected large areas of Sindh (southern Pakistan today) to Islam at the same time. The Maldives remained Buddhist for 500 years, before converting by force too.

The first contacts of the archipelago with Islam took place because of sailors and merchants from Arabia or the Bay of Bengal. But the major actor of the arrival of Islam in the Maldives is Abu al-Barakat al-Barbari. His tomb is located inside the Hukuru Mosque, or Miski, in the capital city of Malé. It seems that this traveler obtained the conversion to Islam of a king who reigned from 1141 to 1166. Nevertheless, the chronicles of Raadavalhi and Tharik, attribute to a Persian, Yusuf Tabrizi, the conversion of the Maldivian kingdom to Islam in 1153. The king becomes sultan following his conversion after twelve years of reign and he sends emissaries to all the atolls to convert the inhabitants to the Muslim faith, without exception. The king himself travels to the island of Nilandhe to call its inhabitants to embrace Islam. It is reported that the conversion of the entire archipelago took place on the 2nd of Rabi ul Akhir of the year 548 AH, the 17th year of reign of Al-Muqtafi, Caliph of Baghdad. From then on, the Maldives became a predominantly Islamic country. The king orders his brother Siri Kalo to build the first mosque in Malé, with the help of Al-Wazir Shanivirazaa. A traveler from North Africa, Ibn Battuta, accredits this conversion of Dhovemi through Abu al-Barakat al-Barbari. Ibn Battûta left a residence in 1340, which attests to his passage. Dhovemi enforced Islamic law. The sultan removed all traces of idolatry from the archipelago and built mosques on many islands, even uninhabited ones.

Archaeology and other scriptural sources at least partially confirm this version. A document called Dhanbidhū Lōmāfānu provides information on the disappearance of Buddhism in Hadhdhunmathi atoll, which was an important religious center. It appears that Buddhist monks were taken to Malé and executed. The satihirutalu (three concentric stone circles crowning a stupa) were destroyed to disfigure the stupas, as well as the statues of Vairocana, which were found in the

266

middle of the archipelago. The state of damage to the manuscripts made by the monks in their monastery suggests that the buildings were burned or razed to the ground so that no trace of them can be found, a recurring tradition in all Islamic conquests.

Islam shapes the daily life of Maldivians. The state applies Islamic law, the Sharia, called in divehi, the sariatu; it serves as the basis for codes of law, interpreted according to the living conditions of Maldivians by the President of the Republic, the Attorney General, the Ministry of the Interior and the Majlis (Parliament). As Friday is the traditional day of the Great Prayer at the mosque, shops and offices close around 11:00 am. They also close for fifteen minutes after each of the five daily prayer calls. During the month of Ramadan, cafes and restaurants are closed during the day, and working hours are reduced.

Most of the islands have several mosques, even if they are sparsely inhabited. Malé, the capital, has more than thirty. Most of the mosques are made of coral stone, painted white and with corrugated iron or thatched roofs. In Malé, an Islamic center of sophisticated architecture was built in 1984 with funds from the Persian Gulf states, Pakistan, Brunei and Malaysia.

The most important festival throughout the year is Kuda Id which marks the end of Ramadan. For one month, adults fast from sunrise to sunset. It is a real test of their faith, in a country where it is so hot and where the eyes are always on water. It is very difficult not to drink water all day long. When the sun sets, a sound produced with a large shell announces to the whole island that it is possible to break the fast. The inhabitants then rush on coconut water or tea and throw themselves on small cookies while waiting for the dinner made of rice and fish curry.

Rhythm of life

The work week runs from Sunday to Thursday. In other words, the weekend consists of Friday and Saturday.

Maldivians begin their working day around 7:30 am in the public service and between 8:30 and 9:00 am in the private sector. Some shops open at 6:00 am. Because the day ends at 1:30 p.m. in the civil service, civil servants often have a second job in the private sector. All businesses and offices closed four times a day for 15 minutes for prayer. Working hours are reduced during Ramadan.

Maldivians use three calendars. The only one that is official is the Islamic calendar still called Hegirian calendar. This book for example is written during the year 1440 of the Hegira. For reasons related to globalization and tourism, the Gregorian calendar is also used. Finally, on some islands, the inhabitants sometimes use a local calendar called the nakaly. It is a calendar based on weather changes, tides, stars, the sun, the moon... This use is lost.

Sports

A distinction must be made between the sports and aquatic activities performed by wealthy tourists and those practiced by natives.

Tourists come to the Maldives to enjoy water sports or visual sensations such as snorkeling, diving, jet skiing, beach volleyball, parasailing, canoeing or windsurfing.

For their part, the local inhabitants, who are less wealthy, tend rather to practice collective and drier sports such as soccer or athletics. Only children play in the sea for a reason related to Islam: it is badly perceived to wear clothes revealing the body of adults, especially when wet.

On almost all inhabited islands, one can see a soccer field more or less developed because, as in many countries of the world, soccer is the national sport. It is organized by the Football Association of Maldives (FAM), founded in 1982. The association is under the supervision of the Ministry of Youth and Sports. In 1986, it manages to integrate the Asian Football Confederation (AFC) and FIFA. In terms of their route to the World Cup, the Maldives have never managed to go beyond the qualifiers. Same situation in the Asian Cup. The country's greatest soccer achievement is its victory in the final of the South Asian Football Championship in 2008.

Figure 114: Crowd in jubilation after the 2008 victory

The influence of nearby India also brings an interest in cricket. It is the Maldives national cricket team that represents the country in competitions in this part of the world. This team has been a member of the International Cricket Council since 2001. On December 11, 2010, the Maldives team won the ACC Trophy Challenge held in Thailand.

Figure 115: Cricket team returning to the Maldives in 2010

The Maldives organizes its own marathon once a year on the atoll of Addu, in the city of the same name.

Figure 116: Addu 2018 Marathon Poster

The Maldives marathon record holder was Ahmed Sharaf who finished the marathon in Rabat, Morocco, on March 5, 2017 in 2 hours 43 minutes and 13 seconds.

A few months later, he was beaten by Muhammad Shifaz at the Kathmandu Marathon on September 16, 2017, which finished in 2 hours 40 minutes and 47 seconds.

As a reminder, the world marathon record is held by a Kenyan with 2 hours 2 minutes and 57 seconds.

Figure 117: Sky view, soccer and cricket fields in Malé

Unsurprisingly, Maldivians have never participated in the Winter Olympics. On the other hand, they have been present at several Summer Olympic Games since 1988 but without ever winning anything as a medal. The level of the Maldives at the Olympic Games is each time mediocre. The delegations consisted of between four and eight athletes only.

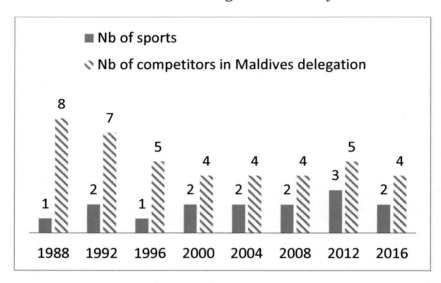

Figure 118: Number of sports and size of delegations to the Olympics

The history of the Maldives at the Olympic Games begins in Seoul 1988 with a delegation of eight athletes. The performances are not there.

Athlete	Proof	Time	Position in qualification
Ibrahim Shareef	100 m	11,49	95th
	200 m	23,17	71st
Ahmed Shageef	400 m	50,61	67th
Abdul Haji Abdul Latheef	Marathon	-	Does not

			finish the race
Hussein Haleem	Marathon	-	Does not finish the race
Ismail Asif Ibrahim Manik Abdul Razzak Aboobakur Mohamed Hanim	4x100 m relay	44,31	26th

At the 1992 Barcelona Olympic Games, Hussein Haleem finished second to last in the marathon but at least he finished the event.

The Maldives is also sending delegations to the Olympic Games in Atlanta 1996, Sydney 2000, Athens 2004 and Beijing 2008.

At the London 2012 Olympic Games, five Maldivians are competing for this 7th participation of the country. Only three sports are disputed by the Maldivian delegation. Mohamed Ajfan Rasheed, the first Maldivian badminton player to participate in the Olympics is the flag bearer at the opening ceremony. He finishes last out of 40 participants in his discipline. Azneem Ahmed, sprinter is in his turn the flag bearer at the closing ceremony. With 10.79 seconds, he breaks his country's record in the men's 100-metre event. Afa Ismail is also present in athletics: Afa Ismail, 12.52 seconds in the women's 100 meters. Finally, in swimming, Ahmed Husam and Aminath Shajan run the 100-meter freestyle for men and 50-meter freestyle for women. Husam was eliminated in 53rd place and Shajan in 63rd place in the qualifiers.

At the 2016 Olympic Games in Rio de Janeiro, four Maldivians are competing. Hassan Saaid and Afa Ismail for athletics and Ibrahim Nishwan and Aminath Shajan for swimming. Saaid manages to climb to 8th place in the quarter-finals of the men's

100m. Ismail breaks her country's record in the women's 200m with 24.96 seconds.

Figure 119: Maldivian Delegation, Rio 2016

In an interview, Aminath Shajan explains the conditions in which she trains: "In the Maldives, we train in the sea because we don't have a swimming pool. Sometimes we train in the middle of all the garbage floating around. And also, sometimes jellyfish sting us." Ibrahim Nishwan adds "we have little light at night, there are waves, garbage in the water. When we take breaths, as we can't see anything, we get water in our mouths ... or other things."

In the women's 100-meter freestyle qualifying event for the Rio 2016 Games, Aminath Shajan finished last (if we don't count the two withdrawals of the Italian and Swedish swimmers). It's a little better for the men's 50-meter freestyle qualifying event with Ibrahim Nishwan's 71st place out of 85.

Moreover, among the rare sports truly invented in the Maldives, we find the Maldivian martial art: hevikan and the Maldivian equivalent of tennis: bashi. Practiced exclusively by women, bashi is a sport whose origins are obscure. Prior to the 1950s, female players used balls and bats made from coconut fibres and wood. Today, it is with tennis balls and rackets that players compete eleven against eleven.

Figure 120: Bashi Match

Figure 121: Hevikan battle, 1907

An ancient Maldivian game, thin mugoali has been played for over 400 years. It is a kind of baseball game.

Mandi is a kind of lacrosse: players use large poles to catch a small stick that they must prevent from falling to the ground.

Finally, bai bala is a kind of wrestling sport resembling Japanese sumo: you have to try to touch the opponent and get him out of the ring.

Transport

Maldivians, as you might expect, do not take the subway or train. Their means of transport are the following (in 2015) :

- 5,269 cars,
- 66,527 motorcycles or scooters,
- 8,157 other vehicles on the road,
- 12,672 miscellaneous boats.

Tourists benefit from the seaplanes of the Trans Maldivian company to move from island to island. Their fleet is 48 seaplanes in 2018. Tickets cost between 250 and 450 US dollars. The crossing can take a handful of minutes and 1h30 for the farthest resorts of Malé.

Figure 122: Malé Airport

Nowadays, island to island journeys for locals are made by ferry. The longest journey takes 15 hours. Prices range from two to ten US dollars. The domestic transportation system is developed by the MTCC company. It is somewhat equivalent to the SNCF in France: the MTCC offers a range of transportation solutions to its 30,000 daily users:

- Ferry authorizing the transport of scooters and motorcycles between Malé and Hulhumalé,
- Ultra-fast shuttles between Malé and the airport,
- Bus to Malé and Hulhumalé,
- Minibus or car rental,
- Wide proposal of intra-atoll ferry links,
- Wide proposal of inter-atolls ferry links.

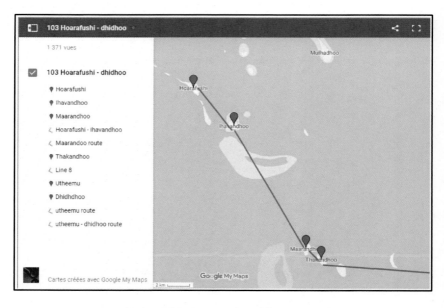

Figure 123: Example of ferry line 103

There are (in 2018) 41 ferry lines whose routes resemble metro lines. The southern atolls (Gaafu and Seenu) are the only ones not served by the public service.

It is anecdotal but Maldivians are not adepts of the bicycle which they consider as the means of locomotion of the poor.

The car is widely used only on about three islands: Malé, Addu and Hulhumalé. At the pump, the inhabitants pay for their diesel about 0.60 euro per liter and gasoline 0.65 euro per liter.

Historically, on the sea, the traditional transport is the doni or dhoni, a type of boat from the Maldives or Sri Lanka. Of a very flared shape, quite comparable to a Viking boat, it measures between 6 and 12 meters, carries a crew of 4 to 8 people and sails.

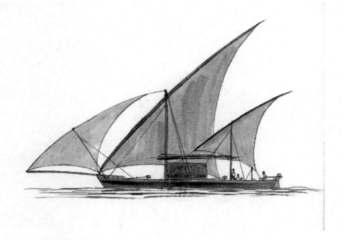

Figure 124: Traditional Maldivian Boat

Finally, on tiny islands, walking is an obvious mode of locomotion.

Education and Universities

Traditionally, children aged three years or older in the Maldives were educated in what is called edhurge, usually in a large room or in the shade of a large tree. The children learned numeracy, dhivehi, some Arabic, and read the Koran.

This type of school no longer exists because it has been replaced by the Western style of schooling. The first Western style school was the Majeediyya School located in Malé since April 9, 1927. It is only since 2010 that girls are admitted there. This school is famous in the country: all the presidents of the Maldives have been students there.

In 1944, the same type of school was created but for girls: Aminiyya School. Since June 14, 2011, it too has become a co-educational school.

Figure 125: School on Medhufushi

In 1976, the government launched a major program to modernize education. This project included teacher training, curriculum development, radio education, textbook development and printing, and adult education. It also aims to erase the gap in level between the capital and the atolls. Under this program, the first school was inaugurated in Eydhafushi in March 1978, then on Kulhudhuffushi in 1979. School construction continued on all the atolls.

In 2002, the Office of the President announced that universal elementary school coverage had been achieved and that, as a result, the literacy rate had increased from 70 percent in 1978 to 98.82 percent in 2002.

In 2011, the National University Act is enacted and provides the impetus for the creation of the country's first university. It was not created ex nihilo: it is the combination of several former institutions.

In 2018, to continue their higher education, Maldivians have the choice of the following schools:

Name	Location	Program
Maldives National University	Malé	Arts, Sciences, Medicine, Tourism, Islam, Commerce
Cyryx College	Malé	Business, Computer Science, Arts and Design, Education
Mandhu	Malé	Information Technology, Tourism, Commerce
Villa College	Malé	Management, Business, Computer Science, Islam, Languages, Sharia, Law, Oceanography
MAPS College	Malé	Accounting, finance, management, hospitality, technology.
Avid College	Malé	Computer Science, Human Resources, Education, Business, Project Management, Psychology
Maldives Business	Malé	IT, Human Resources,

School		Administration, Commerce, Project Management, Advertising, Marketing

Health care system

The health budget of the Maldives is 3.8% of GDP in 2011, or US$545 per capita. For comparison, in France, it is 11.6% of GDP or US$4,086 per capita. This low funding is complemented by the private sector and the participation of NGOs.

There is a severe lack of qualified personnel. There are an estimated 226 doctors, 75% of whom are foreigners, 358 registered nurses, and 204 other nurses without diplomas.

The Maldives has two hospitals in Malé, five regional hospitals, three atoll hospitals, and 40 health centers with beds (mini-hospitals). In the private sector, there are 30 clinics in Malé and 17 in the atolls. Given that there are 200 inhabited islands, this means that some Maldivians do not have access to health care without taking the boat.

The condition of the equipment is deplorable. Many devices need repair.

All of the country's medicines are imported. Extending health care to people outside of Malé has increased the Ministry of Health's expenses dramatically because of the logistics required to get the drugs to all the atolls.

Mental health is not a departmental priority. There are approximately 0.3% patients with mental health problems but no psychiatric hospitals or psychiatric departments in existing hospitals (as of 2011).

If we measure the effectiveness of a health system by life expectancy, then the Maldives has been improving slightly since 2000. Life expectancy in 2014 is 73 years for men and 74 years for women compared to 70 years in 2000.

The infant mortality rate is declining. In 2014, there will be eight deaths of children under one year of age per 1,000 births. To give you an order of magnitude, in France it is 3.6.

Care for pregnant women and babies is good. 95% of births are supervised by trained personnel and 98% of one-year-old children are vaccinated against measles.

Care of pregnant women rarely includes an ultrasound examination for economic reasons, but iron pills are prescribed, blood pressure is taken, women are weighed, and blood and urine tests are performed.

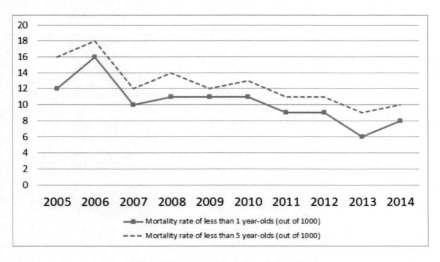

Figure 126: Infant mortality rate

In terms of contagious diseases, remarkable work has been accomplished. The Maldives no longer has any cases of malaria or any inhabitants affected by another mosquito-borne disease, lymphatic filariasis. The next two projects are the fight against syphilis and HIV transmitted from mother to fetus.

Dengue fever remains a problem but causes fewer deaths than before. Other contagious diseases that remain a burden are gastroenteritis and various non-fatal viral diseases.

The most widespread contagious diseases on the islands are acute respiratory infections (flu, ...) with 208,000 cases in 2015. This is almost one person out of two.

In terms of non-contagious disease, the prevalence of tobacco and consumption of sugars and fat and the new sedentary lifestyle of Maldivians has led to the emergence of cardiovascular diseases: 156 deaths per year. Maldivians are smokers at 37% and Maldivian women only 3.4%.

The government plans to equip the country a little better. A future program to set up pharmacies on every inhabited island will give Maldivians equal access to health care.

At the same time, the construction of the Dharumavantha Hospital, the largest building in the Maldives with 25 floors, has become a symbol of President Yameen's health policy. Located in Malé, the building will feature state-of-the-art medical facilities as well as extra-medical but very practical amenities: a chemical storage area (for cancer treatments), a gym, a hydrotherapy center, a nursery and a swimming pool.

Figure 127: Future Dharumavantha Hospital

Priority is now given to the training of paramedical staff in order to support prevention and support. The ministry's ambition in its 2016 program is that every Maldivian should have a healthy lifestyle and easy access to care.

A major innovation is still expected for an efficient health system in the Maldives: a regular means of maritime transport between the islands. The concept of sea ambulance was only introduced in the Maldives in 2014.

Telecommunications

Figure 128: Phone booth on an inhabited island

The Maldives, despite an obvious technical difficulty, is well connected to the rest of the world by telephone and Internet.

In 1995, a law forced the incumbent operator to connect all inhabitants of the Maldives to the telephone. To comply with this obligation, the operator Dhiraagu installed two telephone booths on each of the 200 inhabited islands before the year 2000. 18 years later, Internet access is a common service in the Maldives.

The main islands such as Malé or the one hosting the international airport are connected to the rest of Asia by an 837-meter-long submarine cable to connect the Maldives to the Sri Lanka internet network. This cable was laid on the bottom of the Indian Ocean in 2006. Another cable, the Fiber-Optic Link Around the Globe, also opens up the Maldives.

The rest of the islands are connected either by an antenna that communicates with Malé or by satellite.

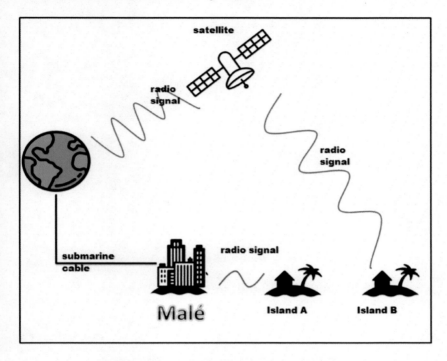

Figure 129: Modes of access to the Internet

Most of the hotels offer wifi (sometimes for free) to their guests at a rather correct rate for islands lost in the middle of the sea. Even in stilted villas, tourists can watch Netflix, read their e-mails or make a video call to make their friends jealous.

Figure 130: Telecommunication antenna on an island

Overall, the Maldives is therefore well connected to the world today.

Indicator	Number of subscribers (2018)
Fixed phones	19 970
Mobile Phones	861 507
Internet subscriptions	318 578

These figures should be compared to the number of inhabitants in 2018, i.e. 512,038.

Entertainment

There is a gap between the entertainment and recreation available to tourists on the resort islands and that available to Maldivians.

In Malé, youth is idle on this piece of land of 580 hectares. The activities are mainly limited to going to the only beach in Malé, Artificial Beach, which is not the most beautiful in the country, playing sports on the soccer or cricket fields, playing tennis or bashi, a local sport. Malé also has several fitness rooms.

Figure 131: Artificial Beach, Malé

Young people enjoy strolling in the small shopping malls of Malé, in the Sultan Park, in the National Museum or meeting in Republican Square.

Meeting places are mainly cafes and restaurants, especially those on the main avenue, Majeedhee Magu road.

There are very few movie theaters. The first one, the Olympus, opened in May 1959, specialized in Asian films.

Figure 132: Olympus in 1959 and 2014

The following ones only opened in 2010 under the impetus of Schwack Maldives Pvt Ltd, which entered the niche of Hollywood and Bollywood film releases.

The largest library in the country is the National Library. It was founded in 1940 when the then Minister of Justice installed a bookshelf in the Malé Courthouse. It contains 15,409 books in Divehi and 46,391 in English.

The National Stadium, also called Rasmee Dhandu Stadium is the largest stadium in the country with a capacity of 11,850 spectators. It is mainly used for soccer matches.

On the rural inhabited islands, the offer of entertainment is even more limited. Google Maps show that all the islands have a soccer field, which shows the importance of this sport as a hobby: it is usually a rectangle of poorly maintained grass on the edge of the island. There are of course beaches, sometimes a library and stores.

Historically, the rural islands are frighteningly silent during the day: this is because men are at sea to catch fish. During the day, the female population silently sweeps through the village alleys, each one around her house. There is never a kindergarten; children play in the alleys or on the beach with what they find. The men relax, play cards or chess in the shade of a tree that serves as the village square. Other forms of board games are popular because they require little physical movement in the overwhelming heat.

In 2018, on the island of Hulhumalé, a first skate park is under construction. It is part of the "young" vocation of the development of this island.

And if there is no other entertainment, there is still the good old television. Thanks to the operator Medianet, people all over the country have access to 180 channels, 85 of them in HD quality: the ten local channels plus HBO, Fox, FX, National Geographic, Sky News, MTV, RT, Bloomberg, Trace Urban, CCTV, BBC World, TV5 Monde, Rai Italia, DW, Aljazeera, France 24, Nickelodeon, ...

At the date of writing this book, there are no nightclubs, amusement parks, escape game facilities, municipal swimming pools, concert halls, theaters, water parks with water slides, racecourses, horseback riding clubs, hiking trails, or zoos in the Maldives.

Media and Newspapers

Historically, TVM, Television Maldives is the public television broadcasting service in the Maldives. It is the only local public channel. Its service started on 29 March 1978. At every prayer hour, programs are interrupted and replaced by a still image of Mecca.

In 2009, the national radio station, Dhivehiraajjeyge Adu (Voice of the Maldives) and TVM were first merged into the Maldives National Broadcasting Corporation (MNBC).

The following year, TVM was renamed to MNBC One and the voice of the Maldives was renamed Raajje Radio.

For a few years, the group put a new channel, Youth TV, on the air for young people. The channel no longer exists.

At the time of President Nasheed's forced resignation, a group of police officers arrived at MNBC headquarters and searched it. A few hours later, content from the privately owned VTV channel was rerouted to MNBC One. In the same day, the channel was renamed, as in the past, TVM and then, to mask the magnitude of the events, they started broadcasting Disney's "Beauty and the Beast".

On February 8, 2012, the company becomes state-owned under the name Maldives Broadcasting Corporation (MBC).

On March 30, 2015, a text voted in Parliament proposes to dissolve the MBC and to establish a new government-led company: The Public Service Media (PSM). The purpose of the operation is to develop and maintain under control the audiovisual media budget, equipment, presses and any technology that allows the broadcasting of news. The text also mentions that the editorial line must remain impartial and independent.

This commitment to independence and impartiality is a travesty. According to Reporters Sans Frontières, six years after the change of President in February 2012, the government has further tightened its repressive policy against the independent press. In August 2016 parliament passed a new law criminalizing defamation and allowing authorities to close a media outlet. Many journalists reported receiving threats. According to a report published by the Maldives Broadcasting Corporation (MBC), political parties were the primary perpetrators. Gangs and religious extremists followed. In April 2017 citizen journalist Yameen Rasheed, who was investigating government corruption and other matters, was stabbed to death. An atmosphere of insecurity and noxious impunity forced journalists to practice self-censorship. The press freedom situation further deteriorated in early 2018 with the declaration of a state of emergency, which allowed the government to intimidate reporters and close independent media outlets.

The Maldives ranks 117th out of 180 countries in the 2017 World Press Freedom Index.

In countries with strong media control such as the Maldives, there is little room for the independent press. Maldivians owe a great deal to the online newspaper Minivan news. Minivan means independent in the Divehi language. With few resources and many death threats and insults, the team of Minivan news, better known under its new name, Maldives Independent has been covering the country's news since 2005. For several events in the recent history of the Maldives, they were the only journalists to report in detail what was happening while the mainstream media minimized or ignored the news. One recalls that during the events of February 7, 2012, public television broadcast La Belle et La Bête all day long under pressure from the instigators of the mutiny.

Food

Maldivians have rice and fish as their staple food.

Rice has always been the staple of the Maldivian diet, yet it does not grow on the archipelago. It is traditionally imported from Bengal, Sri Lanka or India. Small pebbles are often present in rice. Unfortunately, they are added by unscrupulous foreign exporters in order to increase the weight of the bags for free. Maldivians know this and to avoid breaking their teeth, they have the ancestral habit of inspecting the rice several times before cooking it. Women usually spread the rice on large mats on the ground and remove stones and rotten rice grains.

Food in the atolls is often scarce, especially during periods of bad weather because during storms, boats loaded with goods do not dock. Except in Malé, the people of the Maldives are used to the lack of food. During the great periods of famine in the Maldives, velvet leaves (heliotropium foertherianum) were used as emergency food.

Fish is almost the only source of protein. The most popular fish is skipjack tuna (katsuwonus pelamis) also called skipjack tuna, pink tuna or skipjack tuna. Other popular fish are little tunny, yellowfin tuna, frigate tuna, bigeye scad, wahoo, mahi-mahi or bancloche.

Garudiya is a fish broth which is the most traditional dish of the Maldives. Its recipe consists of cutting tuna into several large pieces and placing them in a saucepan. Then add 1.5 liters of salted water and let it cook. Regularly it is necessary to remove the scum above. This dish is eaten with steamed rice or unleavened rolls called roshi. Then it is up to each person to add the flavors he or she wishes: chilli pepper, curry leaves, onions. But the cooking is done exclusively with salted water.

It is also possible to cook the garudiya for a considerable number of hours, causing the water in the stock to evaporate, leaving at the bottom of the pan a kind of black and unattractive mass: the rihaakuru. This condiment is almost reserved for Maldivians for a physiological reason: the concentration of this product in histamine is so high that it would cause a strong allergic reaction in anyone except Maldivians, who in the long run, seem immune. The rihaakaru is served spread on bread, a bit like the British Pot.

Figure 133: Rihaakaru pot

The other form in which Maldivians eat tuna is dried tuna. It is a kind of dry fish sausage. It is simply called Maldive fish (Maldive is singular). It was originally a method of preserving fish for situations of abundant fishing. The tuna is boiled, smoked and then sun-dried until it acquires the appearance and hardness of a piece of wood.

Figure 134: Maldive fish

Traditionally few vegetables are consumed, simply because they do not grow easily on the sand.

Maldivian desserts consist of chewing betel leaves, areca nuts, cloves and lemon. In cakes, the sweet taste comes mainly from coconut.

Figure 135: Typical Maldivian dish

Meat (except pork of course) is only eaten on special occasions.

The coconut plays a big role: shredded, grated, pressed to make milk or as oil for frying. The juice of the still green coconut, called kurumba, makes a delicious and refreshing drink, while raa is the lymph of the palm, which is barely extracted.

Maldivians' starchy foods are imported rice, boiled or crushed into flour, or local tubers such as taro (ala), sweet potato (kattala), cassava (dandialuvi), breadfruit (bambukeyo) or pandanus.

Figure 136: Taro Leaves

Figure 137: Taro root

The mas huni roshi is the traditional breakfast of the Maldives. It consists of a mixture of crushed canned tuna with onions, chilli, grated coconut and lime juice accompanied by some pancakes and sometimes a fried egg or omelette. Maldivians drink tea or espresso coffee and hate filter coffee.

Figure 138: Mas Huni Roshi

Famous Maldivians

It is absolutely improbable for a European to mention the name of a famous Maldivian. Apart from the many Maldivian sultans and politicians, history will perhaps remember the name of Hassan Ugail, mathematician and researcher in computer science at the University of Bradford in England. He is the first Maldivian to receive a doctorate in mathematics. He is, for the moment, the only Maldivian university professor in the field of science. His work focuses on computer graphics and three-dimensional computer imaging representations. His methods of computer graphics representation, storage and transmission of 3D objects are patented in the United States and the United Kingdom.

Figure 139: Hassan Ugail

In September 2011, he invented a new type of lie detector that uses two cameras and a computer to detect slight facial movements associated with the act of lying. Compared to the good old polygraph, his system offers the opportunity to not have to stick a lot of sensors connected by wires on the body of the person whose words are being evaluated. With his device, it will therefore be possible to detect the lies of a person who doesn't even know that he is undergoing a polygraph.

In a totally different register, a Maldivian woman, Raudha Athif is infamous for having been murdered by religious extremists. At the age of twenty-one, Raudha Athif, a Maldivian girl with surprisingly blue eyes, already had a bright future ahead of her. As a young second year medical student at Islami Bank Medical University in Rajshahi, Bangladesh, she was also a model for Vogue India magazine. A brilliant career was in store for her. The young woman was at the heart of this new trend of modern models who represent their origins and cultures through their image.

On March 29, 2017, students find Raudha Athif in her room, lifeless, in the most total incomprehension of her relatives. The model has always been seen smiling and full of life. Her relatives, teachers and parents have never noticed the slightest problem with her. But the facts remain the same: Raudha committed suicide, at least that is the first conclusion. A thousand and one questions still remain unanswered and her family does not know how to answer all these questions about her death. Murder is the most probable lead. A group of extremists who were opposed to her new life were implicated, and they were a way to show their unveiled face. Two autopsies oppose each other: the first concludes that she committed suicide. The second evokes a death by contusion to the head with a hammer while the victim was seated.

Figure 140: Raudha Athif

Social problems

Religious Fundamentalism

All peoples have their collective paranoia. That is to say, a subject that is taboo, primordial and omnipresent at the same time, which provokes irrational reactions. For example, for Americans it is the love of guns. For Russians it is the visceral rejection of homosexuals. In the Maldives, the subject that puts the whole country in a state of collective paranoia is their attachment to Islam and of course its corollary: the rejection of apostasy and other religions.

Maldivians have been Muslims since 1153. They would be wrong to proclaim that they have always been Muslims since they have a Buddhist past, but let's admit that they have been Muslims for a long time. So far, no problem.

The people had embraced this religion without overflowing or extremism for centuries. Older Maldivian women remember very well not being veiled during their youth and even walking around bare-breasted sometimes until they were sixteen years old.

But this gradually changed under the mandate of President Maumoon Abdul Gayoom. Many of his ideas of governance stemmed from his Islamic education obtained in Egypt at Al-Azhar University. During his studies, he understood the power of the mix of Islam + politics. In addition to Islam, he learned Arabic, which allowed him to interpret the Quran directly rather than relying on poor translations of the Quran into Maldivian.

Developing a hard line of Islam in the Maldives, Gayoom was declared "the guarantor of the principles of Islam in the country" by the 1997 constitution.

As a result, the country is becoming even more Muslim than before. A law was passed requiring Muslims to hold Maldivian citizenship. And from then on, madness seized the whole country: destruction of museum pieces testifying to the Buddhist past of the Maldives, suppression in the history books of the mention of an ancient religion in the Maldives before 1153, persecution of people suspected of not being Muslim, dismissal or imprisonment of people who consider themselves atheists or apostates, ...

The effects of the rise of indoctrination immediately bring to mind the mental hold of a cult. The reason for all this: the political instrumentalization of Islam to lead the people. The same parallel could be drawn with France and its obsession with the sacrosanct secularism.

Thus, it is even forbidden to bring in a Bible or any object referring to another religion onto Maldivian soil. Maldivian law therefore officially legalizes xenophobia.

In September 2010, an Indian professor working on the island of Foakaidhoo is to be rescued when an aggressive mob girdled her, tied her up and plans to throw her into the sea all tied up. The angry crowd blames her for drawing a crucifix on a painting in a school on the island. It is, in fact, a simple representation of a compass with its four cardinal points.

In November 2011, the blog of journalist Ismail Khilath Rasheed was closed by the Maldives Communications Authority on the orders of the Ministry of Islamic Affairs, on the grounds that the blog contains anti-Islamic content. Ismail Rasheed is a Sufi Muslim, and called for more religious tolerance. This act of censorship was condemned by the NGO Reporters Without Borders and by Navanethem Pillay, UN High Representative for Human Rights.

On December 10, 2011, blogger Ismail Rasheed is organizing a rally in favor of religious freedom. The rally was attacked and Rasheed's fractured skull came out of it. Following this, he was arrested at the urging of the Islamist party Adhaalath, which then organized a counter-demonstration on December 23, 2011. A website associated with this counter-demonstration calls for his death. Ismail Rasheed is finally released on January 9, 2012 following protests by Amnesty International and Reporters Without Borders.

Figure 141: Ismail Rasheed, bloodied

While the Maldives was traditionally a country of moderate Islam, the arrival in power of President Abdulla Yameen Abdul Gayoom in 2013, in a presidential election with a disputed result supported by Islamists, changes the situation. Influenced by Wahhabi clerics trained in Saudi Arabia and Pakistan, Islamist proselytism is gaining ground, especially in prison circles. Numerous radical sheikhs thus occupy more and more public space: universities, television (their sermons being broadcast once a month on national channels), ... Several NGOs denounce an increase in early marriages in remote islands as well as the growing refusal to vaccinate children. Dr. Mohamed Iyaz, an influential government adviser on Koranic jurisprudence, also praises excision as a religious obligation.

In 2014, a hundred Maldivian women were whipped in public for "acts of fornication".

In 2015, between 50 and 200 departures of Maldivians to the territories of the Islamic State are recorded. While the government has officially condemned the jihad to Syria, activists and opponents criticize its inaction on the issue, some even fearing the establishment of a caliphate in the Maldives.

Status of Women

Basic human rights are routinely violated in the Maldives. Islam is the official religion of the state, and Shari'a law is strictly enforced. Women's rights were the most affected, and the country's backwardness in the area of individual liberties was egregious and worrisome. The country could not truly develop as long as it remained under the grip of religion and certain age-old precepts, such as the whipping of women who had sex outside marriage, including when they were raped.

Several NGOs and the United Nations called on the Maldives to remove the whipping penalty for women having sex outside marriage. In September 2012 a 16-year-old woman was sentenced to whipping for extramarital sex, and her partner received a 10-year prison sentence. In February 2013 a 15-year-old girl was sentenced to 100 lashes and 8 months house arrest for having sex outside marriage. The conviction was based on the girl's confession shortly after she was raped by her stepfather. In August 2013, the Maldivian High Court overturned the decision in August 2013, even though the sentence had not been served: the lashes were to be administered to the girl's 18-year-olds.

The penalty for flogging in the Maldives is whipping the condemned man or woman in public in front of the Malé courthouse, usually a crowded street, in the presence of his or her family to add humiliation. In 2009, one couple was whipped, first the man and then the woman, while they were married when their child was born. It is by calculating the date of conception of the baby that the entourage deduced that the sexual act of procreation had taken place shortly before their marriage. Thus, a happy and loving couple found themselves whipped in public for having a baby. However, at a few miles from Malé, on the resorts, the tourists can give themselves up to all the sexual freedom which characterizes the Westerners on vacation.

The Maldivian government is well aware that these methods are barbaric because it hates that this is made public in order to preserve tourism.

Human Rights

In addition, the Maldives was regularly criticized for its lack of religious freedom. Arrests of bloggers and demonstrators and destruction of Buddhist monuments made headlines.

On April 27, 2014, the government of the Maldives announced that the country would end its 60-year moratorium on capital punishment. Minors guilty of murder could be sentenced to death, in contravention of the UN Convention on the Rights of the Child. The age of criminal responsibility in the Maldives is set at ten years in general and at seven years for certain crimes such as theft, fornication, alcohol consumption and apostasy.

Trafficking in human beings

Human trafficking exists in the Maldives under two main aspects: forced prostitution and forced labor.

A small number of women from Sri Lanka, Thailand, India, China, Philippines, Eastern Europe, former USSR are recruited to be put on the sidewalks of Malé. There are also minors sent from the rural islands to Malé to serve as domestics under the guise of an au pair system.

In the construction or service sectors, the Bangladeshis are the main victims: they are lured by smugglers who promise them very well-paid jobs and eventually fall into the hands of real slavers who confiscate their passports, do not declare them, pay them very little or not at all and subject them to debt bondage: existing since ancient Greece, debt bondage is a way of paying back a debt by directly providing work rather than money or goods. Debt bondage, which very often leads to forced labor, is considered slavery by many countries and by some international conventions, particularly with regard to child labor. Even when they realize their trap, migrants do not return to their country for several reasons: on the one hand, they feel humiliated for having fallen into such a trap. On the other hand, they have often given up everything to come and work in the Maldives: before leaving, they probably sold their homes and sent their wives and children back to their parents. Worse, the migrants themselves pay the smuggler who sends them to the breakers, between $1,000 and $4,000 to have the immense honor of going to work in the Maldives.

A diplomatic source announced the number of 35,000 Bangladeshis working illegally in the Maldives.

To date, the government's efforts to curb human trafficking have been very meager.

The U.S. Department of State thus places the Maldives on its blacklist for human trafficking, alongside Afghanistan in particular.

Unemployment

In the Maldives, the unemployment rate remained stable at 5%. This figure may seem low (9% in France), but it is the situation of young people that gives cause for concern. A quarter of young people are neither employed nor students, according to World Bank statistics. In fact, despite the many hotels that open every year, employment among Maldivians remains low because the construction and hotel sector relies heavily on foreign labor.

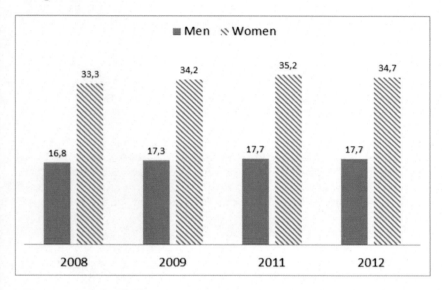

Figure 142: Youth Unemployment Rate

The low wages offered in hotels and the working conditions do not attract young people. Not everyone can work in tourism: it requires personal sacrifice, hard work, a lot of hard work and all with big smiles. Smile. Smiling even when you want to break down into tears. So, it is normal not to find Maldivians in job interviews.

Maldivians have a good level of education and are all predestined for rather intellectual positions that exist only in very small quantities in their country. This is evidenced by the quantity of PhD holders in the Maldives who are theoretically experts in a whole host of fields of study for which there is no application in the country. For example, what use is a PhD in copyright in the Maldives since there is not much to be "copyrighted"?

On the other hand, a tenacious a priori leads hotel managers to believe that Maldivians do not have the skills required for high positions.

The government is looking for solutions to this problem: it began by creating a tax on foreign workers. This tax is intended to increase the cost of employing an immigrant in order to encourage the employment of locals.

Then in April 2018, he obtained a report from the Ministry of Tourism entitled "Factors motivating a Maldivian to work in a hotel complex". The positivism of the title is blatant: the government wants to understand what prevents so many Maldivians from accessing positions in the country's most successful industry.

The document is very informative. It takes the form of a survey of Maldivians working in the resort islands. It shows that 52% of those surveyed work between 8 and 12 hours a day. At the same time, 56% of the respondents consider their housing and integration conditions to be good. If we add this to the respondents who answered "Very good", we see that 92% of Maldivians are well treated in the resort islands.

60% of respondents associate their work with the word freedom.

59% of respondents associate their work with the word food.

The three factors affecting their willingness to work are, in descending order of importance: low wages, lack of consideration, and poor food in the workplace.

Finally, according to the hotel bosses, the five main reasons for resignation are:

1. Fluctuation in salary payment dates,
2. Discrimination between expatriates and locals,
3. The impact on the family,
4. The desire to set up a business,
5. Poor management of personnel by HRDs.

Fight against drugs

In a Muslim country like the Maldives it is not even allowed to talk about alcohol. Alcohol is hard to find by the inhabitants but it is not impossible: bottles of vodka stolen from luxury hotels are sold under the coat for 140 to 350 dollars.

Worse, since the 1990s, there is a scourge that has fallen through the cracks: heroin. This drug, known locally as brown sugar, is causing gangrene in the country and especially in the capital. The idle young people of Malé deal discreetly in alleyways. It is estimated that a third of young Maldivians touch heroin. However, the police are very repressive and violent. The doses cost very little: the equivalent of eight euros.

In fact, Malé offers very few activities to its inhabitants and especially to its young people. It is to fill the boredom that they fall into drugs.

The drugs come from India and then pass through Sri Lanka. It is often drugs cut with other cheap and toxic products.

The police in Malé are in the habit of scrutinizing the arms of the young people they arrest to see if they have injection scars.

This drug-addicted youth sees only two possible ways out of their malaise: at best, to be hired in one of the country's luxury hotels. At worst, to leave the Maldives.

Despite the magnitude of the phenomenon, there is only one detoxification center in the Maldives. After an exhausting detoxification program, patients are sent back to Malé without any follow-up. On their return, the young people find it difficult to escape from their previous life, their friends, their drug dealers. Staying "clean" then becomes an impossible mission.

The Maldivian people have been very ill-prepared for the scourge of drugs. According to the Islamic laws in force in the archipelago, it is forbidden to talk about subjects related to drugs or sex under the age of 18, making any work of prevention impossible.

Waste management

One of the unexpected impacts of tourism in the Maldives is the acquisition of more environmentally friendly waste management methods by the local population. This is commonly referred to as "toilet training. Historically, Maldivians used beaches as open dumpsites but also as toilets. Young women in particular waited until nightfall to relieve themselves on the beaches without being seen, until the invention of flashlights used by peeping toms.

Even today, in 2018, when tourists are allowed to go on excursions to the inhabited islands, they are confronted with the lamentable dirt of the inhabitants' beaches. Some luxury hotels fight against this bad habit because they do not want to see garbage bags or excrement floating to their rich tourists on the island opposite.

This is where the island of Thilafushi comes in.

After having invented the resort island, the Maldives must have invented the garbage island: Thilafushi, a largely artificial island of the Maldives located 6.85 km west of Malé, the capital of the country, between the islets of Giraavaru and Gulhifalhu. Located southwest of the North Malé Atoll, the island is originally about seven kilometers long and 200 meters wide. It is extended to the west by a lagoon surrounded by a large submerged reef. Like all the islands of the Maldives, it is a perfectly flat sandy island; however, human activities have profoundly changed its morphology and composition, and it is now an island in continuous and rapid growth, and could now constitute the highest point of the country: a "mountain" of garbage.

In 1992, the government, no longer knowing how to manage the ever-increasing amount of garbage due to the country's tourism boom, decided to have waste from neighboring islands sent to Thilafushi. Initially, pits with a total volume of 1,060 cubic meters were created to receive the garbage, which was then buried. However, these pits were saturated much more quickly than expected, and in the absence of an alternative solution, the garbage is now dumped on the ground or in the water.

Since then, the 0.43 km² garbage island has been storing 330 tons of waste per day, including about 200 tons of household waste and 100 tons of industrial waste. Each tourist visiting the archipelago - one million annually - produces 7.2 kg of garbage per day, compared to 2.8 kg for a Maldivian; therefore the island grows by one square meter per day.

The consequence of this activity of storing waste without sorting or treatment is an extraordinary level of pollution, both of the soil and water and especially of the air, as part of the waste is constantly on fire, releasing a thick plume of smoke over the island, which sometimes reaches the nearby capital Malé. Oils, mercury, asbestos and lead would thus be dumped into the ecosystem in large quantities without the slightest control.

The exponential growth of the island eventually attracted the interest of some developers: the government opened it to subdivision in November 1997, and 57 companies set up operations there, including a shipyard and warehouses. Today, there are more than 260 businesses on the island. The island has thus become the headquarters of certain polluting industries, such as the treatment of methane or cement. The workers, often from Bangladesh, who live there work twelve hours a day in an environment saturated with toxic fumes for a monthly salary of 255 euros, which is very low even for this country.

Figure 143: Thilafushi, Non-Paradise Island

In 2004, the tsunami ravaged the island and threw most of the garbage and toxic products into the sea, polluting more than a hundred other islands and highlighting the national risk that Thilafushi represents. The Australian and Canadian Red Cross raised nearly $10 million to fund an environmentally friendly and sustainable waste management system, but the lack of government initiative ultimately brought the project to a halt.

The Maldivian government has often been alerted to the ecological as well as health, economic and tourism problems that the island represents, but has never yet taken any real measures to change the situation. In 2008, the World Bank made a loan of fourteen million dollars to launch the Maldives Environmental Management Project, but nothing has changed in Thilafushi. However, an incinerator was created on the island of Vandhoo, on Thaa atoll. In 2011, the unloading of waste is temporarily prohibited on Thilafushi because of its saturation and the drift at sea of a large quantity of waste, but in the absence of an alternative solution the unloading resumes. A contract was also signed with the Indian company Tatva Global Renewable Energy to turn the island into a more modern waste management center, but this project was halted the following year without justification and definitively cancelled in 2014.

Diaspora and emigration

There are several reasons why Maldivians may leave their country temporarily or permanently.

The 2014 census announces that 5,589 people of Maldivian nationality live outside the Maldives. Who are they?

First of all, there are those who work abroad or on the sea, such as sailors.

Then there are the students. As with all small countries, the level of education offered in the Maldives is not always sufficient to cover all university disciplines. Young Maldivians are used to studying in India and Sri Lanka which are great nations in terms of university without being too far away geographically. Universities in Malaysia, Australia or the United Kingdom also attract Maldivians from wealthier families to ensure access to quality studies. On the other hand, students in Pakistan, on the other hand, come to study in another framework: the medersas or madrasas, Muslim theological universities.

Sadder is the political repression. With the country granting almost no freedom of speech or freedom of conscience, Maldivian journalists or bloggers could choose to emigrate to avoid imprisonment or torture. For writing anti-government papers, some journalists were imprisoned, sentenced to death, or simply disappeared overnight; five were under 18 years of age.

Even the former president, Mohamed Nasheed, had to leave the country to hide in the UK after being indicted for terrorism in a mock trial in 2015. For a few months, Mohamed Nasheed campaigned for the 2018 presidential elections ... without setting foot in the Maldives. He then met members of the Maldivian diaspora in Sri Lanka.

Worst reason to emigrate: jihad. The Maldives is the leading supplier of fighters to the Islamic state in Iraq and Syria if we relate this number to the population. Of course, in absolute terms this makes only 200 Maldivians fighting with Daesh, or 1 Maldivian out of 2,000. For comparison, the French in Daesh are 1,700 or 1 Frenchman out of 38,235. Maldivian insurgents are radicalizing mainly in Malé but this can happen in other islands. This radicalization has occurred especially since the beginning of President Yameen's term of office, which is said to be close to the Islamic state.

Unemployment also pushes young people to emigrate. The under 24s represent 45% of the population (2014) and therefore the employment pool is causing severe competition. Maldivians plan to leave the country in order to have access to better incomes, notably by applying for jobs that do not exist in the Maldives. When young Maldivians work abroad, their senior family members often follow them so that they can continue to share time with their children and grandchildren. The inhabitants of Malé in particular are leaving this unlivable capital whose cost of living is prohibitive. The square meters of Malé are expensive. A classic western luxury apartment of 83 square meters with a balcony can be rented for $2,200 USD per month or $26.5/m²/month. Whereas the average salary of Maldivians is 24,000 rufiyaa per month, that is 1,363 euros or 1,551 US dollars.

Type of job	Average monthly salary in rufiyaa	Average monthly salary in euros
Administration	10 000	600
Banks	29 625	1 778
Real estate	34 666	2 080
Accounting	27 610	1 657
Education and Research	1 400	84
Electricity	24 550	1 473
Human Resources	39 645	2 379
Computer science	22 501	1 350
Journalism and Media	24 000	1 440
Justice, lawyers	25 000	1 500
Management	64 767	3 886
Advertising, marketing	18 076	1 085
Mechanics	47 224	2 833
Medicine	17 436	1 046
Production, factories	19 000	1 140
Security, protection	33 506	2 010
Services	7 363	442
Technology	2 000	120
Textile	2 000	120
Tourism, Gastronomy	11 917	715
Translation	10 000	600
Transport and logistics	17 028	1 022

Finally, health is also a starting point. As access to quality healthcare remains difficult in the Maldives, the inhabitants are tempted to pursue their medical careers in Sri Lanka or even further afield. Even the Presidents of the Maldives are still treated abroad. To strengthen the link between the Maldives and its expatriates, in 2013 the government extended medical coverage to Maldivians living in Sri Lanka and India on condition that they visit a list of approved hospitals. In reality, this measure is an admission of failure of the government, unable to improve the national health system, they legalize medical emigration.

Sea level rise

The rise in sea level is a phenomenon observed many times on the geological time scale throughout the Earth; it then leads to a marine transgression. It can be caused by multiple and complex factors that result jointly from the effects of water input (from ice sheets, ice caps and glaciers), the thermal expansion of water due to its temperature, and the distribution of water masses due to the effect of major currents and winds. Sea level has risen about 120 meters since the peak of the last ice age, about 18,000 years ago. In the 20th century, the sea rose by 17 cm. The 2007 Intergovernmental Panel on Climate Change (IPCC) report estimated that the sea could rise by 18 to 42 cm by 2100. This prediction was raised in 2012 to 0.50 to one meter by 2100, in a study published on November 28, 2012 for the 18th UN Climate Conference in Doha.

In 2015, NASA is revising these estimates: the sea level has risen by 8 cm (geographical average) from 1992 to 2015 (and locally up to 22.9 cm), which means that by 2100, an increase of at least 90 cm is expected.

Sea level rise is one of the consequences of global warming, through two main processes: the expansion of sea water (as the oceans warm), and the melting of land ice.

The IPCC suggested that deltas and small island states may be particularly vulnerable to sea level rise. Relative sea level rise may be exacerbated by substantial land subsidence or loss in some deltas. To date, sea level changes have not yet caused serious environmental, humanitarian, or economic losses in small island states.

With an average altitude of 1.5 meters above sea level, the Maldives is one of the countries on probation. Global warming is a palpable reality for this country. Day after day, the rising waters of the oceans engulf the land. Some small islands, inhabited or not, are a few years away from disappearing. Climatologists predict the end of the Maldives in one to two centuries. The height of the oceans is not the only problem: the rise in surface water temperature is causing significant damage to the coral reefs that serve as the protective barrier of the atolls. Erosion of these natural barriers would mean larger waves and powerful currents around the islands. In these cases, tourism would no longer be profitable because no one would be interested in spending their vacations on islands surrounded by rough seas. Global warming also generates costly natural disasters such as tsunamis, cyclones and storms. The UN, in its 1951 resolution on refugees, does not consider climate as a valid cause of emigration, yet Maldivians are leading the way in becoming "climate migrants". Far from fleeing from war or genocide, Maldivians will gradually leave their nation as it sets foot in the water. However, at present, in 2018, there are no statistics proving that Maldivians have left their country because of the climate. Even after the 2004 tsunami, most Maldivians were probably too shocked and too poor to make the decision to leave their country permanently.

In 2008, President Mohamed Nasheed was the first president in the world to consider the total emigration of his people. It is still at the stage of the project: some taxes on tourism are paid into a budget whose purpose is the search and purchase of new land to accommodate future Maldivians after the rise of the oceans. Nasheed told the press at the time, "We can't do anything to stop global warming, so what we have to do is buy land elsewhere. It's a life insurance against the worst". Nasheed likened this search for land to the founding of the State of Israel in Palestine. One can hope he doesn't know what he's talking about by taking such a bad example: 70 years after its establishment, Israel is still in conflict with its neighbors (and vice versa). The three countries considered for mass emigration are India and Sri Lanka by cultural choice and Australia, because it has a lot of uninhabited land.

Former President Abdulla Yameen Abdul Gayoom totally disagrees with his predecessor's massive emigration program and chooses to fight rather than flee, building artificial islands and dikes to stop the waves.

Mythology and folklore

Many myths and legends belong to the oral tradition of the Maldivians. Although some Maldivian legends were already mentioned by Harry Charles Purvis Bell at the end of the 19th century, their in-depth study and publication was only recently carried out by the Spanish writer Xavier Romero Frias at a time when these ancestral tales were beginning to disappear under the weight of Islamic education and the modernization of the people.

Born in 1954, Xavier Romero Frias began investigating the folklore and spoken tradition of the Maldives around 1979. To achieve this, he set himself the goal of learning the two main dialects of the Maldivian language.

After several years of hard work, Romero Frias is completing the translation into English of hundreds of legends and stories about local ghosts and semi-historical tales from several atolls in the Maldives, but mostly from the south and Malé. He then went to India to study Sanskrit and to conduct research on the continental origins of the Maldivian cultural heritage.

Xavier Romero Frias notes and deplores the difficulty Maldivians have in embracing their own identity. He writes "in every head of Maldivian there is a fierce struggle between Maldivian customs and Islamic ideology. Since this conflict is unresolved, there is a widely shared sense of guilt and frustration at being unable to adjust the ancient cultural heritage to the Islamic canvas."

His book, "Folk Tales of the Maldives" is a reference in Maldivian mythology. He compiles 80 Maldivian tales and legends. Their titles are sometimes in Divehi and sometimes in English.

- The Fried Breadfruit Chips
- The Demon King
- The Man Who Burned the Mosque
- Havvā Dīdī
- The First Tunas (or Fiyala Bola Odi Duvvi)
- Boat Number Ten
- The Fruits of Greed
- Amboffulu and Damboffulu
- Telabagudi Koe
- Ukunumana and Līmana
- Mākana Kalō
- Ranna Māri
- Findanpulu and Bondanpulu
- The Skull below the Tree
- The Stingray
- Herra
- The Island of the Lepers
- Debō Dūnige Vāhaka (or The Two-headed Bird)
- Don Hiyalā and Alifulu
- The White Disk
- Fūlu Digu Handi
- The Two Traders

- The Man on the Whale
- Oditān Kalēge and His Wife
- The Dōni Given to Mohan
- The Cat and the Broken Jar
- Bēri
- Kullavah Falu Rani (Queen of the Mangrove Forest)
- Khalidu and Sitti
- Dombeyya
- Mākumbe
- The Monster at the Kitchen Door
- Small Drops of Blood
- Mākana's Treachery
- The Girl in the Shark's Belly
- Delikolu and Alikolu
- Arruffanno Ferēta
- The Scarlet Wake
- The Navigator under the Tree
- Findana and the Cat
- Nadalla Takuru
- Hollavai (Fōlavahi)
- A Heavy Kurumba
- Keula Bēbē Dūña
- Fandiyāru Crab
- The Honour of the Big Seashell
- The Land Crab in the Kitchen
- The Obstinate Mākana
- Satō and the Giant Crab
- Mākana and his Brother-in-Law
- The Vigani That Haunted Toshali Takuru
- Handi Don Kamanā
- Himiccha' eri Furēta (The Monster of Himiti)
- Santimariyambu
- The Legend of Koimala
- The Tree at the Island End
- Māmeli Daita and Her Seven Children
- The Pride of the Fleet

- The Mud Wasp (or Vērehuli)
- The Man Who Learned from Two Books
- The Legend of the Sandara Shell
- The Master Navigator
- The Moon in the Jar
- The Lament
- The Fish That Had More Bones
- The Skin Disease
- Kuda Tuttu Dīdī's Nails
- The Mullet and the Clam
- Rōnu Eduru
- The Cat That Chased Two Rats
- Fanvakkolu and Valikolu
- The Poor Man of Nalafushi and his Cow
- The Awful Giant Fish
- Kalobondāge Diye
- The King of the Sea
- The Palace Bedbug
- Safaru Kaiddā
- Muladovi
- The Sandbank of the Seabirds
- The First Coconuts

Conversion to Islam

Among the legends and tales, there is the "Rannamaari". According to Ibn Battûta, Moroccan explorer of the 14th century, the Rannamaari is a demon that lives in the sea. It haunts the people of the Maldives and remains calm on the condition of a monthly sacrifice of a virgin girl. Each month, a young girl was chosen among the inhabitants, by the king or his advisers. The maiden was to be left alone in a secluded temple by the sea in Malé. At dawn, the girl's family returned to the temple and discovered her lifeless body. The Maldivians were concerned until a passing Muslim gave them a final solution: He asked to go to the temple in place of a young virgin and began to read a few verses from the Qur'an. After that, the Rannamaari never returned. Everyone was happy and began to believe that Allah is the greatest, and then the whole population converted to the Muslim religion.

Coconuts and tuna

Many Maldivian stories and legends reflect the Maldivians' dependence on coconut and tuna. For example, one fable tells that the first inhabitants of the Maldives died in large numbers but that a sorcerer (fandita) made the coconut trees grow from the skulls of the corpses of those who starved to death. Since then, it is said that the coconut tree has an anthropomorphic origin. The tuna is said to have been brought to the Maldivians by a mythical sailor (maalimi) named Bodu Niyami Kalefanu thanks to his proximity to the dagas: a mythological tree which is found at the end of the world and on which tuna would grow.

The end of the world

Of course, the myth of the Maldives being swallowed up is also very present in people's minds. This end of the Maldives, which is quite likely, is similar to beliefs found on the Nicobar or Andaman Islands in the Bay of Bengal.

The foundation of Malé

The origins of the city of Malé are also the subject of mythological tales. It is told that the first inhabitants of the Maldives were Dravidians, which can be briefly defined as inhabitants of southern India, living near the coast, that is to say, Indians and Sri Lankans. It is said that fishermen used to sail to the sandbanks south of Giraavaru Atoll to clean their caught tuna. Because of the large quantities of tuna caught, the waters around this sandbank would turn into a pool of blood (maa ley gandeh). Since "Maa" means big and "ley" means blood, the word "Malé" would have been formed this way.

According to legend, one day a prince from the Indian subcontinent, called Koimala, arrived in Malé on board a large boat. The people of the Giraavaru, already well settled on the same atoll, spotted his ship from far away and decided to welcome him. They allowed Prince Koimala to settle precisely on the large sandbank surrounded by fish blood, previously mentioned. Trees were planted on the sandbank and according to the stories, the first tree to grow was a papaya tree. The inhabitants agreed to be governed by this prince and a palace was built. It was the first building in Malé.

Spirits

Most popular fables in the Maldives deal with evil spirits and their interactions with the inhabitants. These stories always contain a moral at the end. Certain actions are necessary to avoid getting into trouble with the spirits. These attitudes include keeping a secret or avoiding venturing into certain places at certain times.

Spirits can take human form. The evilness of these spirits is often masked by their beauty or youthfulness. Some Maldivian spirits (handi) have the appearance of charming women. These stories of female spirits have their origin in the worship of goddesses in the Dravidian culture.

Other spirits to be expected in folklore are the awful monsters that come from the bottom of the oceans. Legends about sea monsters are part of the basic culture by virtue of the Maldives' ocean environment.

The animals

In Maldivian tales, unsurprisingly, the characters are often fish, crabs, sea birds, such as the heroes Mākana, Findana, Kalhubondage Diye, Fandiyaaru Kakuni, or Don Mohonaai Miyaru. Many are children's stories that are still popular today. Some stories are typical of the Maldives but others are adaptations of foreign tales.

Figure 144: The traitor Heron according to Xavier Romero Frias

Let us dwell on the story entitled "The Traitor Heron". It was told to Xavier Romero Frias by Magieduruge Ibrahim Didi, the most cultured man on Fua Mulaku Island (the old name of Fuvahmulah Island).

Once upon a time, a very sneaky heron, Maakana, landed near a lagoon on the reef at low tide. He looked at the fish swimming in a pond over there and thought, "Those fish look very unconscious to me. I already know how I am going to eat them without too much effort.

Maakana approached the edge of the lagoon and spoke to the fish in a gentle and polite manner, "You look very cramped swimming so close together in this little puddle. This doesn't seem like a good place."

In the same tank, there was a crab on the bottom that said to the fish, "Don't talk to him. He is dangerous, he wants to eat you.

But the fish didn't pay attention to the crab and addressed Maakana, "You're right, it's crowded here. Do you know a better place than here?"

"Of course, I can fly high and, at a glance, I can see the best places on the reef. Not far from here, there is a beautiful blue pool. It is deeper and the water is cooler. It will be a much more pleasant place for you fish to live."

The fish began to feel the warmth of the sun at the zenith in their shallow pond, so they showed interest and asked the bird "how do we get there?"

"Nothing could be easier!" replied the devious bird, while walking in the basin, opening its beak below the surface of the water. "I can carry one fish in my beak at a time. Then I'll come back for the next one.

The crab warned the fish "Don't do that! That sounds like a trick to me.

But the silly fish were so excited that they were already scrambling to be the first to jump into the beak and they didn't even hear the crab's warnings.

Thus, Maakana transported the fish out of the pond one by one. And do you think he was taking them to a better place as promised? Of course not! He brought them to a rock flooded with waves at the edge of the reef and devoured them, smiling with satisfaction at his own intelligence.

In the end, the crab was alone in the basin and Maakana returned, belching and flying with difficulty as her belly was so full. The crab refused to leave, but the bird, eager to have crab for dessert, insisted. "You're going to be so bored alone here in this hot puddle. The fish are having a great time in the big, cool water over there.

With his cunning verve, Maakana managed to persuade even the warned crab and finally the small crustacean accepted to be carried by the bird in its beak.

As they flew, the crab felt the bird squeezing him too hard and protested, "You're hurting me! Hold me softer please!"

But the bird said, "I don't need to be gentle. I'm going to eat you just like I ate all those stupid fish".

Suddenly, Maakana's enormous betrayal jumped out at the crab's eyes and he became indignant from the depths of his soul. Out of anger and also out of desperation, he reached the long neck of the bird with his claws. When he felt able, he pinched the bird's neck with such force that he wounded it to death. Unexpectedly, the crustacean was free of its grip but began to fall.

As the dead bird and the crab began a long fall, the crab thought serenely, "We are above the reef and I might hit a rock. It doesn't *matter if I die. At least I am proud to have given a well-deserved lesson to this vicious bird."*

But what happened was that the crab ended up falling, unharmed, in a beautiful deep blue basin where he spent the rest of his days in good company and peace.

Text by Magieduruge Ibrahim Didi
Translated into English by Xavier Romero Frias
Translated into French for this book.

Arts

Literature

The oldest traces of Maldivian literature are lōmāfānu: Maldivian texts inscribed on copper plates. Several historical texts have been found in this form, the oldest dating from the 12th century. The Divehi characters of the time were called eveyla balhu by the archaeologist Harry Charles Purvis Bell (1851-1937) who described them as very similar to the Sinhalese characters of the Middle Ages.

Figure 145: Lōmāfānu Isdhoo dating from the year 1194

The lōmāfānu " Isdhoo " (pictured above), tells the story of monks from monasteries in the south of Haddhunmathi atoll, who were taken to Malé and beheaded.

In recent history, Husain Salaahuddheen (Hussein Salaahuddin) wrote "Siyarathunnabaviyyaa" which is the most famous book of religious literature in the country. The poet Addu Bandeyri Hasan Manikufaan is considered one of the greatest Maldivian writers. He is the author of "Dhiyoage Raivaru".

Other poets of major importance are Edhuru Umaru Maafaiy Kaleygefaanu, Mohamed Amin, and Bodufenvalhuge Sidi.

Maldivian poetry is called raivaru. It is the oldest form of written literature in the Maldives. The linguist Hussein Salaahuddin defines it as a form of poetry used in ancient times to express desire, thoughts and emotions. Rivaru is famous for its use in communication, entertainment, teaching, counseling, compliments and even satire. In its early days, it was common for women to recite raivaru in coconut forests while gathering wood and coconuts from the ground. They used these exotic rhythms (exotic for us, not for them) to keep auditory contact with the other girls in the group. This was also an excuse for chatting and gossiping. The raivaru were also well known to the teachers. They used them not only to teach literature but also things of life in general. Mothers also recited raivaru to their babies as a lullaby. The men, on the other hand, flirted and indicated their attractions in raivaru. At the foot of large trees, Maldivian men also used raivaru to provoke each other.

No matter how much dust you play with, not always knowing the magnitude of the situation, don't play with fireworks. You could catch fire without warning.

Rivaru have also been used in politics. Educated men recited raivaru at the court of the sultans to ask for favors. The double meaning contained in some raivaru also made it possible to criticize them without the sultans understanding.

There is no dictated structure for writing or reciting a raivaru. Instead, it should be understood that it is a set of short sentences with a conclusion that binds the whole. The length varies between three and twelve lines. The words must be complicated. The raivaru will tend to be difficult to write, difficult to recite and difficult to understand.

It is Edhuru Umaru Maafaiy Kaleygefaanu who took the initiative to define and reform the raivaru. Nowadays, raivaru is taught but hardly leaves the walls of universities. Students no longer find it entertaining or rich. People don't write raivaru anymore and this literary art form is definitely disappearing.

Even if the youth turns its back on the raivaru and does nothing to preserve it, the opinion of the elders is different. They are convinced that the raivaru must be transmitted from generation to generation to avoid its total extinction. Maldivian grandparents encourage their grandchildren to participate in raivaru writing competitions and give them writing tips.

Despite the government's efforts to preserve this tradition, it is already too late. The people no longer perceive the raivaru as creative texts. As the following raivaru indicates:

Knowledge learned once and taught flows from the past to the present through writing. When a new art is encountered, it slowly sinks into history.

Whoever expects to find an abundance of Maldivian literature translated into French or English soon realizes that for some unknown reason, books by Maldivian authors written in a language other than Divehi are almost impossible to find.

One of the rare finds is the book "Dhon Hiyala and Ali Fulhu" by Abdullah Sadiq, published in 1976. It is the story of an extraordinarily beautiful woman (faiiymini) who is taken away from her husband by an evil king. The lovers are reunited again at the end of the book, but their reunion turns short as they are pursued by the evil king's henchmen. Not accepting to be captured a second time, the woman Don Hiyala kills herself and Ali Fulhu follows her in death.

Figure 146: Illustration by Don Hiyala & Ali Fulhu

Cinema

The Maldivian film industry is only forty years old but it plays a major role in the cultural sector. A huge crowd applauds Maldivian films that are beginning to possess internationally recognizable attributes. There are about 70 actors and actresses who have won the attention of the public through their hard work and dedication. In order to reach a global scale, Maldivian cinema needs to develop a little more, especially in terms of acting and screenplays. The magnificent landscapes and beaches are an undeniable asset to set a beautiful scene in films.

"Ahsham" is a Maldivian action film released on December 6, 2015. It is directed by the man who plays the title role: Ali Seezan. The language of the film is obviously Divehi. The production of the film cost 1 500 000 ruufiya, that is to say about 85 000 euros. It is therefore a very limited budget, yet at its release it was pointed out that it was the most expensive film in the history of Maldivian cinema. The publicity surrounding this film insisted on the level of artistic challenge taken up by this film.

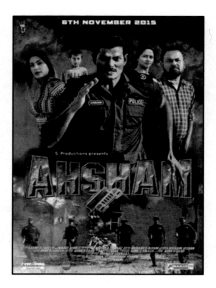

Figure 147: Poster of the movie "Ahsham".

Initially scheduled for November 2015, its release is delayed by the Maldivian police. They wish to view the entire film before its release as several aspects of the film deal with the police.

Criticism is mixed. Ahmed Nadheem of the newspaper Avas applauds the hard work and continuous effort that has gone into this film to make it something the Maldivian public is not used to seeing. It's a "big project" but not a "big film," he said.

The only nominations and victories won by this film are awarded at the eighth edition of the Gaumee Film Awards, a trophy ceremony dedicated solely to Maldivian cinema.

This annual ceremony, also known as the Dhivehi Film Awards is a mini Oscar ceremony that has been held at a very irregular pace: 1994, 1996, twice in 2007, 2008, 2015, 2016 and 2017. It is organized by the National Centre for the Arts (NCA).

The NCA, founded on December 29, 2005, is dedicated to promoting and funding the arts in the Maldives, especially film and music.

In another register, the film "4426" is a Maldivian horror film released on October 18, 2016. It is directed by Fathimath Nahula and Ahmed Sinan, produced by Hassan Sina. It features Maldivian actors Mariyam Azza, Mohamed Jumayyil, Ismail Jumaih, Yoosuf Shafeeu, Sheela Najeeb, Ibrahim Jihad, Mohamed Faisal and Farooq.

Figure 148: Poster of the film "4426".

The media became passionate about this film as its director was already known in the country: Fathimath Nahula is the director of a successful film in the Maldives, released in 2009, "Yoosuf".

The concept of a horror film had never been attempted in the Maldives. The script took four months to write. The actors had to take intensive martial arts classes two months before shooting began.

Exorcism sessions, severed fingers, blood everywhere, possessed girl walking on the walls, the scenes are not original for a western viewer but the work is well done.

The trailer is published on July 16, 2016 and triggers a large surge of favorable opinion. The video is seen 200,000 times a month, which is a record for a Maldivian film.

Upon its release, the criticism continues to be positive. The famous film critic, Ahmed Nadheem of the Avas newspaper called "4426" a masterpiece and praised Nahula for the technical quality distilled in the film. He went on to applaud Ibrahim Jihad's performance and called it "worthy of an award".

The film was screened 25 times at Olympus, a cinema in Malé, to a packed house at each screening and is to date the most profitable Maldivian film of 2016.

Figure 149: Poster of the film "Vaashey Mashaa Ekee".

Ahmed Sinan wins a statuette at the 8th Gaumee ceremony on December 20, 2017.

During this same edition, the film "Vaashey Mashaa Ekee" won the statuette for Best Film. It is a romantic comedy by Ali Shifau starring Mohamed Jumayyil (already present in the film "4426") and Mariyam Majudha. This film simply tells the story of a couple, Natha and Ziyad, happily married for five years. Their couple has everything perfect and everyone envies their story. Then their marriage and their mutual love is put in trouble by the sudden arrival of a newcomer.

Finally, without being strictly speaking a Maldivian film, the film Rogue One, an American science fiction film belonging to the Star Wars saga, directed by Gareth Edwards, released in 2016, was shot in the Maldives.

Figure 150: "Rogue One" movie poster

Star Wars and tropical islands, a priori there is no connection between these destinations and a distant galaxy, and yet! "Rogue One: A Star Wars Story" is inserted just before "Episode IV: A New Hope", the first opus of the saga to be released in 1977.

The country serves as a backdrop to Scarif, a planet studded with chains of islands with beaches and palm trees. Gareth Edwards, the director of the film, wanted to shoot in real places to give more depth to his film Star Wars. The team in charge of special effects then digitally added the various facilities of the Empire, bringing the planet Scarif to life. The result: an original planet whose beauty is only equaled by the real Maldivian landscapes.

It is more exactly in the South of the Maldives, on two islands of the Laamu atoll: Gan, an uninhabited island and Berasdhoo, a deserted island covered with coconut trees, that the action took place.

During the shooting, some extras confessed that they had never heard of Star Wars in their entire lives.

Figure 151: Fictional Planet of Scarif (Star Wars)

Painting

There are few traces of ancient paintings in the Maldives. It is likely that the lack of materials and the dietary concerns of the Maldivians did not allow a wealth of artistic production for centuries except for music.

At most, a few drawings have been found on the island of Fuvahmulah: they represent either magic scenes or astrology diagrams.

Figure 152: Old Maldivian drawing

Figure 153: Maldivian Astrology

But at the present time, the Maldivian artistic scene is intense, especially in contemporary painting. The subjects are naturally those that come to the mind of the men living in the Maldives: the sea, coconut palms, fish, pretty women.

The National Gallery of Malé, located at 131 Majeedhee Magu in Malé, has since 1999 housed a collection of Maldivian works of art, past and present.

Among the most notable painters are Egan Mohamed Badeeu, Samah Ahmed, Ibrahim Arafath, Afzal Shaafiu and Hassan Ziyad.

- Egan Mohamed Badeeu is known for painting triptychs depicting traditional life on the Maldivian islands in a way that brings to mind Paul Gauguin painting Tahiti.

- Samah Ahmed describes his work as a combination of spiritual and emotional experiences. Coming from the Maldives, where the earth's surface represents only 1% of the country's surface, Samah Ahmed considers that it is "the warm blue waters of the tropics" that provide his inspiration. It essentially represents underwater landscapes devoid of fish or vegetation. He orchestrates a skillful play of lights and reflections in the blue water to which he adds, always in the background, a gloomy darkness as if to show the immensity of the ocean which he considers to be the only fear of a Maldivian. The obsession of Westerners for the concept of paradisiacal island or Robinson's life surprises him and he wishes to transcribe this dimension of desire for escape in his paintings.

- Ibrahim Arafath is a figure of Maldivian pop art. His explosive paintings never depict Maldivian landscapes but rather remind us of Andy Warhol's paintings.

- Afzal Shaafiu represents in a style imbued with impressionism, the sea, beaches and clouds of his islands. He also indulges in some deliriums of "flying whales".

- Hassan Ziyad began painting in the 1990s when he made t-shirts and other souvenirs for tourists. He mainly paints landscapes without humans. His paintings have the finesse of real photographs. The landscapes he depicts are both peaceful and sad at the same time.

Many other quality painters are trying to break into the international scene: Striped Coco, Ramy Ink, Kareen,

Psychonautfromaatlantis (Moosa Mamdhuh), Razzan, Manje, Shimhaq98, Bulhaa, Funko, N.R., Ekkay Vishal, Maahy, Maldha Mohamed.

Figure 154: Table by Egan Mohamed Badeeu

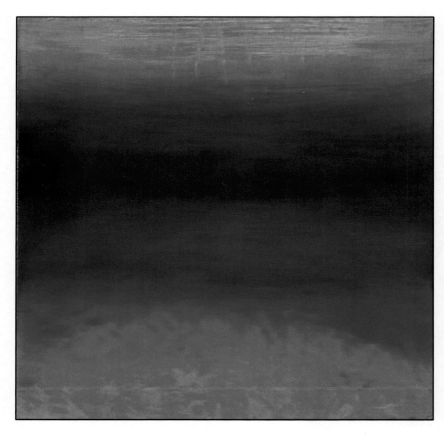

Figure 155: Table of Samah Ahmed

Figure 156: Afzal Shaafiu's Chart

Figure 157: Table by Ibrahim Arafath

Figure 158: Several works by Hassan Ziyad

Figure 159: Afzal Shaafiu's Chart

Figure 160: Table by Maldha Mohamed

Figure 161: Manje's Table

Figure 162: Striped Coco Table

Music and dance

The Maldivians have music in their skin: a long list of traditional dances and songs are part of their history.

Due to the location of the country, the music of the Maldives is marked by Indian, East African and Arabic influences.

The most widespread music in the Maldives is a form of indigenous music called boduberu. This music was introduced by sailors crossing the Indian Ocean. According to historians, it appeared on the archipelago in the 11th century. This music is usually played by an orchestra of 20 people including three drummers and a singer. They are accompanied by a small bell and several drums (they are the bodu beru strictly speaking) as well as an onugadu: a form of bamboo piece perforated with hollows and which is rubbed with a stick.

The songs are typically about heroism, romance, satire. The preludes of the songs are slow paced, oriented to the use of drums and dance. Then, crescendo, two dancers reach and maintain an unbridled rhythm with frenetic movements close to the state of trance.

Another local music, the thaara is orchestrated by 22 men sitting in two rows opposite each other. It can only be played by men and has a somewhat religious meaning. Like the boduberu, thaara songs start slowly and then reach a peak. This music would have come at the same time as the Arabs of the Persian Gulf, in the middle of the seventeenth century.

Later, at the beginning of the 20th century, Sultan Muhammad Shamsuddeen III ruled the Maldives when the youth of the time developed a form of music called langiri, modifying the thaara.

The gaa odi lava is another type of song that is sung at the end of a physical work. It was invented during the reign of Sultan

Mohamed Imadudeen I (1620-1648) for or by the workers who were building the ramparts of Malé.

The bolimalaafath neshun was a dance practiced by women only on special occasions or when giving gifts to the sultan. These gifts, often shells, were kept in carefully decorated boxes or vases: the kurandi malaafath. This dance requires a group of 24 women divided into groups of two to six. They progress towards the sultan by singing patriotic and loyal songs. Since 1968, the country is a republic and therefore there is no longer a sultan or bolimalaafath neshun.

There is another Maldivian dance, the maafathi neshun which is similar to the langiri dance. It is performed by women dancing in rows of ten while waving semi-circular sprays of fake flowers.

Figure 163: Traditional Dancers

We can also mention the combination of singing and dancing fathigandu jehun which is practiced alone or in groups of men holding two short bamboo sticks to accompany the drummer. The lyrics of the songs are usually epics, the most famous being "Burunee Raivaru". This song tells the story of a sultan who left in search of a future wife.

The island of Kulhudhuffushi is known for its local music, kadhaamaali which is played by many drums as well as a kadhaa, a kind of copper dish accompanied by a bar. More than thirty men take part in it, dressed in demon costume (maali).

Maldivians feel an affinity with India because their language is derived from a language of northern India. Most adults watch Hindi films from the 60s or 70s and enjoy listening to the songs in these films. The reason is that beyond the language resembling their own, the rhythms and cadences attract Maldivians. Sound resemblances are diverted: for example, the Hindi words "Ek din" ("One day") are changed to "E kudin" ("These children") in divehi.

Prior to the roll-out of television, the radio programs of the Voice of Maldives were those that broadcast songs in Hindi such as the song "Vakivumuge kurin" ("Before the break-up"). On the rural islands, Hindi songs are still the most popular.

In Malé, on the other hand, as in many big cities in the world, it is western music that appeals most.

Young Maldivians are, of course, producing contemporary music.

In 1996, the group Zero Degree Atoll released an album entitled "Dhoni". This album has its roots in folklore such as the raivaru. The album was a huge success and was followed by a remake in 1997 called "Island Pulse". The members of this group are considered the saviors of the Maldivian musical art and the pioneers of modern divehi music.

The influence of international culture, especially American, has given rise to Maldivian rap, which uses the sounds and video clips of Western rappers. For example, the video " Kamaku Nudhey " of the Maldivian group " Tro, HashTag & Ms.Q ", composed of two men and a young woman, looks a lot like the American clips.

Always in the influence of the globalized culture, the TV show "Maldivian Idol" offers young Maldivians who feel the soul of a singer to come on stage to show what they have in the belly. This program is simply the adaptation of an international television format that takes the name of "Nouvelle Star" in France.

Figure 164: Maldivian Idol Program Logo

The first season ran from January 22, 2016 to May 9, 2016. In front of a jury composed of Ahmed Ibrahim, Ibrahim Zaid Ali and Unoosha, the young Laisha Junaid from Malé won the competition and a prize of 250 000 rufiyaa (14 247 euros). There were 600 candidates in the first season.

Two more seasons took place in 2017 and 2018.

Member of the jury, Mariyam Unoosha, born October 6, 1985 is a very famous Maldivian singer. Immersed in singing from an early age, she is the daughter of two legends of Maldivian music: Shafeega and Mr Naseer. She has the privilege to sing at the Mariah Carey's vow renewal ceremony at the Reethi Rah Resort Island Hotel in 2014.

Figure 165: Unoosha

For her part, the first Maldivian Idol winner, Laisha Junaid, born on October 26, 1997 in Malé, released her first song "Hoadheytho manzileh" on January 26, 2017 and is working on a full-length album. She is recognized in her country as an intelligent and very polite young girl whose dream is to become a doctor.

Agriculture

A country with such a small and fragmented surface area can only challenge those who are interested in it. How have Maldivians been able to feed themselves properly for centuries?

Traditional agriculture

In 1973, the rare tourists of the archipelago noticed that the market stalls of the Maldives are well supplied: taro, manioc, sweet potatoes. But the flagship product is coconut. In addition to this, mangoes, bananas, chili peppers, papayas. At that time, however, there is no trace of any real irrigation system. Agriculture was therefore limited to a rainy season activity. Fortunately, the rainy season in the Maldives extends from April to January. Only the months of February and March represent a form of drought with respectively 38 and 73 millimeters of rainfall against 231 millimeters in November. For comparison, the average monthly rainfall in Paris is 53 millimeters. These islands considered paradisiacal are, in fact, more humid than Brittany.

Annual rainfall in the Maldives	1,901 mm
Annual rainfall in Brest, France	1,210 mm

The Maldives is the land of coconut palms, which make up most of the natural vegetation and historic agriculture in the country. Taro and some other large-leaved plants are the indigenous plants that have been cultivated for centuries. Maldivians always preserved a small area of forest on a portion of each inhabited island. These forests acted as small ecosystems helping to conserve native biodiversity and provide a food supply for the islanders. Then, each inhabitant grew a wide variety of crops on his or her property, such as chilli, sweet potatoes, pineapples, sugar cane, almonds, moringa, millet, maize, breadfruit, papaya, lime, banana, pumpkins, melons, cucumbers, cruciferous (cabbage), taro, areca nut, pepper. Most of these plants had been introduced by man.

Historically it is the women who take care of the vegetable garden. They also raise a few hens for their meat and eggs and goats only for their milk.

Modern agriculture

In the 1980s, the government of the Maldives decided to found an Agriculture Centre to develop modern agriculture and train the inhabitants. Irrigation was introduced, composting techniques were developed and new plantations were introduced on the islands.

A major specificity of the Maldives compared to most countries in the world is its soil. The soil of the Maldives is, as one can imagine, mainly composed of sand. To overcome this constraint, hydroponics, still called above-ground agriculture, has made it possible to grow the impossible: leafy vegetables, melons, cucumbers.

Hydroponics or hydroponic cultivation (or above-ground agriculture), from the Greek πονος (ponos, "work" or "effort") and ὕδωρ (hudōr, "water"), is the cultivation of plants carried out on a neutral and inert substrate (such as sand, pozzolan, clay balls, rock wool, ...). This substrate is regularly irrigated with a stream of solution which brings mineral salts and essential nutrients to the plant. In the case of soil-less crops, the cultivation takes place without soil, thus freeing itself from the constraints linked to conventional land-based crops.

Figure 166: Greenhouse and hydroponics

But this technique got off to a difficult start due to the high cost of installation. This cost was covered by the international community through the UNDP (United Nations Development Programme) fund. This program is part of the UN programs and funds. Its role is to help developing countries by providing advice but also by advocating their causes for the granting of donations. The origins of the UNDP date back to the 1950s with the creation by the UN General Assembly of the Expanded Programme of Technical Assistance (EPTA) and the establishment in December 1958 of the United Nations Special Fund (UNSF). The close activities of these two organizations led the General Assembly to decide to merge them by resolution 2029 and the creation of the UNDP on January [1,] 1966.

Composting was a direct consequence of the establishment of hydroponics. Indeed, the supply of organic nutrients is necessary for crops. In order to avoid the importation of fertilizers, each island had to set up a collection of the organic waste present on site. For example, on the island of Sonevafushi, to date no pesticides or chemicals are used. The virtuous effect of the total isolation of the Maldives from the rest of the world has been the development of a healthier, less chemical agriculture out of a need to reduce costly imports. Hydroponics feeds the plants, the plants feed the people, and the organic waste in turn is composted to go back into the hydroponic pipes. Each island consumes itself! Thus, the island of Sonevafushi manages to produce 95% of the vegetables consumed by its inhabitants. This is a feat of self-sufficiency. The local policy is to cook with food that has traveled "zero kilometers". It is a locavore diet. Locavorism or locavore movement is a movement advocating the consumption of food produced within a radius of 100 to 250 kilometers maximum around one's home. A person who adheres to locavorism is called a locavore.

In greenhouses, an artisanal hydroponic system irrigates plantations that do not lack sunlight with mineral salts. The average number of hours of sunshine is 2,778 hours per year. For comparison, in Barcelona, Spain, this number is 2,524. In Paris, France, this number is 1,661.

Running a farm in the Maldives is humanly difficult. Even in 2015, Maldivian agriculture is very manual for two reasons:

conventional agricultural machinery is expensive to import and is unsuitable because the cultivated areas are tiny. For example, the island of Sonevafushi is 1.41 km long and only 381 meters wide. Also, the island's only greenhouse occupies a sand rectangle measuring 57 meters by 76 meters. This is half the size of an international soccer field.

The work of the farmer(s) consists of checking temperatures and watering the plants. The harvests, also manual, are then transported by a cooperative to the markets of the inhabited islands or to the hotels in the case of islands with a tourist vocation.

In 2013, the FADip program (Fisheries and Agriculture Diversification Program) led by the Ministry of Fisheries and Agriculture has set itself the goal of attracting young Maldivians to these two industries. The mission of this program is to encourage the country to organize itself into cooperatives in order to increase the agricultural workforce and introduce innovative methods or technologies. Two major difficulties were still to be fought very recently:

- Pulling agricultural production at a suitable scale despite the size of the farms,
- Keep highly perishable goods.

The cooperative model, well known in the rest of the world, was a totally new concept for the Maldives until 2013. Traditionally, farmers sold their individual produce directly. A change in the agricultural model is beginning to take shape. By 2018, there are eight cooperatives in the Maldives. Approximately 30 agricultural products are supported, which brings an undeniable dietary diversity.

The majority of the cooperatives work to feed the capital, Malé, the airport and some resorts. In 2018, their market will amount to 500 000 rufiyaa per month or 27 816 euros.

The workforce is about 170 people. To achieve this, starting in 2016, loans are granted to 48 individuals: a total of 6.9 million rufiyaa or 384,000 euros. All cooperatives are accredited by the Ministry and the Maldives Food and Drugs Authority.

For example, the Bizville cooperative on the island of Hoarafushi manages to support sustainable jobs by selling processed products from their hydroponic production: chips, jams, etc. It is important to note that in the infancy of this cooperative, only two years before the writing of this book, the inhabitants of Hoarafushi Island were so unskilled in agriculture that the founder had to train his employees with the help of YouTube videos! These videos, taken on a famous and free platform, made it possible to quickly train future employees in both basic gardening techniques and large-scale agriculture. Bizville is actively recruiting new members and is trying to export its model of success to other islands.

Another example is the Naifuru cooperative, which relies on products with high cultural added value, such as the local culinary specialties of the island bearing the same name. Its founder, Ahmed Yasir, insists on the role that everyone can play in the development of the island: it is necessary to cook, sell, transport and advertise these products both on an island scale and for luxury hotels. These products need to be advertised in order to make the local cuisine attractive to tourists. He put forward the idea of organizing trade fairs to publicize the diversity of local Maldivian products. For decades, Maldivians have been feasting on kudhi gulha still called athujehi or kulhi roshi. These are small flour doughnuts in the shape of dumplings filled with a mixture of tuna, onions, coconut and chilli pepper. The gulha are therefore a kind of tuna accras that serve as appetizers. Their dimensions vary from the size of a ball to the size of a ping-pong ball. The name of the dish, gulha, originally comes from the most caught fish in the Maldives, the gulha, but nowadays cooks opt for canned tuna instead.

A real marketing work awaits this cooperative to make these traditional products known. This includes sending free samples to potential buyers in the global market.

Another world on the island of Faafu Magoodhoo, the F. Magoodhoo Cooperative Society exploits hydroponics, in particular to grow a plant in high demand: lettuce. The conservation of lettuce after its harvest is still one of the major difficulties the cooperative faces today. Keeping them fresh until they are transported to the capital is a challenge they are trying to solve with new packaging. The other highly prized plants on this farm are bananas and eggplants.

On the animal level, a hen farm provides a large volume of eggs. The founder, Ismail Naushaz, also remembers his difficult beginnings: a large quantity of eggs was damaged before they were even sold, which prevented the cooperative from meeting the high demand for eggs from hotels and restaurants.

On the island of Laamu, farmers are actively seeking opportunities to make agriculture on the atoll profitable. This island has decided to collect household waste from other neighboring islands and turn it into fertilizer. Ironically, this means that garbage collection has been put in place to feed the people. Alas, on the compost dump, manpower is scarce. Teams collect the compost, package it and sell it in small fertilizer bags of two to five kilograms, under the brand name LBA. The cooperative also markets seeds and gardening equipment.

On Gaafu Alifu Gemanafushi, the G.A. Gemanafushi Cooperative has focused on fishing as well as fish processing for decades. The fish is cooked and dried by the locals. It also markets rihaakuru, a fish paste. It is a kind of brown paste that is popular but whose productivity is not keeping up with demand at the moment. With a little bitterness, the cooperative's vice-president, Asim Mohamed, deplores the poor prices at which locals used to sell their products in the capital,

Malé. In addition, long payment delays and bad payers have pushed the population to pursue a dream of fair trade. This was the unique motivation for the foundation of this cooperative, on the advice of the Ministry.

In Fuvahmulah City, the Funaadu Development Cooperative Society has as its main mission the elaboration of taro chips called "Olhu Ala". Taro, also known as dream, madeira, madeira root, cabbage or dachine, is a food tuber (root vegetable) from tropical regions produced by plants of the Araceae family, most often from the subfamily Aroideae. The term can also refer to the plant itself, whose other parts (stems and leaves) can also be eaten after preparation because, like the tuber, when eaten raw, they are bitter and irritating due to the presence of calcium oxalate crystals (risk of kidney stones, risk in case of kidney failure). Taro chips are little known outside the Maldives. The taro used is bought from various local farmers and then, as one would do with a common potato, it is peeled, sliced and fried. It is mainly women who are involved in this industry. The cooperative thus sees an opportunity to give women work in the home. The future will also see the diversification of the preparations because at the moment the only flavor offered is plain taro chips. The taro chips undergo a series of food hygiene controls, which allows this product to be placed in the Duty-Free stores at the Maldives International Airport under the brand name "Kanna".

Addu Meedhoo is one of the oldest cooperatives in the country. Their greenhouses are modern and spacious. Various methods are used: always hydroponics, but also pots and soil mixes. This cooperative is the main supplier of the prestigious Shangri-La Resort Hotel in Addu City. The office of Hassan Shaahid, the manager, stands out from those of other cooperatives in the country by its modernity: computer, air conditioning, ... He knows what he owes to the financial support of FADiP and UNDP. The building contains a fresh storage space, which prevents the deterioration of the merchandise. They are also fortunate enough to own a motor vehicle made available to farmers at a much more reasonable rate than commercial transporters.

The biggest challenge for all cooperatives lies in the solidity of the greenhouses. In 2017, one experiment left a bitter taste: from July to December, incessant rains caused considerable losses among farmers. It is still through innovation that the Maldives will have to respond to this kind of problem.

In 2018, 33 types of goods are produced in the Maldives and sold to fourteen hotel group stores. This cooperative formula quickly proved its worth. It is clear to the Minister, Dr. Mohamed Shainee, that this model has yet to flourish on a wider scale.

On a human level, the Minister is also proud to have been able to involve Maldivian women in this agricultural modernization project. The living conditions of all have benefited greatly from the model.

Economy

Historically, the Maldives was famous for cowries, coconut fiber ropes, dried tuna (the famous Maldive fish), coconut seafood and ambergris: an intestinal concretion of the sperm whale, a very fragrant, solid, greasy, flammable substance, with a color ranging from gray to blackish and with a specific smell that was once found most often floating on the oceans or deposited on the coasts.

The Maldives' current economy is quite different.

Index	Value (in 2017)
Currency	Rufiyaa (MVR)
GDP	4.6 billion USD
GDP ranking	165th largest country in the world
GDP growth	4,5 %
GDP per capita	12,530 USD
Population below the poverty line	16 %
Labour force	110,000 people
Exports	145 million USD/year

Imports	1,993 million USD/year

Today's economy is based on tourism, fishing and transportation of goods.

Tourism

It is the most powerful industry in the country. It accounts for 28% of the GDP. It is a new industry for the Maldives: in the 80s, tourism grew by 265 % and then by 115 % in the 90s. More than 90% of public revenue comes from tourism taxes.

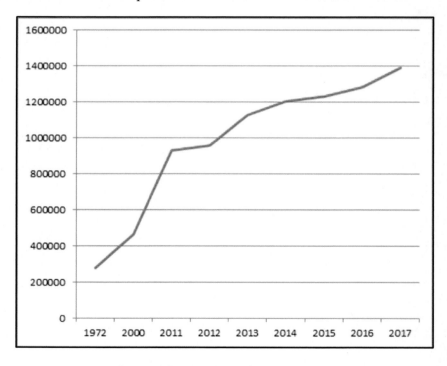

Figure 167: Number of tourists per year

In 2018, we can say that the country has been able to promote its natural charm to attract tourism. The beautiful unpolluted beaches, coral islands, turquoise water and romantic sunsets attract tourists from all over the world. They leave behind approximately 430 million US dollars a year.

1.4 million tourists visited the Maldives in 2017, i.e. about 3,836 tourists arriving every day.

In 2015, hotels sold 6,694,000 overnight stays (1 night = 1 tourist for 1 night).

In 2018, 23 resorts are under construction, including well-known hotel brands such as Waldorf-Astoria, Movenpick, Pullman and Hard Rock Café.

A survey of tourists indicates that their motivations for coming to the Maldives are, in order:

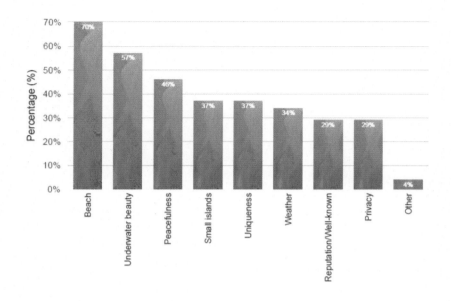

Figure 168: Reasons for visiting the Maldives (%)

Fishing

Far behind tourism, fishing is the second largest industry in the country. As former President Maumoon Abdul Gayoom said, "Fishing is in the blood of our nation. It is innate. From the soil on which we live to the sea that surrounds us, it remains an integral part of our existence. Fishing, our country and its people are one and inseparable forever.

Indeed, the Maldives has an abundant aquatic fauna: tuna, groupers, mahi-mahi, barracuda, rainbow runner, jacks, squirrel fish, and many others.

In addition to its food role, fishing is also a recreational activity for locals but also for tourists. Each hotel offers fishing as an excursion for tourists.

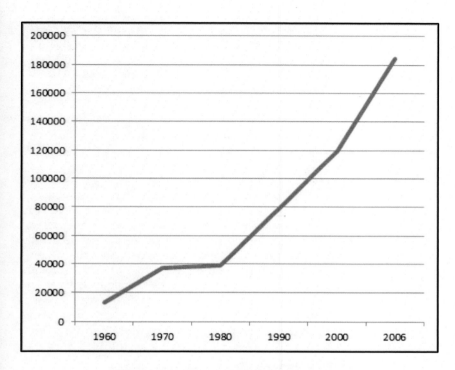

Figure 169: Tons of fish caught per year

There are four harvestable fishing areas:

- Terrestrial areas, i.e. water bodies contained inland. In reality the islands are so small that there are almost no ponds, lakes or rivers in the Maldives. There is no aquaculture either.
- The lagoons. Several collapsed volcanic islands have left behind lagoons totally or partially closed by a ring of coral. These lagoons contain fish.
- The outside of the coral reefs. This is the outside of the lagoons, where the floor becomes progressively deeper. Their waters offer less fishing reserves than the inside of the lagoons.

- The ocean. The open sea. On the surface it is very clearly the main fishing area. The Exclusive Economic Zone (EEZ) of the Maldives covers an area of 900,000 square kilometers. Not bad for a country with a land area of 300 km².

Like everywhere else in the world, the Maldives is facing overfishing. The capacity to rebuild fish populations is largely exceeded, mainly due to tourism.

The export of aquarium fish is also constantly increasing. Approximately one hundred species of fish are exported to aquariums around the world, of which twenty species account for 75% of sales. The use of cyanide for fish fishing is, today, the most well-known destructive practice of aquarists around the world. It is also the most widespread. Bius", which means "stunning" in Indonesian, is the name given to cyanide by local people. It is inserted into a hookah-type device and then released into the reef by fishermen-divers. It is all the know-how of the latter that makes it possible to obtain a profitable technique. Indeed, if too high a concentration of cyanide can kill anything that moves, well-calibrated jets allow divers to easily recover anesthetized fish.

Other Industries

With the exception of fishing and tourism, the industries of the Maldives are anecdotal.

There is agriculture, but it barely manages to fill the Maldivians' bellies or to offer tourists fruit at the buffet of their luxury hotels.

Production plants are few in number. However, there are small boat builders, a few canned tuna production plants, a handful of clothing factories, a bottling plant, and a few factories producing PVC pipes, soap, and furniture.

In banking terms, finance in the Maldives is covered by seven banks and one stock exchange, as well as a regulatory authority: the Maldives Monetary Authority. On the Malé Stock Exchange, the Maldives Stock Exchange, there are only nine companies listed (2018).

Finally, maritime transport has also grown in recent years, thanks in particular to the dynamism of the port of Malé. In the early 1990s, the Port of Malé received a $10 million loan from the Asian Development Bank to help the Maldives modernize this infrastructure. Thanks to this assistance, cargo transiting through Malé has increased from 273,000 tons to one million tons in 2011, which is good but still very modest. For comparison, the port of Marseille in France sees an increase of 82 million tons.

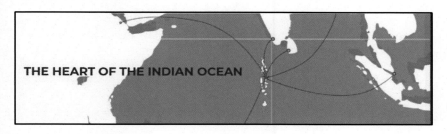

Figure 170: Slogan and illustration of the port of Malé

The strategic position of the Maldives in the Indian Ocean has always helped the Maldives to be a gateway for goods and people. The Maldives is like a crossroads between Africa, India and South East Asia.

The country has grown to a fleet of 60 delivery vessels, all owned by Maldives Shipping Limited.

Imports and exports

The Maldives' trade balance is highly unbalanced: the Maldives exports $34 million worth of goods each month while importing $240 million (figures for January 2018 as an example).

Figure 171: Difference between imports and exports

This imbalance varies greatly from month to month but is always negative and worsens over the years.

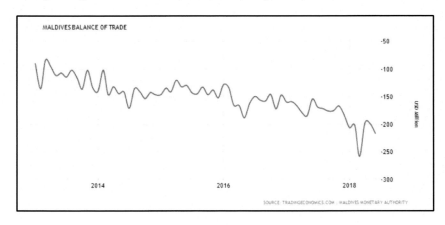

Figure 172: Maldives Trade Balance

The three main countries to which the Maldives sends its exports are Thailand, Sri Lanka and France.

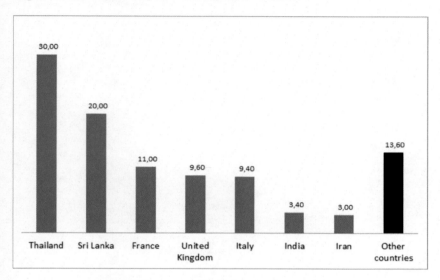

Figure 173: Main Countries for Exports (%)

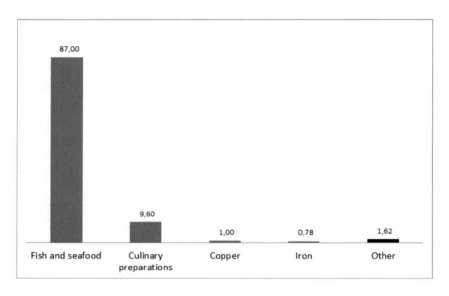

Figure 174: Exported Goods (%)

It is reasonable to say that it is almost exclusively fish that is the source of exports to the Maldives. Thus, exported fish and other seafood products account for 87% of goods while processed fish products account for 9.6%.

According to Trading Economics.com, the main countries from which the Maldives imports originate are the United Arab Emirates, Singapore and India.

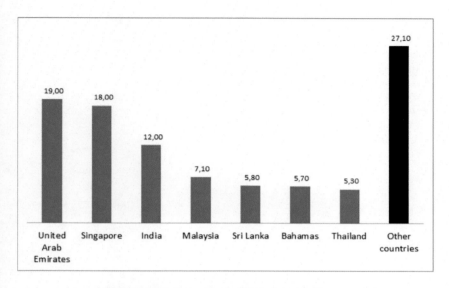

Figure 175: Country of origin of imports (%)

Unsurprisingly, the main imports are petroleum products, appliances, machinery and engines. The Maldives imports surprisingly little food or domestic conveniences. Their imports reflect the need for energy to overcome the isolation, heat, salinity of the water, ...

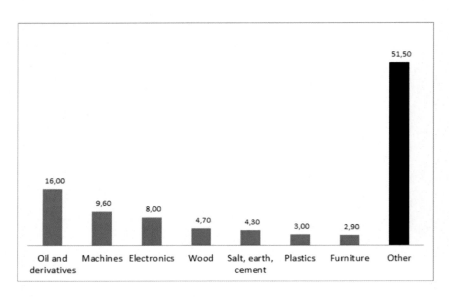

Figure 176: Imported Products (%)

Currency

The Maldivian Rufiyaa or Maldivian Rupee (in Dhivehi: ﷽) is the currency of the Maldives. The establishment of the currency is controlled by the Maldives Monetary Authority (MMA). The ISO 4217 code for the Maldivian Rufiyaa is MVR, the abbreviation rf is also used.

A rufiyaa is divided into 100 laari. The word rufiyaa is derived from the Hindi word rupayā (rupee).

1 EURO = 17.505 RUFIYAA

Or

1 RUFIYAA = 0.057 EURO

The first coins called rufiyaa were struck in 1970. The previous currency of the Maldives was the "Laari". Nowadays, the rufiyaa cents are called "laari". The coins have inscriptions in English since the late 1970s.

The current series of banknotes was designed in 1983 in denominations of 2, 5, 10, 20, 50 and 100 rufiyaa. The 500 banknote was added in 1990. The smallest bill, the 2-rufiyaa bill, was withdrawn from circulation and replaced by a coin in 1995.

In October 2015, the Maldives Monetary Authority released a series of plastic (specifically polymer) banknotes to commemorate the 50th anniversary of the country's independence. The 1,000-rufiyaa banknote was invented on this occasion.

Switching from paper to plastic for printing banknotes is a very modern measure that has appealed to Australia since 1996 and many other countries since then. They are more difficult to imitate and do not deteriorate much with use. Moreover, it is very convenient to have plastic banknotes in a country surrounded by water.

Figure 177: Polymer rufiyaa bills

Figure 178: Rufiyaa Coins

For economic reasons that are difficult for the layman to understand, Rufiyaa is absolutely non-exchangeable in any other currency in the world. This means that a tourist is not allowed to leave the country with Rufiyaa coins or banknotes. It also means that a person who receives a salary in Rufiyaa can only spend it in the Maldives. This is why the dollar reigns supreme in the hands of tourists and hotel employees.

Fiscal system

Simplicity

Like any nation, the Maldives has taxes, but in the opinion of many economists, its tax system is the simplest in the world. Individuals don't have to bother with their income tax returns because it doesn't exist. They don't have to worry about housing tax, property tax, ...

In fact, only companies pay taxes.

Researchers from the World Bank and the auditing firm PWC imagined from scratch a flowerpot manufacturing company with 60 employees, a building and a van. They then read the tax code of every country in the world to find out how long it would take this fictitious company to fill out its tax form. Their conclusion was that in the Maldives, it would take less than an hour.

In comparison, in the United States, it would have taken 187 hours. And in Brazil, the worst country in the world in terms of tax complexity, it would have taken 108 days.

The Maldives Inland Revenue Authority was formed on August 2, 2010 to modernize the tax system. It has only 282 employees. It is headed by a seven-person commission appointed by Parliament.

Its efficiency allows it to better enforce tax laws and collect more and more tax, as this curve shows.

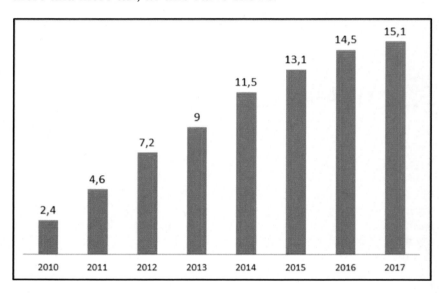

Figure 179: Taxes collected (in billions of rufiyaa)

List of taxes

There were only nine taxes in the Maldives.

- **The tax on tourism goods and services.** Launched on January 1st, 2011, it is imposed on hoteliers, tourist boats, and some services dedicated to tourists. It has been replaced by the following tax.

- **The tax on goods and services.** Launched in October 2011, it extends the tax on tourism to the entire economy. It levies 6% of the economy's revenues.

- **Tax on profits.** It came into force on July 18, 2011. It consists of levying 15% of company profits that exceed the 500,000 rufiyaa (approximately 28,424 euros).

- **The tourism tax in the Maldives** is a tax that exists all over the world. It consists of charging eight US dollars per tourist per night. In fact, this tax was repealed on December 1, 2014, making stays in the Maldives less expensive.

- **The tourist housing tax.** Hotels must pay a tax of eight dollars per square meter of occupied space, per year.

- **The green tax.** Effective October 1st, 2016, it is only for foreign tourists staying in a hotel, hostel or cruise ship. It consists of paying six dollars per day per tourist (3 dollars if the tourist sleeps in an inn).

- **Employment tax.** It is a tax that aims to penalize foreign employees by levying 3% of their salary. Since October 1st, 2016, it therefore targets all immigrant workers.

- **The tax on bank profits.** This tax is only imposed on banks. They must pay 25% of their profits. In exchange, they are exempt from another tax: the tax on profits.

- **The airport taxes.** It is a tax that requires 25 US dollars per foreign passenger passing through Malé airport or 12 US dollars for a Maldivian passenger. Exempt persons are those who only stopover in Malé, as well as diplomats and babies under two years old.

Army

Although there is no participation in any major war in the history of the Maldives, the country has an army.

However, there are three historical events that can be considered as conflicts that required an army in the Maldives:

- The expulsion of the Portuguese garrisons in 1573,
- The attacks of the Kingdom of Cannanore from 1573 to 1773,
- The 1988 coup d'état.

The Maldivian army is called the Maldives National Defence Force (MNDF). It is an army as small as its country, with a budget of $45 million a year, making it the 131st largest army in the world.

Its primary responsibility is to meet all internal and external security needs of the Maldives, including in its exclusive economic zone.

Figure 180: Emblem of the Maldivian Army

History

The Hagubeykalun are the first reference to an organization for the defense of the Maldives, shortly before the reign of Muhammad Thakurufaanu Al Auzam (1573 - 1585). This sultan reorganized the security forces of the time and appointed a dhoshimeynaa wazir, i.e. a minister, to head the army (lashakru). As a reminder, Muhammad Thakurufaanu Al Auzam, better known as Sultan Al-Gazi Mohamed Thakurufaan, is the hero of the war against the Portuguese. It is precisely following this victory that he focused on the need for an effective army in the Maldives.

The army owes its present form to the initiatives of Sultan Ibrahim Nooraddeen Iskandhar (1888-1892). This sultan was impressed by a group of young men practicing military marching while they were at the Sultan's Palace to learn martial arts. The sultan gave his blessing to their new learning and facilitated their training. This same group of men later began to accompany the Sultan during his royal travels. During his short reign, the sultan enlists a selection of young people and teaches them hevikan (the Maldivian martial art) and makes them participate in royal ceremonies. On April 21, 1892, a new security force was created by royal decree. The Sultan appointed himself Commander-in-Chief of the security force. This new force was authorized to bear arms and the Palace granted them certain special privileges.

On January 10, 1979, after years of progression and evolution, the Ministry of Public Security and the National Guard were renamed Ministry of Defense and National Security Service (SNS) or National Security Service (NSS) in English. The police, for its part, remained fully included until the Ministry of Home Affairs named it the Maldives Police Service on September [1,] 2004 and declared it a "civil service".

After the secondment of the police from the NSS, the missions and duties of the NSS must be reviewed. This review envisages a completely new structure. The very core of the armies is being rethought and redesigned. The name Maldives National Defence Force (MNDF) is adopted on the 114th anniversary of the Maldivian army on 21 April 2006 in the presence of President Maumoon Abdul Gayoom.

According to estimates, the Maldivian army is composed of 3,500 soldiers. This figure is never officially revealed.

Branches of the army

Coast Guard

The geography of the Maldives means that the country has only maritime borders. In fact, most of the country's security concerns are based on the sea. 90% of the country is water and the remaining 10% is scattered over an area of 415 km x 120 km. The country's location and scattered shape provide ideal conditions for smugglers.

Figure 181: Maldivian Coast Guard

For this reason, the functions assigned to the MNDF to maintain surveillance over Maldivian waters and provide protection against poaching intruders in the exclusive economic zone and territorial waters are a huge task from a logistical or economic point of view. To carry out these functions, the Coast Guard plays a vital role. To provide responsive security, patrol boats are stationed at several regional headquarters throughout the territory.

The Coast Guard is also responsible for responding to distress calls at sea and conducting timely search and rescue operations. Oil spill control exercises are conducted regularly each year to prepare for this type of disaster. Finally, the Coast Guard is responsible for transporting troops and equipment across the country. They may also be in charge of escorting and protecting a VIP (very important person).

Marine

The Marine Corps (new name of the Rapid Reaction Force) is the Maldivian army corps going into ground combat (as their name does not indicate). Formed just in 2006, the Marine Corps are deployed in several strategic or vulnerable locations to increase their protective power over the country. It is a mobile, lethal unit with a high strike force and combat capabilities. Once again, it is the amphibious nature of the country that required its infantry to be trained for the sea. Marines are trained and equipped to fight with equal power at sea, or on land in any weather and terrain, in rural or urban areas.

Their secondary functions are the fight against terrorism as well as non-combative functions such as the provision of humanitarian assistance after a disaster.

Special Forces

Special Forces (SF or SF) are an elite unit within the MNDF. They are trained to fight in all conditions and at anytime, anywhere in the world. They are involved in situations where conventional infantry faces an obstacle.

The Maldivian special forces are only dated February 9, 2009. Their first task is the fight against terrorism and intervention operations at the national level. Their other types of missions are hostage-taking, sabotage, raids and intelligence.

Special forces undergo an intense and meticulous year-long training that requires strict physical agility, mental well-being and intelligence. They have the opportunity to train with reputable Special Forces from other nations.

Services

It is the division of the army that supports the others. It is in charge of facilitating the provision of equipment and services to the entire organization. These services include the following support functions:

- Communications, electronics and information technology,
- Transportation,
- Clothing (uniforms),
- Power supply,
- Army band.

Corps of Engineers

This is the division responsible for engines and other equipment to be maintained or repaired: boat engineering, air conditioning, design of steel structures, firearm modifications.

But they are also the builders of the army: they are in charge of repairing or building buildings.

Protection Panel

This unit is responsible for the protection of the Head of State as well as visiting foreign dignitaries. Its creation is the immediate repercussion of the coup d'état of November 3, 1988 against President Maumoon Abdul Gayoom. At that time, it was the Indian army that saved the Maldivian President.

Military Police

Section 43 of the 2008 Armed Forces Act states that the ministry must establish a military police within the military itself that will be responsible for investigating any wrongdoing by a member of the armed forces.

The existence of a military police within the military is crucial to ensure the conduct and discipline of all soldiers. This newly created police force will help ensure law enforcement within the military and expand its sense of respect for human rights. For anyone familiar with the recent history of the Maldives, this "human rights" turn of events in the Maldives is astonishing.

Air Force

It is only on January 1st, 2013 that the President of the Maldives impulses the creation of an air force, the Maldives Air Wing or Aviation Security Command.

Its mandate is to protect and safeguard Maldivian airspace, monitor suspicious activities in Maldivian waters and conduct search and rescue operations.

Since 2010, the Maldivian army had a helicopter offered by India: a Dhruv. The HAL Dhruv is a versatile medium helicopter designed by the Indian company HAL in collaboration with Messerschmitt-Bölkow-Blohm to succeed the Indian Army Alouettes. It began service in the Indian Army in 2002 and has been exported to Burma, Israel, Nepal and Bolivia. The Dhruv is available in different versions, some of which are civilian.

In total, in 2018, the air force fleet will amount to ... two Dhruv helicopters. It is small but this fleet is similar to those of the armies of countries of the same size. For example, the army of Belize (population 360,000 and a military budget of $35 million) has only one helicopter and two airplanes.

Training Institute

This is the unit that manages the training and coaching. They are in charge of improving the professionalism of the troops, in particular by drawing inspiration from foreign armies.

Fire Fighters

The Fire and Rescue Service carries the responsibility of responding to fire situations. For the moment, it is only available in Malé and its surroundings.

Medical Service

As its name suggests, it is responsible for providing medical services to the men and women of the MNDF army.

The future of the Maldives

Since 1972, the country has been in the midst of modernization. From a country covered with coconut fiber houses, the Maldives has become an amusement park for the rich, building dream villas, suspension bridges, underwater restaurants, cities trying to imitate Monaco, and even skyscrapers.

The future of the Maldives will lie in its ability to solve its current problems. These are mainly ecological, religious, tourism and political. The country's reputation is a precious asset that the country must protect in order not to scare away its only source of capital: it is the government's responsibility to take care of tourism.

On the one hand, the fight against religious fundamentalism will be the only guarantee of a wider international opening. Indeed, it can be observed that the more a foreigner becomes aware of the strict application of Sharia law in the Maldives, the less inclined he is to go there. How do you explain to a tourist that he spends his vacations in a country capable of whipping raped women in public places or executing a child? It is not only the image of the country that needs to be looked after, it is its entire relationship to Islam. This work has been carried out for several years by the MDP, the Democratic Party. It will be necessary to convince the country to adhere to the idea that it is indeed the tourist, mostly non-Muslim, who finances the so good standard of living of the Maldivians.

The segregation of tourists and residents is also a subject to be re-examined. It is likely that the CDM in power since 2018 will revisit this concept because it prevents the redistribution of economic benefits to the people. From the point of view of the country's image, the foreign tourists who are most attached to ethics or the discovery of cultures will be hindered in their desire to go to the Maldives as long as this segregation is not lifted.

On the political level, great things are to be accomplished in order to give a little grandeur to the Maldivian people, until now too infantilized. Few Maldivians are famous. Few elections take place calmly. Few investors intend to establish projects in the Maldives. Few Maldivians perform sporting feats. These indicators show that the country does not find its place on the world map. For lack of political will, the country is known only for its beaches.

But besides, how long will the country be able to count on its beaches? The Maldives faces the same lack of future as oil-producing countries: their main resource is exhaustible. The oil of the Maldives is tourism but what will they do when the country is no longer attractive? Global warming, pollution, and coral death could well turn dream beaches into a nightmare. No tourist wants to visit a country surrounded by concrete dikes. No one wants to swim in the middle of garbage or meet a sewage pipe while snorkeling.

Successive governments will have to find a way to preserve their annuities and, more importantly, prepare for the long-term future. For, whatever their efforts on a local scale, the rise in ocean levels is a global affair that concerns Malé, Manhattan or Arcachon as well. The role they can take on is a position that is currently vacant: world leader in the fight against rising sea levels. The Maldivians will have to take up their pilgrim's staff and invite the rest of the world to open their eyes to global warming, especially large countries like China. But precisely, China has just built a bridge of Sino-Maldivian friendship: isn't this an opportunity to get help from someone greater than oneself? Having as an ally a country whose surface area is 32,204 times its own, and incidentally one of the biggest polluters in the world, will perhaps make it possible to take the necessary future decisions, namely: either to stop or reverse global warming, or to buy a 298 square kilometer piece of land to relocate the entire population.

A more aggressive attitude would be to take the rest of the world to the International Criminal Court for failure to assist countries in danger, or even for passive genocide. But this would solve nothing.

To go further

Five men share the common thread of having lived in the Maldives and of having copiously documented the country in widely spoken languages. Their writings deal with the religion, culture, politics and folklore of the Maldives.

- Ibn Battuta
- François Pyrard
- HCP Bell
- Xavier Romero Frias
- J.J. Robinson

Ibn Battuta

Ibn Battûta, born on February 24, 1304 in Tangier and died in 1377 in Marrakech, is an explorer and traveler of Berber origin who traveled nearly 120,000 kilometers between 1325 and 1349.

From 1343 to 1344 he lived in the Maldives. In these islands he became a cadi (judge), then he married several daughters of viziers. More than a simple observer, Battûta will then impose a strict interpretation of Islam by regulating divorces and by obliging women to stay with their husbands. He also tries to impose the hijab, without success, because he notes that the Maldivian women walk around bare-breasted, with a simple skirt!

He returned briefly to the Maldives in 1345 to visit a baby of whom he was said to be the father.

In the book "Travel, India, Far East, Spain & Sudan, vol. 3", his two trips to the Maldives are detailed. It is often about Islam, women and the culture, especially the culinary culture of the country.

François Pyrard

François Pyrard (born about 1578, Laval - died about 1623, Paris) is a French polyglot navigator and explorer.

Warned of the enormous profits made by Dutch companies in the Moluccas (Indonesia), in 1601, the Company of Saint-Malo, Laval and Vitre armed two ships, the Corbin and the Croissant to seek a way to the Indies and show it to the French. François Pyrard is part of the voyage aboard the Corbin. The aim is to propagate the Catholic faith and to increase the political and economic power of France.

On July 3, 1602, the ship struck twice with force on a reef and immediately lay down on its side. The Corbin was wrecked in the middle of the night on the reefs of the Maldives because of the inexperience of the captain and the drunkenness of the entire crew.

At first shipwrecked then collected and well looked after by the king of the Maldives, Pyrard stays five years in the archipelago.

In the book " Voyage de François Pyrard de Laval " published in 1615, his stay is detailed.

HCP Bell

Harry Charles Purvis Bell, nicknamed HCP Bell, was a British civil servant born in India in 1851 and died in 1937.

Trained as an archaeologist, HCP Bell made several trips to Sri Lanka and the Maldives even after the end of his career. His major works on the subject are: "The Máldive Islands: An Account of the Physical Features, Climate, History, Inhabitants, Productions, and Trade" published in 1882, "Excerpta Máldiviana" and "The Máldive Islands: Monograph on the History, Archaeology and Epigraphy".

In these works, HCP Bell translates old historical texts that he obtains from the sultans. He is also interested in the alphabet and the origins of the Maldivian language.

Xavier Romero Frias

Xavier Romero Frias, born in Barcelona in 1954, is a Spanish anthropologist, writer and cartoonist, specializing in the culture of the Maldives.

Arrived in the Maldives in 1979, he settled on the island of Fua Mulaku (old name of Fuvahmulah), in the south of the archipelago among the inhabitants of the island whose language he learned and studied the customs. After twelve years he collected, translated and annotated a large part of the oral tradition of the Maldives. Fifteen years later he continued his research in India where after twelve years of study he found clues that allowed him to elucidate the sources of Maldivian traditions.

Frias' books are all banned in the Maldives without any explicit reason, but it can be assumed that they reveal too many non-Muslim beliefs for the government's taste.

His major books are "The Maldive Islanders: a study of the popular culture of an ancient ocean kingdom" published in 1999, "Folk Tales of the Maldives" published in 2012 and "The Old Alphabet of the Maldives (Divehi Akuru - 1)".

J.J. Robinson

J.J. Robinson is an Australian-British journalist born in 1983. A graduate of Columbia University's prestigious School of Journalism (New York), he is head of the Minivan News, the only independent newspaper in the Maldives from 2009 to 2013. During these four years, Robinson did not hesitate to immerse himself in the political saga of the Maldives and even witnessed the forced resignation of Nasheed in 2012.

His book "The Maldives: islamic republic, tropical autocracy" is one of the few English-language analyses of the Maldives' political and economic system.

Table of illustrations

The illustrations in this book belong solely to their respective owners.

Sources

Article " 7 countries invited to observe Maldives presidential election "
http://www.xinhuanet.com/english/2018-06/26/c_137282122.htm

Article "7 unique indigenous tribes of South Asia".
http://www.wionews.com/edge/7-unique-indigenous-tribes-of-south-asia-6534

A story from kelaa's kandoofaa" article
https://ideaskelaa.wordpress.com/2017/08/24/of-famine-and-food-security/

Article "About the unemployment report by HRCM".
https://maldivesresortworkers.wordpress.com/2009/08/19/about-the-unemployment-report-by-hrcm/

Article "Ancient Flags of Maldives".
http://www.academia.edu/12172383/Ancient_Flags_of_Maldives

Article " Bashi : the most popular game you've never heard of "
http://momentum.travel/entertainment/bashi-popular-game-youve-never-heard/

Article " Gayoom speaks out on feud with Yameen "
https://maldivesindependent.com/politics/gayoom-speaks-out-on-feud-with-yameen-why-did-he-let-things-go-this-far-127236

Article "Heroin flooding Maldives".
https://www.rnw.org/archive/heroin-flooding-maldives

Article "Maldives blocks access to international media".
https://www.epochtimes.fr/les-maldives-bloquent-lacces-des-medias-internationaux-opposition-492863.html

Article " Jellyfish stings no bother for swimming's plucky minnows "
https://www.nst.com.my/news/2016/08/163243/olympics-jellyfish-stings-no-bother-swimmings-plucky-minnows

Article "Sunscreen threatens corals".
http://www.webplongee.com/actualite/divers/creme-solaire-coraux.html

Article "The day the Maldives is engulfed".
https://usbeketrica.com/article/le-jour-ou-les-maldives-seront-englouties

Article " Maldives: the first underwater nightclub in the world ".
https://www.nouvelobs.com/rue89/rue89-nos-vies-connectees/20130209.RUE3063/maldives-la-premiere-boite-de-nuit-sous-marine-au-monde.html

Article "French tourists desert the Maldives".
https://www.tourhebdo.com/actualites/destination/les-touristes-francais-desertent-les-maldives-446099.php

Article "The China-Maldives Friendship Bridge open to traffic".
https://www.tresor.economie.gouv.fr/Articles/2018/09/11/le-pont-de-l-amitie-chine-maldives-ouvert-a-la-circulation

Article " Maldives Film Industry - something more to do in Maldives "
http://www.themaldivestravel.com/maldives-film-industry-something-more-to-do-in-maldives.html

Article " Maldives situation worse than previously understood "
https://www.firstpost.com/world/maldives-situation-worse-than-previously-understood-says-european-think-tank-raises-concerns-on-upcoming-presidential-election-5150191.html

Article "Maldives tourism, how it all started".
https://www.kuredu.com/maldives-tourism-how-it-all-started/

Article "Abdulla Yameen, authoritarian president of a postcard country".
https://www.ouest-france.fr/monde/maldives/maldives-abdulla-yameen-president-autoritaire-d-un-pays-de-carte-postale-5981815

Article "Maldives: 19 months in prison for former President Gayoom".
https://www.la-croix.com/Monde/Maldives-19-mois-prison-president-Gayoom-2018-06-13-1300946852

Article " May the Maldives be with you "
https://www.exotismes.fr/blog/maldives/vu-a-la-tv/star-wars-rogue-one-maldives.jsf

Article "Nahula's productions now available on Sun Play".
https://en.sun.mv/43930

Article " The greatest Maldivian visual artists of the 21st century "
https://hani-amir.com/blog/2016/7/20/the-greatest-maldivian-visual-artists-of-the-21st-century

Article "Traditional coral housing in Maldives".
https://cruisingmaldives.blog/2016/04/18/traditional-coral-housing-in-maldives-1/

Article " SURFERS ARRESTED IN THE MALDIVES..."
http://www.surfatoll.com/surfersarrestedinthemaldives/

BFMTV article "These places that could disappear".
https://www.bfmtv.com/planete/ces-lieux-qui-pourraient-disparaitre-les-maldives-paradis-menace-898652.html

Article de blog " What can be broken, must be broken "
http://zueshan.blogspot.com/2010/12/raivaru.html

Article de la BBC " Two arrested over abusive Maldives wedding ceremony "
https://www.bbc.co.uk/news/world-south-asia-11654600

Article de presse " Unlikely allies: Nasheed and Gayoom team up "
http://www.catchnews.com/international-news/unlikely-allies-nasheed-and-gayoom-team-up-to-restore-democracy-in-the-maldives-55877.html

Slate Article "Watch a Maldivian beach illuminated by the light of the sun"....
http://www.slate.fr/life/82529/plage-maldives-illuminee-planctons-luminescents-bleu

Slate's article "The Turbo-is taxes".
https://en.wikipedia.org/wiki/Maldives_Inland_Revenue_Authority

Le Figaro article "How the Maldives fell into chaos".
http://www.lefigaro.fr/international/2018/02/06/01003-20180206ARTFIG00196-comment-les-maldives-ont-bascule-dans-le-chaos.php

Le Figaro article "The hidden face of the Maldives paradise".
http://www.lefigaro.fr/international/2012/02/17/01003-20120217ARTFIG00550-la-face-cachee-du-paradis-des-maldives.php

Article du Monde " Underwater ministerial meeting in the Maldives ".

https://www.lemonde.fr/planete/article/2009/10/17/conseil-des-ministres-sous-marin-aux-maldives_1255193_3244.html

Trailer of the movie "4426".
https://www.youtube.com/watch?v=A26U0rvKHSQ

Blog " A year of reading the world "
https://ayearofreadingtheworld.com/2012/12/06/maldives-free-books/

Blog " Maldives Complete
http://blog.maldivescomplete.com/

Blog " The truth about expat life in the Maldives "
http://travelpilz.com/expat-life-in-the-maldives/

Map of North Malé Atoll
http://carnets-de-voyages.net/index.php/asie/plongee-aux-maldives/map-of-north-male-atoll-maldives/

Map of the Maldives
https://maldivesfinest.com/location-map

Clip of the song "Kamaku Nudhey".
https://www.youtube.com/watch?v=ynZxmeIVFBk

Speech by President Mohamed Nasheed at COP15
http://archive.ipu.org/splz-f/cop15/nasheed.pdf

Document " Factors that motivate maldivians to work in resorts "
http://www.tourism.gov.mv/downloads/reports/survey_final_report.pdf

Document " The Maldives: One year after the tsunami "
http://statisticsmaldives.gov.mv/tsunami-reports/

Documentary " The Island President
http://theislandpresident.com/

Official Documentary of the Ministry of Agriculture
https://www.youtube.com/watch?v=p1A4U9Rj2dI

Video documentary "Agriculture in Maldives".
https://www.youtube.com/watch?v=bOV99obl-Fk

Document " Statistics of utilizations of electricity in Malé "
http://statisticsmaldives.gov.mv/yearbook/statisticalarchive/wp-content/uploads/sites/3/2018/02/11.1.pdf

Official list of resort islands

http://www.tourism.gov.mv/downloads/lists/tourist_resorts_list.pdf

Common Plants of Maldives" book
https://books.google.fr/books?id=pBpfDwAAQBAJ

Book "Cultures of the World", Times
https://archive.org/stream/maldives00ngch

Dhon Hiyala and Ali Fulhu" book
http://www.maldivesroyalfamily.com/pdf/don_hiyala.pdf

Book "Folks Tales of the Maldives".
https://www.diva-portal.org/smash/get/diva2:876644/FULLTEXT01.pdf

The Maldives: Islamic Republic, Tropical Autocracy" book
https://www.amazon.com/Maldives-Islamic-Republic-Tropical-Autocracy/dp/1849045895

Book "India, Ceylon, Bhutan, Nepal, The Maldives".
https://archive.org/details/indiaceylonbhuta00grey

Page " 40 things to do in the Maldives "
https://www.dreamingofmaldives.com/blog-des-maldives/40-choses-a-faire-aux-maldives-vous-ne-vous-ennuierez-jamais-aux-maldives/

Page " Energy consumption on the Maldives "
https://www.worlddata.info/asia/maldives/energy-consumption.php

Page " The development of the resort islands "
https://journals.openedition.org/etudescaribeennes/862

Page " Maldives - Housing " from Nations Encyclopedia
http://www.nationsencyclopedia.com/Asia-and-Oceania/Maldives-HOUSING.html

Page " Cyanide fishing: a reality still in the news "
http://www.recifs.org/modules.278.html

Muhammad Shirin Maghribi's page on poetry-chaikhana.com
http://www.poetry-chaikhana.com/Poets/M/MaghribiMuha/index.html

Maldives page in worldatlas.com
https://www.worldatlas.com/articles/major-islands-of-the-maldives.html

Maldives page on the Global Security.org website
https://www.globalsecurity.org/military/world/indian-ocean/mv-air-wing.htm

Maldives page on the PopulationData.net website

https://www.populationdata.net/pays/maldives/

Maldives page on Reporters Without Borders portal
https://rsf.org/fr/maldives

Bardot Ocean" page
https://www.bardotocean.com/pages/swac-sea-water-air-conditioning-by-bardot-group

Maldivian Olympic Committee page
http://www.nocmaldives.org/

Facebook Page " Maldives Lifestyle "
https://www.facebook.com/lifestylesmv/photos/a.901306039930767.107374
1829.901042273290477/1337572419637458/?type=3

Fandom Star Wars page of " Scarif "
http://fr.starwars.wikia.com/wiki/Scarif

Official page of Gan Airport
http://www.ganairport.com/

Trans Maldivian Airways official page
http://www.transmaldivian.com/

Official "UNDP" page
http://www.undp.org/content/undp/fr/home/about-us.html

Official page of the restaurant "Ithaa
http://conradhotels3.hilton.com/en/hotels/maldives/conrad-maldives-rangali-island-MLEHICI/amenities/restaurants-ithaa.html

Web Page " Commonwealth Health Online "
http://www.commonwealthhealth.org/asia/maldives/health_systems_in_maldi
ves/

Maldives web page on Trading Economics.com
https://tradingeconomics.com/maldives

Web page of the Ministry of Fisheries and Agriculture
http://www.fishagri.gov.mv

Official web page of the Presidency of the country
https://presidency.gov.mv/

Wikipedia page of " 2003 Maldives civil unrest "
https://en.wikipedia.org/wiki/2003_Maldives_civil_unrest

Wikipedia page of " 2005 Maldives civil unrest "
https://en.wikipedia.org/wiki/2005_Maldives_civil_unrest

Wikipedia page of "2007 Malé bombing".
https://en.wikipedia.org/wiki/2007_Mal%C3%A9_bombing

Wikipedia page of " 2011-12 Maldives political crisis "
https://en.wikipedia.org/wiki/2011%E2%80%9312_Maldives_political_crisis

Wikipedia page of "2018 Maldives political crisis".
https://en.wikipedia.org/wiki/2018_Maldives_political_crisis

Wikipedia page of "Abdul Majeed Didi".
https://en.wikipedia.org/wiki/Abdul_Majeed_Didi

Wikipedia page of "Abdulla Yameen".
https://en.wikipedia.org/wiki/Abdulla_Yameen

Wikipedia page of " Ahsham "
https://en.wikipedia.org/wiki/Ahsham_(movie)

Wikipedia page of "Arakkal kingdom".
https://en.wikipedia.org/wiki/Arakkal_kingdom

Wikipedia page of " Black Friday (Maldives)
https://en.wikipedia.org/wiki/Black_Friday_(Maldives)

Wikipedia page of "Boduberu".
https://en.wikipedia.org/wiki/Boduberu

Wikipedia page of "Capital punishment in the Maldives".
https://en.wikipedia.org/wiki/Capital_punishment_in_the_Maldives

Wikipedia page of "Naturally cold water air conditioning".
https://fr.wikipedia.org/wiki/Climatisation_%C3%A0_l%27eau_naturellement
_froide

Wikipedia page of "Malabar Coast".
https://fr.wikipedia.org/wiki/C%C3%B4te_de_Malabar

Wikipedia page of "Dhadimagi Kilhi".
https://en.wikipedia.org/wiki/Dhadimagi_Kilhi

Wikipedia page of "Dhuvaafaru".
https://en.wikipedia.org/wiki/Dhuvaafaru

Wikipedia page of " Flag of the Maldives
https://fr.wikipedia.org/wiki/Drapeau_des_Maldives

Wikipedia page of "Economy of the Maldives".
https://en.wikipedia.org/wiki/Economy_of_the_Maldives

Wikipedia page for "Education in the Maldives".
https://en.wikipedia.org/wiki/Education_in_the_Maldives

Wikipedia page of "Fishing industry in the Maldives".
https://en.wikipedia.org/wiki/Fishing_industry_in_the_Maldives

Wikipedia page of "Folklore of the Maldives".
https://en.wikipedia.org/wiki/Folklore_of_the_Maldives

Wikipedia page of " HAL Dhruv "
https://fr.wikipedia.org/wiki/HAL_Dhruv

Wikipedia page of "Hassan Nooraddeen II".
https://en.wikipedia.org/wiki/Hassan_Nooraddeen_II

Wikipedia page of " History of the Maldives "
https://en.wikipedia.org/wiki/History_of_the_Maldives

Wikipedia page of "History of the Maldives".
https://en.wikipedia.org/wiki/History_of_the_Maldives

Wikipedia page of " Hulhumalé "
https://fr.wikipedia.org/wiki/Hulhumal%C3%A9

Wikipedia page of " Hulhumalé "
https://en.wikipedia.org/wiki/Hulhumal%C3%A9

Wikipedia page of "Human trafficking in the Maldives".
https://en.wikipedia.org/wiki/Human_trafficking_in_the_Maldives

Wikipedia page of "Ibrahim Mohamed Solih".
https://en.wikipedia.org/wiki/Ibrahim_Mohamed_Solih

Wikipedia page of "Islam in the Maldives".
https://fr.wikipedia.org/wiki/Islam_aux_Maldives

Wikipedia page of "Italian auxiliary cruiser Ramb I".
https://en.wikipedia.org/wiki/Italian_auxiliary_cruiser_Ramb_I

Wikipedia page of "Khadijah of the Maldives".
https://en.wikipedia.org/wiki/Khadijah_of_the_Maldives

Wikipedia page of "List of sultans of Maldives".
https://en.wikipedia.org/wiki/List_of_sultans_of_the_Maldives

Wikipedia page of "Majeediyya School".
https://en.wikipedia.org/wiki/Majeediyya_School

Maldives Inland Revenue Authority" Wikipedia Page
https://en.wikipedia.org/wiki/Maldives_Inland_Revenue_Authority

Wikipedia page of "Maldives National Defence Force".
https://en.wikipedia.org/wiki/Maldives_National_Defence_Force

Wikipedia page of " Maldives "
https://fr.wikipedia.org/wiki/Maldives

Wikipedia page of " Maldives "
https://en.wikipedia.org/wiki/Maldives

Wikipedia page of "Maldivian Cuisine".
https://en.wikipedia.org/wiki/Maldivian_cuisine

Maldivian Diaspora" Wikipedia page
https://en.wikipedia.org/wiki/Maldivian_diaspora

Wikipedia page of "Maldivian Idol".
https://en.wikipedia.org/wiki/Maldivian_Idol

Wikipedia page of " Maldivian Language "
https://fr.wikipedia.org/wiki/Maldivien

Wikipedia page of "Maldivian Literature".
https://en.wikipedia.org/wiki/Maldivian_literature

Wikipedia page of "Maldivian Rufiyaa".
https://en.wikipedia.org/wiki/Maldivian_rufiyaa

Wikipedia page of " Maldivian "
https://fr.wikipedia.org/wiki/Maldivien

Wikipedia page of " Malé "
https://fr.wikipedia.org/wiki/Mal%C3%A9

Wikipedia page of "Mohamed Nasheed".
https://en.wikipedia.org/wiki/Mohamed_Nasheed

Wikipedia page of "Mohammed Waheed Hassan".
https://en.wikipedia.org/wiki/Mohammed_Waheed_Hassan

Wikipedia page of "Muhammad Fareed Didi".
https://en.wikipedia.org/wiki/Muhammad_Fareed_Didi

Wikipedia page of "Muhammad Imaaduddeen VI".
https://en.wikipedia.org/wiki/Muhammad_Imaaduddeen_VI

Wikipedia page of "Muhammad Shamsuddeen III".
https://en.wikipedia.org/wiki/Muhammad_Shamsuddeen_III

Wikipedia page of "Muhammad Thakurufaanu Al Auzam".
https://en.wikipedia.org/wiki/Muhammad_Thakurufaanu_Al_Auzam

Muliaage" Wikipedia page
https://fr.wikipedia.org/wiki/Muliaage

Wikipedia page of " United Nations Development Programme "
https://fr.wikipedia.org/wiki/Programme_des_Nations_unies_pour_le_d%C3%
A9veloppement

Progressive Party of Maldives" Wikipedia page
https://en.wikipedia.org/wiki/Progressive_Party_of_Maldives

Wikipedia page of "Rufiyaa".
https://fr.wikipedia.org/wiki/Rufiyaa

Wikipedia page of "2004 Indian Ocean Earthquake and Tsunami".
https://fr.wikipedia.org/wiki/S%C3%A9isme_et_tsunami_de_2004_dans_l%27
oc%C3%A9an_Indien

Wikipedia page of " Administrative subdivision of the Maldives
https://fr.wikipedia.org/wiki/Subdivision_administrative_des_Maldives

Wikipedia page of " Theemuge "
https://en.wikipedia.org/wiki/Theemuge

Wikipedia page of "Thilafushi".
https://fr.wikipedia.org/wiki/Thilafushi

Wikipedia page of "Green Turtle".
https://fr.wikipedia.org/wiki/Tortue_verte

Wikipedia page of " Tourism in the Maldives "
https://fr.wikipedia.org/wiki/Tourisme_aux_Maldives

Trans Maldivian Airways" Wikipedia page
https://en.wikipedia.org/wiki/Trans_Maldivian_Airways

United Suvadive Republic" Wikipedia Page
https://en.wikipedia.org/wiki/United_Suvadive_Republic

Wikipedia page of "Wildlife of Maldives".
https://en.wikipedia.org/wiki/Wildlife_of_Maldives

Wikipedia page of "List of Maldives atolls "
https://fr.wikipedia.org/wiki/Liste_des_atolls_des_Maldives

Fuvahmulah Wikipedia page
https://en.wikipedia.org/wiki/Fuvahmulah

Wikipedia page of Villingili (Malé)
https://en.wikipedia.org/wiki/Villingili_(Mal%C3%A9)

Wikipedia page of Xavier Romero Frias
https://en.wikipedia.org/wiki/Xavier_Romero_Fr%C3%ADas

Wikipedia page of the " Cauri ".
https://fr.wikipedia.org/wiki/Monetaria_moneta

Wikipedia page of the movie "4426".
https://en.wikipedia.org/wiki/4426

Photos of traditional dances
http://www.eydhafushitimes.com/live/pictures/36272/

Ministry of Health statistics booklet
http://www.health.gov.mv/Uploads/Downloads//Informations/Informations(73).pdf

Satellite shots
https://www.google.fr/maps

Report " Exclusive Investigation (M6) : The Maldives, a paradise in danger ".
https://vimeo.com/151621970

Reportage from France 2 " Maldives: The home of luxury
https://www.youtube.com/watch?v=LzlyDCrDSbs

Site " Everyculture.com
http://www.everyculture.com/Ja-Ma/Maldives.html

Sales site of uninhabited islands
https://www.privateislandsonline.com/

Site of the National Bureau of Statistics
http://www.planning.gov.mv/

Site Housing Development Corporation
https://hdc.com.mv/hulhumale/

Official website of the show " Maldivian idol ".
http://maldivianidol.mv/

Official website of the hotel Centara Ras Fushi
https://www.centarahotelsresorts.com/fr/centara/crf/

Official website of Kurumba Hotel
http://www.kurumba.com/keeping-paradise-pristine

Official website of the Maldives
https://www.maldives.com/

Official website of the MTCC
https://www.mtcc.com.mv

Official website of the port of Malé
https://port.mv/

Article " Sharaf breaks 27-year-old national marathon record "
https://raajje.mv/en/news/6009

Addu City" Wikipedia page
https://en.wikipedia.org/wiki/Addu_City

Official page of Addu Marathon
https://raajje.mv/en/news/6009

Wikipedia page of " Paradise Island "
https://fr.wikipedia.org/wiki/%C3%8Ele_paradisiaque

Wikipedia page of "Maldives at the 1988 Summer Olympics".
https://en.wikipedia.org/wiki/Maldives_at_the_1988_Summer_Olympics

Wikipedia page of "Maldives at the 1992 Summer Olympics".
https://en.wikipedia.org/wiki/Maldives_at_the_1992_Summer_Olympics

Wikipedia page of "Maldives at the 1996 Summer Olympics".
https://en.wikipedia.org/wiki/Maldives_at_the_1996_Summer_Olympics

Wikipedia page of "Maldives at the 2012 Summer Olympics".
https://en.wikipedia.org/wiki/Maldives_at_the_2012_Summer_Olympics

Wikipedia page of "Maldives at the 2016 Summer Olympics".
https://en.wikipedia.org/wiki/Maldives_at_the_2016_Summer_Olympics

Page Wikipédia de " List of countries by Human Development Index " https://en.wikipedia.org/wiki/List_of_countries_by_Human_Development_Index

Blog " Dhivehi Observer Maldives News "
http://doreview.blogspot.com/2009/08/

Official page of the National Library
https://nlm.gov.mv/en/about/history/

Official MediaNet website
https://medianet.mv/channel

Article " Maldivian Ancestry in light of Genetics "
http://maldives-ancestry.blogspot.com/2013/05/maldivian-ancestry-in-light-of-genetics.html

Article " The race of his life: An introduction to the Maldives' latest ... "
https://maldivesindependent.com/feature-comment/the-race-of-his-life-an-introduction-to-the-maldives-latest-presidential-hopeful-139100

Article "Maldives: the leader of the opposition claims victory"...
https://www.france24.com/fr/20180923-maldives-chef-opposition-salih-revendique-victoire-presidentielle-yameen

Wikipedia Page " Sea level rise "
https://fr.wikipedia.org/wiki/%C3%89l%C3%A9vation_du_niveau_de_la_mer

Article " Maumoon Abdul Gayoom: Former Maldives president released on bail "
https://www.bbc.com/news/world-asia-45700948

Wikipedia page of "Islands of the Blessed".
https://fr.wikipedia.org/wiki/%C3%8Eles_des_Bienheureux

Wikipedia page of " Desalination "
https://en.wikipedia.org/wiki/Desalination

Article Maldives restores the death penalty for children more ... "
https://www.sudouest.fr/2014/05/22/les-maldives-retablissent-la-peine-de-mort-pour-les-enfants-de-plus-de-7-ans-1562961-4710.php

Wikipedia page of "Dhives Akuru".
https://en.wikipedia.org/wiki/Dhives_Akuru

The author

Lionel Bolnet is a French computer engineer and writer born on July 14, 1984. His short stay in the Maldives in November 2011 at the height of the Maldives honeymoon trend pushed him to know this country better. He has endeavored to write the most complete book on the subject on the market by compiling a huge number of sources.

Made in the USA
Coppell, TX
24 June 2021

58032880R00252